Motion, Emotion, and Love

Benemia
Cucurucu
lucia mia.
Bernoualla.
Che buona mi sa.
BALLI DI SFESSANIA
di Jacomo Callot
Jac. Callot In. fe.

Motion, Emotion, and Love

The Nature of Artistic Performance

THOMAS CARSON MARK

GIA Publications Inc.
Chicago

ALSO BY THOMAS CARSON MARK

What Every Pianist Needs to Know about the Body

Spinoza's Theory of Truth

G-8250

GIA Publications, Inc.
7404 S. Mason Ave.
Chicago, IL 60638
www.giamusic.com

Produced by Marquand Books, Seattle

Library of Congress Cataloging-in-Publication Data
Mark, Thomas Carson, 1941–
Motion, emotion, and love : the nature of artistic performance/
by Thomas Carson Mark.
p. cm.
ISBN 978-1-57999-901-8 (alk. paper)
1. Music—Psychological aspects. 2. Music—
Philosophy and aesthetics. 3. Emotions in music.
4. Love in music. 5. Music—Performance. I. Title.
ML3830.M32 2012
791.01—DC23
2012027551

Printed in the United States of America

For Barbara Conable

Contents

Acknowledgments

I am grateful to the artists, famous and not so famous, who through their performances have enriched my life with the experiences I attempt to explain and rationalize in this book. In such things lie our humanity and our hope for the future.

I want to thank the friends and colleagues who have made valuable comments on this book: Lisa Andrus-Rivera, Richard Louis Brown, Gretchen Corbett, Arthur C. Danto, Winthrop Hall, Laura Helper-Ferris, Bridget Jankowski, Jennifer Johnson, Peter Kivy, Graham Mark, T. Richard Nichols, Paul Roberts, Sue Taylor, David Vining, and Jeanne Weisman. The Callot etchings are reproduced through the courtesy of Richard Louis Brown. I first undertook this book at the urging of Barbara Conable. She has followed its progress from the beginning and been a tireless source of encouragement, criticism, and suggestions. Without her interest and enthusiasm, I doubt I would have completed the project.

A Note on Pronouns

I do not wish to be accused of sexism, but neither do I wish to burden the text with cumbersome expressions or shifts in mid-sentence from a singular subject to a plural pronoun. Therefore, I have arbitrarily decided that pianists and dancers are almost always "she"; actors and performers whose field is unspecified are almost always "he."

Gian Fritello.
Ciurlo.

Preface

When I was completing my previous book, *What Every Pianist Needs to Know about the Body,* it occurred to me to dress it up by inserting at the beginning a wise saying by a famous pianist or philosopher. I looked for a suitable quotation but didn't find one that seemed exactly right. So, following the venerable philosophical tradition of appealing to imagination when facts and arguments are lacking, I made one up. I thought a bit about my pseudo quotation, decided I liked it, and used it:

Piano playing is motion, emotion, and love.

Every now and then a passing thought turns out to be more significant than it appears at first, which is what happened in this case. After the book was published, I realized that my aphorism has wide implications for all varieties of artistic performance, not just piano playing. *What Every Pianist* dealt almost entirely with motion, which it approached from a practical point of view, and it scarcely touched on emotion and love. I saw that exploring the roles of motion, emotion, and love in artistic performance would fill another book.

This book is aimed at performers of all kinds—musicians, actors, and dancers—as well as their audiences, and for performers and audiences alike it will have practical value. However, speaking clearly about artistic performance requires a framework for the discussion, so I must undertake some conceptual or philosophical consideration of such questions as how a work of performing art is related to a performance of that same work, whether performers are artists in their own right, and what the nature is of intentional action as it relates to performance. These are interesting topics in themselves, some of which deserve more extended examination than I give them. Philosophers may feel that my discussions leave many questions unanswered, which is doubtless true, but my interest is in performance, not theory, and I examine theoretical topics only as far as necessary to illuminate performance. Despite the forays into philosophy, the book is practical in intent. Understanding the nature of artistic performance makes a practical difference because how we think about what we do – what we take ourselves to be doing – influences the way we go about it. Thinking about performance in the ways I shall describe can transform a person's practicing, rehearsing, performing, and teaching. It can also transform the experience of the audience. Although the discussion focuses mainly on performers, it is equally relevant to their audiences.

The subject matter of this book is important for all performers, but I myself am a musician, a pianist. Consequently, the examples that usually occur to me come from musical performance – piano playing in particular. I try to point out the application of my ideas to other kinds of performance, but I have not attempted to conceal that I approach these questions first as a pianist. It seems better to use examples of something I know from the inside than to invent examples from varieties of performance of which I have little personal experience. If the ideas set forth here have the importance I think they have, then actors, dancers, and musicians other than pianists will have no trouble supplying examples more illuminating and useful to their own enterprise than any I could devise.

I first addressed the concept of performance years ago in a paper I could not resist calling "Philosophy of Piano Playing."* A friend urged me to write a book about performance and I made a few desultory attempts, but soon abandoned

* "Philosophy of Piano Playing: Reflections on the Concept of Performance," *Philosophy and Phenomenological Research*, 41:3 (March 1981), 299–324. The paper is available on my website, www.pianomap.com.

the project. Shortly afterward, I left academia and returned to the piano, which had been my focus seventeen years earlier, before I entered graduate school in philosophy. In time, I moved to Oregon, where for nine years I organized and performed in a chamber music series. I taught piano, learned to rehabilitate injured pianists, wrote *What Every Pianist*, and read about the astonishing neurological discoveries that reveal some of the ways the brain works. Throughout this period I continued to reflect on the concept of performance, and when it occurred to me that motion, emotion, and love captured much of the essence of artistic performance, I was ready to undertake an utterly different book from anything I could have envisioned earlier.

Capⁿ. Bonbardon.
Cap. Grillo.

The Etchings

The twenty-four etchings that decorate this book comprise a set, *Balli di Sfessania,* by Jacques Callot. Callot was born in Nancy, in Lorraine, now northeastern France, in 1592. He began training in Lorraine, travelled to Italy where he studied, probably with Antonio Tempesta in Florence, and also worked for the Medici court. He returned to Nancy in 1621 and remained there until his death in 1635. The *Balli di Sfessania* etchings were done shortly after his return from Italy. His name is no longer familiar to most of us, but Callot is an important figure in the history of art. He made important innovations in the technique of etching, and his work was widely sought after and collected. Rembrandt owned many etchings by him.

The *Balli di Sfessania* etchings are usually described as depicting characters from the commedia dell' arte, a form of improvisatory comedy that began in Italy before 1550 and by 1600 was popular throughout Europe. Troupes traveled from place to place, generally performing on makeshift stages at carnivals and fairs; some troupes became famous and performed at royal courts. The productions consisted of a mix of song and dance, acrobatics, rehearsed scenes, and improvised dialogue, with a lot of humor, much of it bawdy. Plots followed a few standard story lines (young lovers aided by pert serving girls to overcome the resistance of miserly, tyrannical parents or guardians, for example) and used a number of stock characters – the blustering captain, the pedantic doctor, the clown, the comic servant. Many of the male characters wore masks, and the costumes of comic males often included a prominent phallus (often emphasized by a cloth draped from it), depicted in some of the Callot etchings and in keeping with the bawdy humor of the commedia dell' arte.

The word *sfessania* in the title has mystified many commentators, and some scholars now doubt whether the *Balli* etchings actually depict commedia dell' arte figures. It appears that by the fifteenth century a dance called the *moresca,* which could include furious gestures, wild poses, and mock battles, was popular throughout Europe. In Naples, at the turn of the seventeenth century, a form of *moresca* was known as the *sfessania.* Callot is not known to have visited Naples, but he spent some years in Florence and many of his images fit the descriptions we have of this dance, so it is plausible that it, not the commedia dell' arte, is the principal subject of the *Balli di Sfessania* series of etchings.* For our purpose in this book, nothing hinges on settling that question. Whatever their historical subject, the etchings are marvelously gestural, full of movement and energy, and they are a perfect accompaniment to a book on motion, emotion, and love in artistic performance.

* Donald Posner advocates this interpretation of the etchings in "Jacques Callot and the Dances Called *Sfessania,*" *The Art Bulletin,* 59:2 (June 1977), 203–216.

Cap: Esgangarato.
Cap:o Cocodrillo

Fracischina.
Gian Farina.

1 • *What Is Artistic Performance?*

Carved across the façade of Butler Library at Columbia University in New York City are the names of some famous authors: Homer, Herodotus, Sophocles, Plato, Aristotle, Demosthenes, Cicero, Vergil.* Those names say something about the books to be found in the library, but they also represent a civilization: the historical, literary, and artistic traditions that define our culture, which it is the business of the university to preserve and carry forward. Fifty blocks south of Columbia University is Lincoln Center for the Performing Arts, its plaza flanked by the David H. Koch Theatre, Avery Fisher Hall, and the Metropolitan Opera House. Those buildings, like Butler Library, represent the traditions of a civilization, but they do not have names carved on them. Lincoln Center was designed and constructed in the 1960s, when it was not fashionable to decorate public buildings with the names of famous individuals.

Had Lincoln Center been contemporaneous with Butler Library, Avery Fisher Hall might have been adorned with the names of Bach, Beethoven, and Brahms; the Metropolitan Opera House with Mozart, Verdi, and Wagner; and the Koch Theatre, a venue for drama and ballet as well as opera, with Shakespeare, Molière, and Petipa. Each building would honor some of the greatest creators of works of performing art and identify itself as a place dedicated to the preservation and performance of their works. Names like those do, in fact, appear on many theatres, concert halls, and opera houses built in the

* So spelt on the Library. According to *The Columbia Encyclopedia,* "The spelling *Virgil* is not found earlier than the 5th cent. A.D."

nineteenth and early twentieth centuries. The Paris Opéra, an extreme example of elaborate architectural decoration, was completed in 1874 and has on its façade not only the names but the gilded busts of various composers, including Rossini, Mozart, Beethoven, and Meyerbeer. Such names raise a question, however. Why should we honor those individuals rather than Artur Rubinstein, Jascha Heifetz, Maria Callas, Margot Fonteyn, Luciano Pavarotti, Laurence Olivier, Sarah Bernhardt, or Rudolf Nureyev? Why should we choose composers, playwrights, and choreographers instead of musicians, actors, and dancers? Shouldn't a center for the performing arts display the names of famous performers? Why can't performers have their names in stone as well as lights?

Performers give us some of the most memorable and significant experiences of our lives, and I suspect we can all recall performances we will never forget. Some performances from long ago that remain fresh in my mind are Judy Holliday, alone on the apron of the Schubert Theatre in New York, quietly singing "The Party's Over." Or Edward Villella in a series of death-defying leaps in the New York City Ballet. Or Beverly Sills in the first act duet of *Lucia di Lammermore*, where she seemed to be a creature whose very breath emerged as music. Such moments have enriched and shaped my life. Naturally, other people will recall other performances, and not necessarily on Broadway or at the Metropolitan Opera. The soprano in church singing "Nearer My God to Thee." The first time hearing the Beatles or the Stones or Thomas Lauderdale in performance. Being moved to tears by an actor playing King Lear or Willie Loman. And every high school has its silver-voiced young soprano or budding virtuoso on guitar or drums; they offer a heartfelt performance and chills run up our spines.

None of this should surprise us. Giving ourselves over to the work of gifted performers is part of being human. The prehistoric campfire had its storyteller or dancer, the Greek amphitheatre its tragedian, the Renaissance its commedia dell' arte buffoon and comic pedant. As a musician and former professor of philosophy, I am stimulated to ponder why performances can move us so profoundly. What is it performers do that so engages us? I shall propose answers to these questions in the course of this book.

Everyone agrees that Shakespeare, Sophocles, Bach, and Beethoven, who created works of performing art, are artists on the same exalted level as Michelangelo, Cervantes, Rembrandt, or Monet, who created works of nonperforming art. But the *performers* of the works of Shakespeare, Sophocles, Bach, and Beethoven are rarely put in the same category. A person asked to name some of the greatest artists of the twentieth century is more likely to mention Picasso, Stravinsky, or Joyce than to mention Rubinstein, Heifetz, Fonteyn, or Olivier; indeed, the very suggestion that performers be included might seem odd to some, because the artistic status of performers is by no means clear. We refer to them as artists, but what do we mean when we describe them that way? Are they creative artists or mere interpreters? Should we regard someone as an artist whose activity consists mainly or entirely of performing works by others? If we do maintain that performers are artists, then what are their artworks? What do they create? These questions rarely receive careful scrutiny, perhaps because people assume they know the answers. But the answers are not really obvious.

In this book I shall examine these and closely related questions. Eventually I shall offer arguments to establish the artistic status of performers. I shall claim that they are indeed artists in their own right and make clear what their artworks are. That is, I shall insist that although a performance presents an artwork—a sonata, a work of choreography, or play—which is the work of one artist—Beethoven or Balanchine or Shakespeare—it also offers *another* artwork that is the work of the performer. Two artworks are present simultaneously. In addition, I shall insist that the performer's work is as complex, demanding, expressive, and profound as any other kind of artwork. Those arguments must wait, however, until the final two chapters of the book. For the moment I simply assume that performers are artists, leaving until later a full account of what makes their creations special. Performers are, after all, commonly designated as artists, so I am following ordinary usage in this.

Assuming that performers are artists, there is no reason to suppose them inferior as a class to the creators of the works they perform. Granted, some composers are greater artists than some pianists, and some playwrights greater than some actors, but surely, the opposite can be true as well. Some pianists are greater artists than some composers, and some actors are better than some playwrights—at least that is the opinion of drama critics, who often claim about a new play that the actors are better than the material they have to work with. To suppose that composers and playwrights are necessarily superior as artists would be to revert to the opinion, common in earlier centuries, that the arts can be classified hierarchically, with some inherently higher ranking than others. But that is not a tenable position. It is tempting to conclude from this that when carving names on centers of performing art there is no compelling reason to choose the names of composers but not pianists, dramatists but not actors, choreographers but not dancers.

However, that conclusion is a bit hasty. One thing separates performers from creators of works of performing art, and justifies a name carver in choosing Beethoven and Brahms rather than Rubinstein and Horowitz. The works of Beethoven and Brahms are available to be presented in the concert hall, whereas Rubinstein and Horowitz are dead and their works—their performances—no longer exist. Their playing is preserved on recordings, but recordings are reproductions, not their actual artworks. Carving the names of legendary performers would be a tribute to their memory, but it would not refer to anything that can now occur in the hall. It would be like putting up the names of composers whose works have all been lost.

Practitioners of the performing arts include composers, musicians, playwrights, actors, choreographers, and dancers. But there are differences between the activity of composers, playwrights, and choreographers, on the one hand, and that of musicians, actors, and dancers, on the other. Composers, playwrights, and choreographers create works of performing art. By "work of performing art" I mean an artwork that is intended to be performed: performance is the intended means of communicating the work to its audience. Musicians, dancers, and actors perform works of performing art. They do not create the works they perform. A pianist is not a composer; she does not produce a sonata but a performance of a sonata. A dancer produces not a ballet but a performance of a ballet. It is admittedly possible for the same individual to fill both roles; a pianist can compose her own sonata and a dancer can choreograph her own ballet, but the roles are nevertheless distinct, and usually carried out by different individuals.

One difference, alluded to earlier, between performing artists and those who create works of performing art is that the performer's artwork is over as soon as it is complete. What Beethoven is alleged to have said to the violinist who fingered the Opus 59 quartets – "These works are for future ages" – is not something a performer can say; it is impossible to perform for future ages. A performer cannot leave an *œuvre,* a body of work that remains after he is dead. Obviously I shall have something to say about works of performing art and the artists who create them, but that is not the focus of this book. The artists whose activity we shall examine are the performers, not the creators, of works of performing art. This is a book about artistic performance.

In identifying our subject as artistic performance I am using the phrase "artistic performance" in a particular sense. People often use the adjective "artistic" to indicate the aesthetic merit of a performance or to distinguish one performance from another. They may say that a performance was "highly artistic," meaning that it was exemplary in expressivity, grace, or precision, or of two performances that although both exhibited technical mastery, one was more "artistic" than the other. I believe this is the sense of "artistic" that occurs in the appraisal of certain sports, as when a gymnast or a figure skater is given a score for "artistic impression." I offer these examples to make clear that I shall use the phrase differently. I shall use "artistic performance" to refer to occasions in which there is both a performance and an artwork being performed. A pianist, for example, performs a sonata. When that occurs, there is a performance, by the pianist, and an artwork being performed, namely the sonata. This concept of artistic performance is narrower than the concept of performance generally, because not all performing, even if it is very difficult and demanding, counts as artistic performance in this sense. Jugglers and tightrope walkers are performers, and they typically possess and display astonishing skill. But there is no artwork that a tightrope walker performs. His skill is exhibited for its own sake, not embedded in an artwork. His performances, therefore, are not artistic performances in the sense I am specifying.

In order to explain what artistic performance is, we must make clear the relation between a work of performing art and a performance of that same work. To do that, we must say something about the nature of works of performing art. Now, the precise nature of a work of performing art—the manner in which it exists (if "existence" is the proper term here)—is a controversial philosophical question. Some people claim that a work of performing art is a kind of abstract entity, like a concept or a Platonic idea, but others disagree. We need not take sides on the question. Our interest is not in the works themselves but in performances of them, and it will be sufficient for our purpose simply to point out that whatever they may be "in themselves," works of performing art are not physical objects and they cannot be perceived by the bodily senses. I shall explain both these points.

Let us take Chopin's Fourth Ballade as an example of a work of performing art. Chopin completed the Fourth Ballade in Paris in 1842 and it has been in existence ever since. But the ballade has not existed *in Paris*, or indeed, in any other place; it is not like the Statue of Liberty, which has existed in New York Harbor, and nowhere else, since 1886. The Fourth Ballade does not have a location in space. Nor, clearly, is it the same as any of its performances. A performance has a beginning and an end, and lasts only a few minutes, whereas the ballade has existed for some 170 years. Moreover, the ballade exists even at moments when it is not being performed, and could even exist if it never had been performed. There are works of performing art that have been completed by their creators but never performed.

The ballade is also not the same as the score, or any copy of the score, since it could exist if all copies of the score were lost or destroyed. Many pianists know the Fourth Ballade from memory and could still play it even if all copies of the score somehow disappeared. Therefore, existence of the ballade does not depend on existence of the score. Nor does it even depend on a score having been prepared. Mozart is said, in some accounts, to have composed entirely in his head and then to have written down the completed work later. If that is true, then the work existed, presumably in the same manner as any other work of performing art, from the moment of mental completion, although it was not accessible to anyone but Mozart until a score was written out. We know that Mozart performed some of his piano concertos without ever having written out the entire piano part, although of course he had to supply written parts to the players in the orchestra. As Alfred Einstein put it, "He knew perfectly well what he had to play."*

A work of performing art does not have a definite location, but a performance of that work does occur at a particular time and place. When a performance occurs of the Fourth Ballade, it is surely correct to say that the ballade is present at that time and place. But two pianists could play the Fourth Ballade simultaneously in different cities, and if that happened we would have to say that the ballade was present in two places at once. This simply reinforces the point that the ballade is not a physical object. Physical objects have definite locations and cannot be in two places at once.

As a nonphysical object, the ballade cannot be perceived by the bodily senses. That is, however we characterize the

* *Mozart: His Character, His Work* (New York: Oxford University Press, 1945), p. 313. See also the example of the Bach ricercar, below p. 13.

elusive object that has existed continuously for 170 years and can be present in different locations at the same time, we cannot perceive it directly. Nevertheless, we do apprehend works of performing art through the bodily senses. This comes about because works of performing art can be embodied, made perceptible to one or more of the senses, which is what occurs in performance. In performance a work of music is presented as a series of actual sounds. Unlike the work of music, sounds have a location in time and space. Whether or not we consider them to be physical objects, they are certainly physical occurrences, perceptible to the sense of hearing. Thus, when someone performs a work of music we can say that the work is presented in a manner perceptible to the sense of hearing, which is the manner of presentation for which it was composed.

The sounds that embody a musical work constitute what I shall call an *instance* of that work. When a pianist plays the Fourth Ballade, the sounds emerging from the piano, taken together, are an instance of the Fourth Ballade. A similar account applies in other performing arts. A work of choreography is realized by a series of bodily movements. Like sounds, movements are perceivable physical occurrences. When a dancer performs a work of choreography, her movements constitute an instance of the work, which now occurs in a form perceptible to the sense of sight. A play is realized when certain speeches occur accompanied by appropriate actions. Those speeches and actions constitute an instance of the play. The score of a work of music can be thought of as a set of instructions specifying that certain sounds should occur in a certain order. Likewise, the text of a play can be thought of as a set of instructions specifying a particular sequence of speeches and actions, and a work of choreography as a set of instructions specifying a series of bodily movements.

My use of the word "instance" to designate individual realizations of works of performing art in an appropriate sensuous medium may seem idiosyncratic, but I do not know a better word. We have no handy vernacular term with which to designate individual perceptible realizations of works of performing art. So I am adopting the word "instance" to refer to those individual realizations, and I hope that readers will become accustomed to it. Because there is no generally recognized term for referring to instances of works of performing art, people often use the word "performance" when they are really referring to an instance. That can be a source of confusion.

A work of performing art can receive any number of instances. Numerous pianists can perform the Fourth Ballade, in various places, at different times or at the same time. To do that, they push down the keys of a piano and produce sequences of sounds that satisfy the instructions in the score and each of those sequences is an instance of the ballade. Since each instance offers a sequence of all the sounds specified in the score, we can say that the ballade is fully present in any one of its instances. If two instances occur simultaneously in different places, then the *ballade* is present in two places at once, although each *instance* is a separate occurrence. All works of performing art have this feature. A work of drama can be given numerous instances by being enacted on different occasions by different actors; a work of choreography can likewise be given instances on different occasions by different dancers. The work is fully present in each of its instances, but each instance is unique.

I shall sometimes say that any instance of a work of performing art *is* that work, by which I simply mean that each instance offers the complete work. If dancers execute the movements prescribed by Balanchine in *Jewels*, then there is nothing else that must occur, nothing else the dancers must do, in order for their movements to constitute *Jewels*. Similarly, any instance of *King Lear*—any sequence of the proper speeches and appropriate actions—constitutes *King Lear*. No instance is more truly an instance than any other, because anything that counts as instance gives the actual work.

Although two instances of the same work may not differ insofar as they are both instances, they can differ in other respects. An instance of the Fourth Ballade produced by one pianist may be faster than an instance produced by another pianist, with different dynamics, different tone quality, and different emphasis. Two instances of a play use different scenery and different stage direction; they may be utterly unlike one another visually and yet be instances of the same play. I shall refer to differences between two instances of the same work as differences of *interpretation*. Two pianists who play the Fourth Ballade in different ways are playing the same work, but under different interpretations.

I am not eager to engage in lengthy arguments that would divert us from our principal subject, but I should point out that determining what counts as an instance can be complicated and subject to divergent opinions. Many works of performing art include instructions about how instances should be produced. Works of music, for example, generally specify particular instruments. Someone could insist that the manner of producing the sounds is essential to whether a sequence of sounds counts as an instance. On this view, it is not an accidental feature of the Fourth Ballade that it is a composition for *piano*. Someone else might say that what matters is not the manner of production but the quality of the sounds, that is, what they sound like. *Sounding lik*e a piano would then be sufficient. There are at least five possibilities.

An instance of the Fourth Ballade might be: 1) Any sequence of sounds with the pitches and rhythms specified in the score – sounds produced in any manner on any instrument. Sounds from an organ or a synthesizer would count, even though they are not very similar to piano sounds. 2) A sequence of *piano* sounds – i.e., sounding like a piano – produced in any manner. Sounds from an organ would not count, but sounds from a CD player would. 3) A sequence of sounds actually coming from a piano. A CD player would not count, but a player piano would. 4) A sequence of sounds coming from a piano actually played by a person. This might seem to exhaust the possibilities, but as we shall have occasion to discuss, people can play mindlessly, without attention. There is therefore another, more stringent possibility: 5) A sequence of sounds coming from a piano played by a person with full awareness and intention. The position I take in this book is that all of these except the first count as instances, but only in the last case, number five, do we have a performance, and then only if there is an audience or a "virtual" audience.*

Just as what counts as an instance can be controversial, so can the distinction between instance and interpretation. It seems obvious that two instances can differ from one another in various ways—in what I am calling interpretation—while still being instances of the same work; indeed, this happens frequently. Nevertheless, the differences between two instances might be so great that we would no longer say they were mere differences of interpretation, we might say instead that one of the instances did not count as an instance at all. I believe this does occasionally happen, but I do not think there is any way to draw the line precisely. The question is one of taste and judgment, on which people disagree. For example, when Angela Hewitt plays Bach on the piano I consider that she is producing an instance of Bach's music, even though Bach composed for harpsichord, not piano. For me, therefore, the difference between Bach on the piano and Bach on the harpsichord is one of interpretation. Other people insist that to be an instance, the sounds must come from a harpsichord. I disagree, but I do not know a conclusive argument to prove the point. There are other cases, however, where I do think that a performance goes to such an extreme that what it offers no longer counts as an instance. I once heard a movement of a Beethoven symphony played by an ensemble of accordions, and in my opinion the result was not an instance of Beethoven.

Works of performing art become available to their audience in the intended way when they are actually performed. I say they "become available in the intended way" when they are performed, not that they must be performed in order for us to become acquainted with them at all. A person can become

* I argue in chapter 6 that directing one's activity toward an audience is an essential part of performance, although I concede that a person could perform for an absent audience.

acquainted with a play by reading it.* Similarly, some musicians can read scores silently, as other people read novels. Nevertheless, these works are intended to be performed, not merely to be read silently. Because they are intended to be performed, we could say that they include the idea of performance by way of intention and that in this sense the concept of performance is part of the concept of a work of performing art.

Let us digress briefly here to consider improvisation. Nowadays, improvisation is relatively uncommon, although some musicians do practice it. Jazz musicians, as everyone knows, use improvisation, and so do church organists, who must be able to improvise to fill portions of the service whose length is not known ahead of time. In the eighteenth and nineteenth centuries, improvisation was more widespread than it is today. Beethoven and Bach were legendary improvisers. Improvised performance is rare nowadays among classical musicians, but there are some who include it in their programs. The Venezuelan pianist Gabriela Montero offers entire concerts of improvisations on themes supplied by the audience, and Robert Levin is known for his improvisations of the cadenzas of classical concertos. Improvisation has been an important element in other performing arts than music. The Italian commedia dell' arte, depicted in the etchings in this book, used a combination of rehearsed routines and improvised dialogue.

Improvisation might seem to count as an exception to the separation I have been making between a work of performing art and a performance of that work, because in an improvisation the work appears to have no existence separate from the performance. In fact, however, the account I have offered does leave room for improvisation. I pointed out earlier that creating a work of performing art and performing it are separate activities, although a person can engage in both of them, as when a pianist composes and then performs her own sonata or a dancer choreographs her own ballet. Both these activities

* Because of this, plays can be regarded as works of literature as well as works of performing art. In this book, however, I treat them as works of performing art.

occur in improvisation also. What distinguishes improvisation is that they occur simultaneously. Creating the work occupies the same stretch of time as performing it; the creation, in this case, is not done ahead of time. Nevertheless, we can still make a distinction between the work and the performance.

Take musical improvisation. The music created in an improvisation is ordinarily performed only once, that is, it is given only one instantiation. But there is no necessity that this be the case; it could, in principle, be played again and instantiated a second time. Indeed, additional instances do occur when an improvisation is recorded. Every time the recording is played, it gives another instance of the music that was created in the improvisation. The *performance* was a single event, but the *music* can be heard over and over. The easiest way to preserve music created in an improvisation is to record it, but that is not the only possible way. The performer might memorize the work while improvising, and then play it again. Legend has it that Bach improvised the three-part ricercar in the *Musical Offering* and later wrote it down from memory.* Or a listener with an extraordinary ear and memory might learn a piece just from listening, and then play it or write it down. Mozart, famously, had this ability, and according to Abram Chasins, so did the great twentieth-century pianist Josef Hofmann.† I conclude that although improvisation is special in that the creation and the performance of a work occur simultaneously, we can still distinguish the work from a performance of the work. The work admits of numerous instances, even if it actually receives only one, whereas the performance is necessarily a unique event.

Works of performing art are not the only artworks that can be realized in numerous instances. The same is true of literary works such as novels. Novels are like works of performing art in that they are not physical objects, and they are not perceivable to the bodily senses. We become acquainted with a novel

* This example was suggested in a personal communication by Peter Kivy.

† *Speaking of Pianists* . . . (New York: Knopf, 1958), 16.

by reading a printed copy, but the novel itself is not the same as its copies, because destruction or loss of all the copies would not necessarily amount to destruction of the novel. Someone might know it from memory, and would still know it even if all copies were lost or destroyed, just as pianists who know the Fourth Ballade from memory could play it despite loss of the score. Knowing a novel from memory would be a remarkable feat, but examples are easily come by. In ancient Greece, the Homeric poems were passed on by oral tradition, and there were individuals – rhapsodes – who made a profession of reciting them from memory. In addition, there have been people who memorized the Bible. (Julien Sorel in *Le rouge et le noir* is a fictional example, but there have been real cases.) A novel, therefore, is not the same as its copies, any more than the Bible or the Homeric poems. Since a literary work is not a physical object and is not perceivable to the senses, it must be embodied in some perceptible form in order for us to become acquainted with it; that is to say, it must be given an instance. For the Homeric poems, in ancient Greece, that could mean being recited by a rhapsode whose recitation made the poem perceptible to the sense of hearing. Nowadays, almost all instances of literary works are printed copies that make the works available to the sense of sight.*

The instances I have described so far are all sequences of some kind. Instances of a novel are sequences of printed words, instances of works of music are sequences of sounds, and instances of works of choreography are sequences of

* As the text makes clear, works of literature can be made available in more than one way. The same holds for works of music, which can be made available through a score, perceptible to sight, or through sounds, perceptible to hearing. Which of these modes of access should count as an instance depends on which is the intended means of presenting the work to its audience. Works of music are intended to be heard, so the sounds, not the score, are the instance. Works of literature, nowadays, are normally intended to be read, not to be listened to, so their instances are sequences of printed words. But as the example of the Homeric poems makes clear, these conclusions are not matters of necessity, they can vary at different times in history. (I considered some of these points in "Philosophy of Piano Playing," pp. 302–3.)

movements. However, some artworks have instances that are not sequences. Etchings and other types of graphic art can have numerous instances. An etching is not the same thing as any of its individual prints. Each individual print is an instance of the etching, but a print is not a sequence. Therefore, it is not true for all artworks that admit of multiple instances that each individual instance is some kind of sequence, although that is the case in the performing arts, which are, after all, our concern here.

A work of performing art must receive an instance in order to be apprehended by its audience in the intended way, but, obviously, instances do not just happen, they are the result of human action. They have to be made on purpose. That is where the performer comes in. The performer *produces* or *makes* an instance of the work being performed. In the case of the Fourth Ballade, the performer is a pianist who makes the sounds that Chopin specified, one by one, in the proper order, by depressing the keys of a piano. For a work of choreography, the performer is a dancer who executes the proper bodily movements one after the other in the proper order. For a work of drama, the performer is an actor.

A performer produces an instance of a work, but the instance is not the same as the performance. Performance, as I shall use the term, is an *activity*, or a period of activity. In the case of a pianist, it is the activity of depressing keys on a piano to produce sound. An instance of a work of music is a series of sounds; the performance that produces those sounds is a series of human actions. The two occur simultaneously, but they are not identical. Human actions are bodily movements directed by intention. "Mental" activities such as deciding, paying attention, and the like are also properly described as human actions. Sounds, by contrast, are patterns of sound waves that travel through the air and give rise to the experience of hearing. Sounds are perceivable to the sense of hearing; a dancer's movements are perceivable to the sense of sight. But the activity of producing those sounds or movements is not perceivable, or at any rate it is perceivable only in part. We can perceive a pianist's fingers moving to depress the keys; bodily movement is perceivable. But performing is not mere bodily movement, it is human action, that is, bodily movement directed by intention. Intention is essential – mere movement without intention is not performing – but it is not perceivable to the senses. I conclude that the instance and the activity of producing it are not the same. The instance is a perceivable embodiment of the work, it is the work in a form available to one or more of the senses, whereas the activity of producing that instance – the performance – is a series of bodily movements directed by intention and it includes essential nonobservable elements. Both components of performing, the bodily movement and the intention that directs it, will be central topics throughout this book.

Performances are not enduring objects, they are events, as are actions. Like any other events, they occur, they end, and they are over. We may talk casually of repeating an action or a performance, but that is not really possible. We can't do the same individual action again, because every action occurs at a particular time and once it has occurred, that moment in time has past. All we can do is carry out another action similar to the first. A repeat performance is *another* performance. The product of the performance is an instance of the work performed, and it, too, whether it is a sequence of sounds or a sequence of bodily movements, is unique. Sound waves occur at a certain time and place and then they dissipate. We can produce similar sounds at another time or place, but we cannot repeat the numerically identical sounds. Likewise with movements. Performances, therefore, and the instances they produce, are not repeatable. Interpretations, on the other hand, can be repeated. A work of performing art can receive more than one instance under a particular interpretation, and it is possible, in principle, for different performers to give separate instances under the same interpretation.

The following definitions summarize the conclusions reached so far. A *work of performing art* is an artwork created with the intention that it be performed; performance is the intended means of making the work available to an audience.

An *instance* is an individual realization of a work of performing art in an appropriate medium perceivable to one or more of the senses. *Interpretation* refers to the ways in which two instances of a single work may differ from one another while remaining instances of the same work. *Artistic performance* is the intentional activity of producing an instance of a work of performing art, with the purpose of making that work available to an audience.

Every performer is necessarily an interpreter of the work being performed. This goes counter to what some people assume to be the goal of a performance. The ideal performance, they say, is one in which the performer disappears completely, becoming transparent, as it were, and presenting the work "in itself," without any intermediary. Now, in one sense this does happen: the performer does set the actual work before the audience, as we saw earlier when we observed that the Fourth Ballade is fully present in each of its instances. But it does not follow that the work is or could be presented *uninterpreted*. That is not merely an ideal unattainable in practice, it is a conceptual impossibility. The reason is that although every instance of a work of performing art does present the work itself, and in that way sets it before the audience, it necessarily presents it under an interpretation, because the score or script underdetermines every detail of every instance that complies with it. In a work of music, every note could be played slightly louder or softer, every portion could go slightly faster or slower, there could be expressive pauses – or not – and all of these variants could still comply with the score. Similarly, in a work of dance or drama, a particular bodily movement or a particular vocal inflection may comply with the instructions for the dance or the script of the play, but it is always possible to imagine a slightly different movement or a different vocal inflection that would comply also. Consequently, every instance of a work of performing art offers only one of the ways the work can be realized; other instances could be different.

Now, according to the definition offered earlier, respects in which two instances differ from each other are differences of interpretation. Therefore, since every instance is made up of elements that could have been otherwise, every instance is under some interpretation or other. When a performer produces an instance, every part of it can be seen as the result of a choice among possibilities, which means that the performer chooses among interpretations. He may make these choices consciously, or he may not, but if he does not choose consciously, he still chooses by default, since each detail of the work he presents will have a definite character that could have been otherwise. If a performer does choose consciously, he is deciding exactly how he wants the work to go. When he has reached clear conclusions about that, we can say that he knows how he wants the work to go, or, equivalently, that he has an interpretation in mind.

It appears to follow from the foregoing discussion that the performer has two principal tasks: 1) to produce an instance of the work and 2) to develop an interpretation, that is, to decide exactly how he wants the work to go, and to verify that the instance he produces does realize his intended interpretation.

An obvious question at this point is: How do motion, emotion, and love, the trio of concepts that provide the title of this book, illuminate these tasks of the performer? Anticipating a bit, and very roughly, we shall see that motion pertains mainly to the first of the performer's tasks, the production of an instance, and emotion to the second, the development of an interpretation. The role of love is less immediately clear, and for the moment I shall simply assert without argument that love is a prerequisite for the proper exercise of the other two tasks. It provides a context in which motion and emotion can operate effectively. In the remainder of this introductory chapter I briefly consider motion, emotion, and love, showing why each of them is crucial in artistic performance and why they merit the extended treatment I propose to give them.

Motion

When Jack descended the beanstalk he brought with him a golden harp, stolen from the giant in the sky. He set it on a table, said, "Play!" and it played beautiful music. That was all he had to do. He did not have to *learn* to play the golden harp or spend hours practicing. There was no "technique" of golden-harp playing. That is because his harp was a magic harp. Ordinary musical instruments do not respond to verbal commands or wishful thinking. You can't say, "Play!" and expect music to emerge; you have to do something to the instruments – touch them, pluck them, hit them, blow into them – to make sound. But touching, plucking, hitting, and blowing are bodily movements; that is, we make music by moving our bodies. This point is not controversial or doubtful; it is perfectly evident that musicians produce sound by physically manipulating their instruments. Actors and dancers likewise move their bodies to perform; that their activity consists of bodily movement is even more obvious than it is for musicians. Actors and dancers know this, and they consciously train movement. In this they differ from many musicians, who, although they must move their bodies to play or sing, do not ordinarily train movement as movement. Of course, teachers of instrumental technique do offer advice about what movements to use for different effects, and musicians practice those movements, repeat them to make habits of them, and refine them to achieve subtlety and variety. Many musicians also practice technical exercises.

Nevertheless, musicians do not ordinarily think of themselves as movers – much less, at any rate, than actors or dancers do. If you ask a group of musicians to characterize their professional activity by filling in the blank in this sentence: "Musicians ________ for a living," you find that they rarely offer a verb describing physical movement. Actors and dancers are quicker to offer movement verbs. Perhaps the reason musicians tend not to think of their activity in terms of movement is that they communicate through sound, not directly through bodily movement the way actors and dancers do. Musicians do move, and the quality of their movement is intimately connected to the quality of the sound they produce, but since it is the sound, not the movement, that *is* the music, they may pay less attention to the movements that produce the sound. Whether or not that is the correct explanation, the fact remains that many musicians do not think of their music-making as movement involving the entire body, and they admit, if asked, that they are unaware of their bodies as they play.

That all performers, musicians as well as dancers and actors, perform by moving their bodies may not seem to be especially consequential; it is, one might think, merely an obvious but not very important fact. On the contrary, it is immensely important, both theoretically and practically. Just consider: *everything* performers do, including speaking and singing, they do by moving their bodies. Bodily movement is their artistic medium. Therefore it ought not to be a surprise that much of this book is a sustained attempt to explore implications of the seemingly commonplace observation that performers perform by moving their bodies. Recognizing that performance consists of bodily movement and focusing on movement both in itself and in relation to the artistic or emotional content of the work alters a person's practicing and performing. Chapter 2 introduces the concept of the body map to show how the way we think of ourselves, even if our thoughts are not consciously formulated, determines the way we move. A Body Mapping* approach, in which a performer examines his body map and modifies it as necessary to make it consistent with his actual anatomical structure, is a powerful tool for performers, even for those who, like dancers, already do think of themselves moving their bodies to perform. The approach improves movement, and it can help performers avoid or recover from stress injury.

The body map is a physiological reality as well as a pedagogical tool, and chapter 3 treats it in relation to recent discoveries about the way the brain works and the way it changes throughout our lives. Such topics may seem to be a digression with little practical relevance for performers, but they have implications for rehearsing and practicing. Indeed, as a pianist I believe that these neurological discoveries have more to tell us about how to play, practice, perform, and teach than does much traditional piano pedagogy, rooted in nineteenth-century misconceptions about the body, which still occasionally passes for wisdom. After all, when we practice and rehearse we are teaching ourselves the movements that we will use in performance, and since the body map governs movement, a person's body map will influence this process, whether the person is aware of it or not. Knowing something about the body map and its foundation in the brain can make practicing and rehearsing far more efficient and effective and improve the quality of performance. I take up practicing—the training of movement—in chapter 4, which builds on the conclusions from chapters 2 and 3 to explain more fully the relation of voluntary movement to the body map that governs it.

* The expression "body map," which I define in chapter 2, is common to many disciplines; neurophysiologists, for example, may speak of the body map. "Body Mapping" (upper case) refers specifically to a pedagogical approach in which a person examines and refines his body map, and it is a proprietary term of Andover Educators.

Although performance is movement, it is not *mere* movement. A vivid way to bring this out is to consider the pianola, a piano-playing machine popular around 1900. The pianola had felt-covered "fingers" that extended over the keyboard of an ordinary piano. Activated by a pneumatic system in the pianola, the "fingers" depressed the keys of the piano. Apparently, the pianola could bring sounds from the piano that were remarkably similar to the sounds produced by the famous pianists who recorded for it, which means that it depressed the keys by movements essentially identical, from the piano's point of view, to the movements of a pianist. But however closely the sounds resembled those of a pianist, we have not the slightest inclination to say that the pianola *performed* the music. It is easy to construct analogous examples for dance and drama. Imagine a computer-driven mechanical doll that could move and produce words. However much the doll looked and moved like a dancer or an actor, even if it could be programmed to dance Odette/Odile or enact the role of King Lear, its movement, I submit, would not count as a performance.

It is obvious why neither the movement of a pianola nor the movement of a mechanical doll would be a performance. Performance requires *voluntary* movement. The movement must be an *action*. Involuntary or automatic or mechanical movement is not performing. If we realized, watching our mechanical doll, that it was a doll we were watching, we might admire the skill of whoever made it, but we would not say that the doll was performing. Likewise, if we learned that a pianist was playing in a drug-induced or hypnotic trance, with no awareness of what she was doing and (therefore) no conscious control or choice, we would deny that she was performing the music. Moving mindlessly, automatically, or involuntarily is not performing.

The chapters on motion may seem to pertain more to performers than to those in the audience, who observe the movement but do not engage in it. But all of us, whether we are performers or not, move our bodies constantly in our daily lives. We move to accomplish various tasks, some easy, some difficult, some requiring skill, and some, like using the computer, that are highly repetitive and carry the risk of injury if done improperly. We sometimes move carefully, with full attention, and sometimes casually or automatically, with our minds elsewhere. Particularly in connection with exacting or repetitive tasks, we can profitably apply the information in the chapters on motion to our daily activities, whether our movement has an artistic purpose or not.

Emotion

Many works of performing art have an expressive or emotional content, and it seems plausible that the goal of performing such works would be to enable the audience to experience the feelings or emotions they express. Some works bring about emotions that have names, like pity and fear, which Aristotle claimed were the appropriate emotions for tragedy, but sometimes, especially in the case of music and dance, which are less overtly descriptive than drama, the response is not an emotion that can be named. Indeed, it is not clear that "emotion" is always the best word to use in describing the response to a work. Sometimes people's responses are like exclamations—"How beautiful!" Sometimes they are physical, as when people find tears in their eyes at a fine performance although they are not really inclined to weep, and sometimes they seem more abstract than emotional, as when we contemplate the structure of a fugue by Bach or a ballet by Balanchine. Despite these caveats, let us take as our point of departure the idea that works of performing art generate a response in their audience that includes, or may include, an element of emotion or feeling.

Generating a response does not appear to be just an accidental by-product of performing, but to be essential; it is what performances are *for*. But simply producing an instance may not be sufficient to generate a response. A pianist might play "perfectly"—play all the notes and follow all the instructions in the score—and yet fail to bring about any significant feeling in the audience. Similarly, a dancer might give a "perfect" performance as the White Swan—she flawlessly executes all the movements—but miss the pathos and tragedy that most people think the role should evoke. Now, failure to bring about a response is a serious flaw. Someone who says of a performance that "it left me cold" or "I was unmoved" is not calling attention to an inconsequential detail; on the contrary, the complaint is fundamental. The person is saying, in effect, that the performance was poor, that the performer did not do the job. Complaints such as those do occur, yet, by hypothesis, the performer in these examples is following the instructions in the score or script, thereby producing an instance of the work. So what is missing?

To see what is missing we must take a detour. For the problem is not that the performer has neglected to include some particular ingredient which, when added, will yield a good performance. The problem lies rather in the way I have described the situation. To speak, as I have been doing, of an artwork "generating a response" is not acceptable, even though we often hear it and similar expressions. People say that artworks "produce," or "generate," or "evoke," or "cause" feelings, or that they "speak" to the audience. Such expressions seem to imply that all the audience need do is receive the message, or experience the feeling, thus assuming a largely passive role. It is up to the artwork (aided, in the case of performing art, by the performer) to bring about a response. But this is not an illuminating way to think of the situation. It likens art appreciation to an exercise in behaviorist psychology, with the artwork serving as a stimulus and the audience responding to the stimulus. On such a view, if a performance is ineffective it means that the performer should have been more expressive (so as to give a more effective stimulus) or the audience should have been more receptive (so as to have the proper response). We need to approach the question differently. I shall argue that the performer *uses* emotion and feeling to prepare and present the work of performing art, and the audience likewise uses emotion and feeling to apprehend it.

Let us reject the model of stimulus and response and substitute the model of sharing, or, better and more simply, of setting the artwork before the audience. We can still say—because it is clearly true—that many artworks have emotional content, but the performer does not present that content as if to generate (or stimulate) a response, instead he presents the artwork as something to be aesthetically appraised. The audience uses feeling as one tool to make that appraisal, and the result, sometimes, is an emotional experience for the audience. To see that this differs profoundly from the stimulus/response model, we must consider more closely what is involved in setting a work of performing art before an audience.

Clearly, to set the work before the audience the performer must produce an instance of it. But as we saw earlier, every instance is necessarily under some interpretation or other. Therefore, the performer must settle on an interpretation, which amounts to deciding exactly how he thinks the work should go. How does he decide how it should go? There is no brief or fully comprehensive answer. He starts, of course, with the score or the script, but does not stop there. He may read critical articles or analyses, he may receive advice or comments from colleagues or directors or audience members. Any of these things may be helpful, but none of them is necessary, nor are they separately or jointly sufficient to ensure a good performance.

What *is* necessary is that the performer examine the work, study it, develop and refine his grasp of what it means or symbolizes or expresses and this cultivated apprehension is what he attempts, by performing, to set before his audience. It is here, in his coming to understand the work, that emotion and feeling enter the picture. The performer uses emotion and feeling to arrive at an interpretation. But he uses them in a special way. He does not simply bathe in an emotional state, and imagine that the authenticity of his feeling will somehow be transmitted, nor does he receive feelings passively. He uses his feelings to apprehend the work and guide him to a satisfying interpretation. When the performer examines the work this way, he is approaching it aesthetically, and as Nelson Goodman pointed out,

> In aesthetic experience the *emotions function cognitively.* The work of art is apprehended through the feelings as well as through the senses. . . . Emotion in aesthetic experience is a means of discerning what properties a work has and expresses. . . . Cognitive use [of emotions] involves discriminating and relating them in order to gauge and grasp the work and integrate it with the rest of our experience and the world"*

There is a further complication. The performer makes cognitive use of emotion and feeling on two levels. When he works out an interpretation, an understanding of how he wants the work to go, he is forming an intention. But intentions are not always realized; they can fail. He must therefore take an additional step, and appraise the success of his movement in realizing his intention. To do that, he must contemplate his activity from the perspective of the audience. He must occupy the position of the audience even while attending to the movements that constitute his performance. He must learn to relate his movements to their effects and evaluate them from that point of view. This is a vital part of practicing and rehearsing, and every performer, even in the solitude of the practice room or the rehearsal studio, needs to have it constantly in mind. Dancers are aware of this—dance studios have enormous mirrors so that the dancers can appraise the effect of their movements. In examining his work from the point of view of the audience the performer is evaluating it aesthetically; he uses the feelings his activity produces to evaluate that activity and inform him of the success or shortcoming of what he is doing. This is a second case of using emotions cognitively. Thus, performers use feelings and emotions on two levels, once to reach an understanding of the work and again to evaluate their realization of that understanding.

* *Languages of Art* (London: Oxford University Press, 1969), p. 248. Italics in original.

If the performer arrives at an intention about how the work should go, and if he executes movements that realize his intention, then he has set the work before the audience, under the interpretation he had in mind. This does not guarantee that the audience will be appropriately moved. *That* depends on the audience apprehending the work. It becomes the audience's turn to engage in aesthetic appraisal, using *its* feelings cognitively to understand and experience the work. To properly apprehend the work, a member of the audience cannot be a passive recipient, but must actively engage his mind and feelings. Nelson Goodman articulated the insight that emotions function cognitively in aesthetic experience in *Languages of Art*. That book appeared in 1968, so the insight is not exactly new. Nevertheless, I believe it is unfamiliar to many people, and perhaps it seems counterintuitive. I shall explore it further, with arguments and examples, in chapter 5.

Love

It might seem that if a performer produces an instance of a work under the interpretation he intends, his job is finished and the rest is up to the audience. The audience may embrace the work and the performer, or not, but in either case the performer, having done his job, is off the hook. In fact, the situation is more complex. The purpose of a performance is that the feelings expressed by the artwork become part of the selves, that is, part of the experience of the audience. This involves an intent on the part of the performer to communicate, to share, which means that performance is directed outward, it is action done *for* another.

Not only does the performer perform for the benefit of the audience, the audience must feel that such is the case; it must feel included. The performer's intentions in this regard are communicated, in subtle ways to be sure, but the subtlety of the communication does not make it any less important. Successful performance depends very much on the audience feeling that the activity on the stage is aimed at *it,* not merely offered impersonally as an object of contemplation.

Not only does the performer communicate with the audience, the audience also communicates with the performer, as any actor will attest who has performed the same role on different nights for different audiences. Therefore, the relationship of performer and audience is not simply that of giver and recipient, it is an *interaction*. This interaction turns out to include several features that are also characteristic of loving relationships: other-directed action, mutual acceptance, self-exposure, and reciprocity. I believe this analogy with loving relationships should be taken seriously; I claim that there exists—or should exist—a love affair of sorts between performer and audience.

Love enters the picture in other ways as well. It is essential in the relation of performers to one another in an ensemble and also in the relation of a performer with himself, where it takes the form of self-love or self-esteem. I am not referring to conceitedness or arrogance, but to the sense of security within himself that a performer must have if he is to take his responses and feelings seriously and make them the basis of his communication with the audience. Doing so is essential if his performance is to be other than cold and lifeless, yet it requires courage and a sense of self-worth, which I consider to be a kind of self-love.

I shall explore the concept of love in chapter 6, but we can see already that love is not a peripheral or inessential ingredient in performance. It is more like a prerequisite for the effective deployment of all the topics covered under motion and emotion—it provides a context in which they can function. It is vital for the success of a performance; motion and emotion are empty without it.

The argument of chapters 3–6 will put us in a position, in chapter 7, to address the questions raised earlier about the artistic status of performers. Although performers are sometimes regarded as mere interpreters, not creative in their own right, and are said to be subservient to, or in the service of, the artists whose works they perform, I argue that they are more than just interpreters. It is inappropriate to think of them "serving" the artists whose works they perform, or, if they can in one sense be said to serve those artists, that is not all they do, nor is it the most important thing they do. Performers are creative artists in as true and legitimate a sense as any other artists, and I make clear what their artworks are.

In chapter 8, I show how the artworks of performers have a relation to the activity of producing them that is different from what we find in nonperforming art, and because of that they offer a kind of artistic experience unavailable anywhere else. I ultimately claim that in artistic performance the foundations of consciousness are shaped into an artwork, although that claim is opaque without the preparation of the intervening chapters. Finally, I conclude – though once again the conclusion depends on the intervening chapters – that performance offers an experience more intense and more coherent than the rest of ordinary life; our experience is shaped into an artwork, and performance makes art out of the conditions of human existence.

Bello Sguardo.
Couiello.

2 • *Motion I: The Body Map*

Everything performers do, they do by moving their bodies. But although performance is movement, it is not just any kind of movement. Performing must be voluntary and intentional; reflex or involuntary movements are not performing. For the moment, we can characterize intentional movement as movement guided by thought. Most of the time, the thought that guides our intentional movements is just the simple awareness of the goal or purpose of the movement. We think of "opening the door" or "drinking coffee," not about the bodily movements that go into those actions. To open the door, I merely reach out and open it; I don't consciously think, "Now I need to extend my arm, now I need to flex my fingers to grasp the doorknob, now I need to rotate my forearm to turn it," even though I must do those things to open the door. I *can* think those things, and I can do them intentionally, but usually I don't.

A casual attitude toward movement, under which we move our bodies without attending to the exact manner in which we do it, is sufficient for most daily activities but may not do for highly repetitive activities or tasks requiring refined, precise movements. Performers engage for hours every day in some of the most complex and demanding physical movements of which humans are capable. They cannot afford to take a casual attitude. They must pay close attention to their bodies, their movement, the relation between thought and action, and the way the structure of the body and its possibilities of movement relate to conscious intention. So let us look a little more closely at how I open the door.

We could call the movements that go into opening the door—extending my arm, flexing my fingers around the handle, and so on—the *cause* of the door opening. Equivalently, we could say that naming those movements amounts to explaining "how to open a door," since if someone could extend his arm, flex his fingers, and the rest, but happened not to know how to open a door, I could explain to him how to open the door by saying, "First extend your arm to bring your hand to the handle, now flex your fingers around the handle," and so on. Each of those movements, as I mentioned, is something I can do as a voluntary action. I can extend my arm whenever I wish; likewise I can flex my fingers. But suppose I try to explain *those* actions in the same way I explained how to open the door. What is my answer to "how do you go about extending your arm?" I can't give an analogous explanation. I can give a list of voluntary movements that bring about the opening of the door, but I can't give a list of voluntary movements that bring about the extending of my arm. I can extend my arm whenever I wish; I may say that I "know how" to extend my arm; but I don't know how in the sense of being able to explain how I do it, or teach it to someone who can't do it. How does it happen, then, that I have the capacity voluntarily to extend my arm? The answer is: because I have a body map.

What is the body map? We can illuminate it as follows, using a different example. Imagine yourself at your desk with a cup of coffee at hand. Occasionally, you sip your coffee. Sipping coffee is something you do often. You can do it while paying only partial attention, without interrupting your work. Nevertheless, it requires coordinated movements of many parts of the body. Consider what happens. You reach out by extending your arm at the shoulder and elbow joints, your hand approaches the cup, your fingers grasp the handle. Bringing the cup to your lips requires movements at the wrist, elbow, and shoulder joints different from those of reaching and grasping. If the cup is far enough away that you must incline your body to reach it, then grasping it with your arm extended and bringing it to your lips will require coordinated postural adjustments throughout your torso. Each of these movements requires the activation of appropriate muscles, in the proper sequence, and the simultaneous release of others. Physiologically, the process is enormously complex, but none of the components just mentioned – the simultaneous activation and release of appropriate muscles – is anything you consciously *do*. Your brain, outside your conscious awareness, sends the appropriate neural signals to the various muscles. To do that, however, it requires information about the body: information about the size of the body and its parts, how the parts connect to each other, and how they can move. Possessing that information, it can direct the complex movements of sipping coffee. The essential point for us is this: the brain contains information about the structure, size, and function of the body and its parts. That information, used to govern movement, is what I am calling the *body map*. We are not directly aware of our body maps, although, as I shall explain, we can discover their contents, but whether we are conscious of them or not, we clearly do possess body maps. That my brain contains a body map is proven by the fact that I can act. I can move my body, therefore whatever information my brain requires to enable me to move my body must be present in it.

In describing the body map as "information in the brain, used to govern movement," the qualification "used to govern movement" is vital because the brain also contains information about the body that is *not* used to govern movement. For example, an anatomist knows a lot about the body and this information is stored in his brain. But the information may simply be factual knowledge, not used to govern movement. If the anatomist does not use his body efficiently, despite his store of accurate information about the body, then some of the information contained in his brain is not used to govern movement, and in that case, according to the concept of "body map" I have offered, the information is not part of his body map, even though it is about his body and is contained in his brain.

The brain must possess the proper information about the body *before* a person can act in a particular situation. This is clear because people can perform actions they've never performed in the past and get them right the first time. If I see a new, oddly designed coffee cup, I don't have to practice picking it up before I can drink from it, I can do that immediately. If I encounter a ditch across my path I can step over it or jump across it, even though I may never have encountered a ditch of that precise width before. In daily life we constantly perform actions that are not exact replicas of previous actions, but we couldn't perform them if our brains didn't possess appropriate information about how the body works. Nevertheless, we are not born with that information. Babies have to practice such activities as reaching out, touching things, picking things up. They are developing their body maps as they do this. With each movement they are exploring their bodies, discovering the structure, size, and function of the various parts. When this information is stored, it becomes a body map that can guide future movements.

The concept of the body map as I have presented it requires some refinement. There is a problem with describing the body map as "information in the brain used to govern movement," because the word "information" suggests truth or accuracy. But the brain does not always direct movement according to accurate information. Sometimes it directs movement according to an inadequate, inaccurate, or mistaken assessment of the body. How this can happen will emerge as we proceed; for the moment it is enough to use the word "representation" in place of "information." A representation, unlike a piece of information, can be true or false, so the word "representation" leaves open the question whether the representation is accurate. I shall therefore modify my definition of the body map, and call it the "representation in the brain that governs movement."

Taking a Body Mapping approach to movement and the training of movement is a powerful tool for performers and teachers. The approach involves systematically examining the content of one's self-representation, comparing that content with anatomical reality, correcting any inaccuracy, and relating that revised self-image to one's actual movement. Even though the body map is not an object of conscious awareness, there are ways to discover and to modify it. Developing an accurate, adequate body map makes practicing and training far more efficient and effective. It helps overcome technical and expressive limitations, and improves every aspect of performance. Dancers and actors do consciously train movement, but they nevertheless confront problems that can be addressed by improving the body map. Musicians, in general, are less attentive to movement as such than actors or dancers and they are consequently less likely to know how to attend to the overall quality of their movement—its ease and freedom from tension. Performers who are inattentive to their quality of movement can easily develop inefficient habits that affect their performance and put them at risk for stress injuries like tendonitis and carpal tunnel syndrome. Stress injuries are far more common among performers than many people realize, but most of the stress injuries that plague performers are avoidable and curable. Developing an accurate, adequate body map enables performers to avoid injuries, or once injured, to recover.

That the concept of the body map should be as useful as I have claimed may seem surprising, even implausible. In fact, it is not implausible at all. I shall show this by means of an extended example. The example will make clear on an intuitive level how the body map develops, how a body map can be inaccurate or inadequate and lead to problems, and how correcting the map can resolve the problems. Since one purpose of the example is to let you experience the way thinking affects the quality of movement, I urge you to try the following:

Allow your hand to hang loosely at your side. Then raise your hand by bending your arm at the elbow joint. Move your hand up and down that way several times. If you watch your hand as you move it up and down, you see that your hand and forearm move together, the forearm remains straight and pivots at the elbow joint. What you see is not surprising. It is consistent with what I presume you believe about the structure of your arm, namely that there are rigid bones in your forearm, they attach to your upper arm bone at the elbow, and the movement of bending your arm occurs at the elbow joint. Besides being consistent with your beliefs, what you see reflects the facts of your anatomy. There *are* rigid bones in your forearm, they *do* attach to your upper arm bone at the elbow, and the motion of bending your arm *does* occur at the elbow joint.

But what if the facts were otherwise? For example, imagine an arm that does not have a rigid upper arm bone joined at the elbow to rigid forearm bones; instead, it has a single long bone extending from shoulder to wrist, part of which–the part corresponding to the forearm–is flexible, made of cartilage, perhaps, instead of bone. Someone with an arm like that would not bend his arm just at the elbow, the way we do, he would bend the entire forearm portion, making it into a curve, like a banana. He would raise his hand by *bending his forearm*, not by flexing at the elbow joint. Well, imagine that you have an arm like that. Raise your hand again, but this time, as you raise your hand, try to bend your entire forearm all along its length. Do that several times and notice how it feels. You agree, I expect, that it feels different from simply bending your elbow joint as you normally do. It feels like more work. It is probably slower as well. Move your forearm back and forth in the ordinary way, without trying to bend it into the shape of a banana, and contrast that feeling with how it feels when you do try to bend it into a banana. Alternate the two ways of moving your arm, attending to the different feelings. Notice that although they *feel* different, the two ways of moving may not *look* very different. A casual observer might not be able to tell whether or not you were trying to bend your forearm into a banana (although a trained observer could probably see the difference).

Obviously, you do not change your anatomy if you think that your entire forearm bends and try to move it that way. What you do is activate the muscles that *would* bend it that way, were it flexible. In other words, thinking of bending your forearm into a banana causes you to activate certain muscles in addition to the ones needed just to flex at the elbow joint. It causes you to work harder, to move with tension instead of ease, which is to say that it changes the *quality* of your movement. From this example it is clear—and this is an important point—that the way we think of our structure affects the quality of our movement. This can be true even when the outward appearance is unrevealing. That is, two movements, one governed by an accurate body map and the other by an inaccurate map, might be of very different quality, one free and the other tense, and yet they could appear similar to an observer.

I have been supposing in this discussion that you have a choice: you can move your forearm in the ordinary way, or you can try to bend it into a banana. In addition, you know which of those movements you are intending and you can compare one with the other. What makes this possible is that both ways of moving are in your repertoire and you can switch from one to the other. But what if that were not the case? What if you *only* thought of your forearm as flexible, and *always* moved it with the extra effort of trying to bend it into a banana? In that case, the movement of trying to bend your forearm into a banana would be your ordinary movement and would just feel normal. Since you would have nothing to compare it with, you wouldn't think of it as an unusual way of moving, to you it would just be "moving my arm." You would be activating more muscles than necessary merely to move your arm, but you wouldn't know that or think of your arm as tense. It wouldn't occur to you to ask whether you were moving your arm with tension or not.

The example I have offered may seem far-fetched, but the situation I am describing is actually very common. Many people habitually move their bodies in ways that involve unnecessary tension; sometimes it's as if they were trying to move in anatomically impossible ways, as in the example we are considering. Of course, people do not consciously try to defy their anatomy. But we do not learn to move by studying anatomy books, we learn by doing. We try out various movements to discover which ones get a desired result. We imitate what we see around us. We are surrounded by good and bad examples, and consciously or unconsciously we adopt what we see in our family, our friends, and the rest of the population, which becomes the basis of our movement. Sometimes people develop peculiar habits. Barbara Conable, an Alexander teacher who has worked with many injured musicians, describes the case of a woman who patterned the movement of her head on that of her beloved childhood Barbie doll.* Since human heads do not connect to human bodies the way Barbie heads connect to Barbie bodies, the result, for this woman, was a pain in the neck. My example of a person moving his arm by trying to bend the entire forearm may be fiction, but it is not unrealistic. Indeed, experiments by Jaron Lanier have shown that, stimulated by virtual reality techniques, people's brains can adapt to even stranger self-representations than these – oneself with lobster legs sprouting from one's body, for example.†

Suppose, then, that when you move your forearm you always try to bend it into a banana. Perhaps, like the woman with her Barbie doll, you once had a plastic doll whose arms were flexible not just at the joints but along their entire length, and you came to believe – or to wish – that human arms moved the same way. So you began, quite unaware, to direct movement according to that representation. Eventually you developed a fixed habit, and now, whenever you bend your elbow, you engage the muscles that would bend your forearm, were it flexible, into the shape of a banana. We could say that you have "mapped your forearm from your plastic doll," or that you have "mismapped your forearm as a banana."

Mismapping your forearm that way could be perfectly benign. You could go through life with that mismapping and never encounter any problems, but it would depend on your activities, on how often and for what tasks you bent your arm.

* *How to Learn the Alexander Technique* (Portland, OR: Andover Press, 3rd ed. 1995), 38.

† Lanier's work is described, without documentation, by Sandra and Matthew Blakeslee in *The Body Has a Mind of Its Own* (New York: Random House, 2007), 149–51.

If you only bent your arm to accomplish ordinary daily actions, the mismapping might never become an issue, but under other conditions it could be harmful. Suppose, therefore, that you take up juggling, which requires frequent rapid bending at the elbow. With the enthusiasm of a convert, you practice diligently every day, always, of course, with this unconscious mismapping of your forearm, and therefore always flexing your elbow with tension. After some weeks or months, you notice that your arm is sore. But you don't think much of it. Perhaps you say to yourself, "No pain, no gain," and reflect proudly that the pain in your arm is proof of your dedication. Perhaps you recall that your arm has been sore in the past after episodes of hammering or gardening but recovered in a few days. So you continue to juggle.

Your arm feels worse. Weeks go by and it doesn't get any better. You consult a doctor, who examines your arm. Perhaps he takes an X-ray and runs some tests. Then he says, "Well, there's really nothing wrong with your arm. You've probably got a bit of tendonitis. Give it a rest for while. Take an anti-inflammatory if it gets bad." He sees you out and his receptionist says, "That will be two hundred dollars."

What the doctor told you is true. There isn't anything medically wrong with your arm. That is, you're not ill, you haven't suffered traumatic injury, and you do have tendonitis. Of course, you knew all that, or at least suspected it, before consulting the doctor. Nevertheless, you feel reassured. You go home, take some pills, rest over the weekend, and continue to juggle.

A few weeks later, your arm is as bad as ever so you go back to the doctor. He offers the same diagnosis as before. Perhaps he advises longer rest, or physical therapy. Then he says, "Maybe you should give up juggling. Find another hobby." You are aghast. Give up juggling? Out of the question! Juggling has become essential to your life. So you consult another doctor. The second doctor says much the same thing as the first. Discouraged, you look elsewhere. You consult a chiropractor. Then an acupuncturist. Then a physical therapist, a naturopath, a psychologist, a nutritionist. None of them gives you lasting relief, and after a while you are desperate enough to try anything—hypnosis, faith healing, aroma therapy, psychics, reflexology, magnets in your shoes. Anything. You have become a credulous patron of any outlandish quackery.

The scenario I have sketched will seem distressingly familiar to any musician—or any friend or relative of a musician—who has been injured. But the cause of your tendonitis and the reason for its persistence are perfectly obvious. Your tendonitis is caused by tension in a repetitive activity that you engage in for hours every day, week after week. But notice—and this is important—the cause of the injury is not *juggling*. Many jugglers never encounter any problems. The cause of the injury is the *way* you juggle, not the activity itself. Nor does your injury come from juggling *too much*. It is misleading to describe your problem, or performers' injuries in general, as an *overuse* injury. Musicians (and computer users, writers, and others) do not become injured from playing (or typing or writing) *too much* but from playing (or typing or writing) *incorrectly*, where "incorrectly" means "using movements unsuited to the demands of the task."

The last point is worth a digression, since people often describe musicians' injuries as "overuse injuries," which is unfortunate since it suggests that what the musician needs to do to recover is play less. But merely cutting back doesn't usually work very well. Injured musicians need to change the way they play, not just the amount. That is not to say that there are no such things as overuse injuries. Some tasks, like lifting fifty-pound bags of flour, require a lot of muscular exertion, and there is doubtless a limit to how often or for how long a person can do them safely. Exceeding that limit could appropriately be called "overuse," and if exceeding the limit led to injury, the injury could be called an "overuse injury." Other tasks, however, like playing a musical instrument, or writing, or using a computer, are not like that. Those tasks are repetitive, but require very little force. If a person uses appropriate movements—tension-free movements that permit a high rate of repetition—such tasks can be performed with no limits of time.

Returning to our example: You have tendonitis because you have undertaken a repetitive activity that requires frequent bending of your elbow, and every time you bend your elbow your brain directs a movement that involves tension throughout your forearm. The reason your tendonitis persists is that the cause has never been addressed. No one has said, "Your arm hurts because you try to bend your entire forearm. Stop thinking of it as flexible. Think of it as it really is: rigid bones in the forearm connected to a rigid upper arm bone, with motion at the elbow joint. You'll move differently and it will stop hurting." Equivalently, someone could say, "You've mismapped your elbow joint and the movement of your forearm. Correct the map, and you'll bend your elbow differently, without tension. It may *look* much the same, but you'll be moving it without tensing the muscles in your forearm, and your tendonitis will heal."

Granted, it would require a perceptive teacher to recognize that you've mismapped the motion of the forearm and elbow joint. Unfortunately, few musicians and teachers—and few physical therapists, for that matter—are trained to look at movement from this point of view. And even after the mismapping has been pointed out and you've experienced a way to move your forearm without tension, new movements may not replace the old ones immediately. Most likely, you'll have to be vigilantly attentive to your movement for a while, until new movements become habits—that is, until the new movements become sufficiently established in your brain to replace the body map that dictated bending your entire forearm. When that happens, you will have a revised body map that will dictate movement in accord with your actual structure instead of movement that your structure makes impossible.

The example I have offered is fanciful in the sense that I do not know whether anyone has ever actually mismapped his arm in the particular way I have described, but it does illustrate the general pattern of musicians' injuries. Almost all musicians' injuries can be regarded as movement problems: they come from moving with tension in a repetitive activity. But since the body map directs the way we move, we can equally well describe such injuries as mapping errors–mistaken representation of the structure, size, or function of the body and its parts. When the map is corrected to conform to anatomical reality, the injury resolves. Conversely, any treatment of injury that does not change the body map–that is, any treatment that does not identify the movements that caused the injury and replace them with better movements to accomplish the same task–is ineffective. Nevertheless, you would doubtless find it odd, even bizarre, if you came to me, your arm sore from juggling, and I said, "You're in pain because you've mismapped your forearm." After all, you're probably not aware of ever having mapped your forearm at all, so what can it mean to say that you've *mis*mapped it?

Although the brain directs movement according to an internal representation, the representation needn't be conscious. You may not consciously think of bending your entire forearm, even if that's how you characteristically move it. Now, in our example the representation that guides your movement, besides being unconscious, is false. That is, it represents your forearm bending even though your forearm cannot actually do that. Moreover, you may know intellectually that bones are rigid structures that do not bend. Thus, it is possible for the representation that guides your movement to be wrong even though your conscious understanding of your anatomy is correct. The woman who patterned her movement on her Barbie doll may have known perfectly well, in her conscious mind, the differences between human and Barbie anatomy, but she still had a pain in the neck.

We must, therefore, consider the body map in relation to conscious awareness, and observe, first of all, that the body map is not an object of conscious awareness. The instructions in my brain that dictate how I actually do move my arm constitute my body map, but what I am aware of when I move my arm is just my arm moving, not the instructions in my brain that activate the muscles that move my arm. Now, when I move my arm I may be aware of its movement, and, in addition, I

probably have some beliefs about the structure of my arm and how it moves. If my conscious beliefs about how my arm moves coincide with the instructions in my brain that direct my movement, then my beliefs can be said to be consistent with my body map, and my body map, though I am not directly conscious of it, can be said, in turn, to be consistent with my conscious belief. But this need not always be the case. My conscious beliefs may stand in opposition to my body map – that is, my conscious beliefs about the structure and movement of my body may not coincide with the way my brain actually directs my movement. An example would be a person with accurate knowledge of anatomy and correct anatomical understanding of what counts as tension-free movement, who nevertheless moves badly. In that case, the person's conscious beliefs would not be consistent with his body map; the two would stand in opposition. Such situations occur frequently.

Although the body map is not an object of conscious awareness, we can discover its contents indirectly. There are several ways to gain access. We can do it by learning enough anatomy to understand how the body is constructed, how it moves easily, and then, with that in mind, observing our movements and the movements of other people.* Another way to discover the content of the body map is to draw the body, or parts of the body. For example, people who ordinarily stand with their weight thrown backward will usually draw the weight-bearing portions of their spines further toward the rear of the body than the true position. People who pull their head and neck forward will usually draw the point where the head rests on the top of the spine closer to the back of the skull than it really is.†

Sometimes we can discover the contents of a person's body map by extrapolating from the observed motion. For example, seeing you move your arm with tension, I might wonder, "What concept of the arm would cause a person to move that way? It's as if he were trying to bend his entire forearm. . . ." I continue to watch and ponder, and I see that you always move that way. I would then know from observation that you have a body map that dictates tensing your entire forearm when you bend at the elbow. This is a faulty body map, in the sense that it directs a movement with unnecessary tension. A good map would dictate easier, noninjurious movement. At this point, although I know from its effects that your map is faulty, I do not know its contents, though I presume that it includes a misrepresentation of your anatomy. My next step is to discover the relationship between your faulty body

* A helpful book is *Anatomy of Movement* by Blandine Calais-Germain (Seattle: Eastland Press, 1993).

† Although having people draw their bodies is usually an effective way to reveal the contents of their body maps, I suspect that it works best with people who have never learned to draw. Take the example of someone who pulls his head and neck forward. If that person had studied drawing, he would probably have learned something about the proportions of the head; that the ear is approximately in the middle, front to back, and that the distance from the corner of the eye to the ear is equal to the distance from the chin to the ear, and so on. Such a person might draw heads accurately, even though he habitually pulled his own head and neck forward.

map and your conscious awareness, so I ask you, "Do you think that the entire forearm bends?"

There are several ways you might reply. You might say, "Of course it bends, how else could it move?" Such an answer would show that not only do you have a faulty body map, your conscious beliefs about your body are faulty as well. That is: the representation that guides your movement (unconscious) and the beliefs you have about your structure (conscious) agree with one another, and both are wrong. In this situation, I would first try to persuade you that the forearm does not really bend along its entire length. I could appeal to anatomy books and models to show you the actual structure of your arm and encourage you to palpate your arm to verify what you had learned.

Having corrected your conscious beliefs, I would next address the unconscious representation that guides your movement. I would try to guide you to a tension-free movement of your arm, which you could compare to your ordinary use. I would, in effect, be putting you in the position described earlier (p. 37) in which a person has two different ways of moving in his repertoire and can compare them. I would have given you the experience of what tension-free movement feels like. Such movement, up to now, has not been your ordinary movement, but you find that you can move that way when you pay attention. In time, with attention and repetition, you could come to move that way always, in which case we would say that you had changed your body map, bringing it into agreement both with your actual structure and your newly corrected conscious beliefs.

A different response you might make when I ask you whether you imagine that your entire forearm bends, would be, "Of course not. Everyone knows that the bones in the forearm are rigid and do not bend." In that case, I would need to point out that although you know the facts, you do not move according to them. In this case, your conscious beliefs disagree with the unconscious representation that guides your movement. Your conscious beliefs are true, but the unconscious representation is false. When you come to understand that your habit up to now, guided by your unconscious representation, has been to attempt to move contrary to your structure and contrary to your conscious understanding of your structure, and when you can experience a different way of moving and verify that it is less tense than your previous movement, you will be in a position to correct your body map.

I have offered two scenarios. In one, a person is surprised to discover that his anatomy is what it is, since he has moved and imagined it otherwise (if he's imagined it at all). In the other scenario, the person knows something about his structure but is surprised to discover that he attempts to move contrary to that structure. (This is quite common among physicians who play musical instruments.) Both scenarios involve a poor body map. They differ in whether the person's conscious beliefs about anatomy are correct or not.

Two other scenarios are possible, both involving a good body map. Again, the difference between the two lies in differences in the person's conscious beliefs. Someone may have a good body map and true conscious beliefs about his structure, or a good body map and false conscious beliefs about his structure. The first of these cases is obviously the most desirable condition, and, in fact, it occurs frequently. Many performers move very well (i.e., have good body maps), and also have accurate conscious understanding of their structure and its movement. This condition is the goal of rehabilitation, since if a person can develop an accurate, adequate body map as well as accurate conscious understanding, injury will not be a threat and the person can practice and perform with confidence.

The second case, in which someone has a good body map but false conscious beliefs about the body, also occurs frequently. Some people move well instinctively or automatically, but because they have never encountered problems they have not been obliged to examine *how* they do what they do and their conscious beliefs about the body in movement may have nothing to do with anatomical reality or with the way they actually use their bodies. This might never cause problems, because if someone moves freely, without tension (because of an accurate, adequate body map), that person is unlikely to develop physical symptoms from playing, however bizarre his conscious beliefs about the body. Nevertheless, although the situation is benign in itself, it sets the stage for two potential problems. The first potential problem is that the person undertakes to teach, which can be bad, even disastrous, for the student. That is because the person (by hypothesis) moves well but cannot accurately describe his own movement. Since he doesn't *know* what he does, there is no way he can teach his good movement except by demonstrating, hoping students can learn by observation and imitation. Now, there is nothing wrong with demonstration as a teaching method; on the contrary, it can be very effective, partly for physiological reasons that will emerge in chapter 3. But it can be inefficient and it carries a risk, for if the demonstrator undertakes to *describe* what he does and invokes his false conscious beliefs about how the body works, his students may try to move according to those false beliefs and develop dreadful habits. The second potential problem for someone who moves well but has false conscious beliefs about the body is that he may himself try to move according to his false beliefs, thus undermining his initially good body map.

The possibility just described, of someone undermining his good body map by consciously appealing to beliefs that turn out to be false, brings us to an important point. Possession of a good body map is no guarantee that a person will always retain a good body map. It is entirely possible for a person with a good body map to acquire bad habits—which amounts to replacing the good body map with a poor one. In fact, this happens frequently. Most young children have good body maps. They move very well, although they can't describe what they do. All too often, however, their body maps later become corrupted. Whether from bad instruction or from being surrounded by bad examples or from some other cause, they develop bad habits. For example, a child may stand nicely in balance but then, under the influence of the myths about posture that inculcate a mistaken conception of "standing up straight," he may develop a back-oriented habit and become vulnerable, in time, to back trouble. (By "back orientation" I mean the habit of standing or sitting with weight thrown back of balance, as if the weight-bearing portion of the spine were further back than its true location.)

Accurate anatomical information about the body in movement contributes powerfully to correcting or improving one's body map. But information alone is rarely sufficient. Someone who wants to improve must not only know how his body *should* move, he must become aware, through direct sensation, of how he actually *does* move it. Only then will he be in a position to compare his actual movement to the freest movement permitted by his structure. Learning to make this kind of observation generally requires deliberate training and practice, because most people are not accustomed to attending to the quality of the movements they use to perform specific tasks. They are aware of their intention, that is, they know what they want to accomplish, and they generally know whether they succeed or not, but they do not ordinarily attend to the way they move to realize their intention. For example, if a pianist intends to play an E-natural, and does play E-natural, she knows she played it. She knows it because she can hear it. But as long as she hears E-natural she may not look any further into the quality of the movement used to play E-natural. Nevertheless, that information is important, and it is available.

When the brain directs the body, nervous impulses travel from the brain to other parts of the body and generate movement. But the body also sends information back to the brain. That is how the pianist can hear the E-natural; sound vibrations from the piano enter her ears, sending signals to her brain, which says, "E-natural. That's right." Hearing is an example of sensory information, and sensory information is usually considered to be of five kinds, corresponding to the five senses: hearing, sight, taste, touch, and smell. Now, information about how my forearm feels when I try to bend it does not fall under any of the five senses. Nevertheless, it is sensory information. There are, in fact, nervous receptors, mostly in the muscle spindles, that send information to the brain about our position and our movement. If you and a friend each hold one hand above your heads so that you can see your friend's hand but not your own, you know at once whether your hand is in the same position—fingers straight or bent, open or closed—as your friend's hand. You know it because you can feel the position of your hand. But you don't feel it through taste or smell or sight or any of the canonical five senses. This means, however, that the list of five sense modalities that we were taught as children is incomplete. We actually have more than five senses.* In particular, we have a movement sense, which is as truly a sense modality as any of the others. Scientifically, the movement sense is called the "kinesthetic" sense or *kinesthesia.* Etymologically, the word means "feeling movement." The kinesthetic sense provides information about position and movement and also about the quality of movement—whether it is tense or easy. Many structures and bodily habits that people often ignore, such as the balance of the head on the spine, freedom or tension of the hip joints or the lumbar vertebrae, can become objects of awareness through the kinesthetic sense.

The kinesthetic sense is vital for performers. Performers move their bodies to perform, so it seems reasonable that they would rely on the sense modality that informs them of their movement. Nevertheless, many people, including many performers, do not cultivate the kinesthetic sense, even when it would be desirable—or vital—for them to do so. Perhaps that is because they are not consciously aware that they have a kinesthetic sense. It has no colloquial name in English, and one can easily overlook something that doesn't have a name. Perhaps it is because people are so preoccupied with the results of their actions that they do not pay attention to the means—the movements—by which the results are obtained, as in the example of the pianist who notices whether she plays E-natural but does

* Some authorities expand the traditional list of five senses further, adding not only a sense of position and movement, which I am calling kinesthesia (it is also called proprioception), but also a sense of hot and cold (thermoception), a sense of pain (nociception), and a sense of balance (equilibrioception).

not appraise the quality of her movement. Whatever the explanation, ignoring the information supplied by the kinesthetic sense can lead to problems for performers, as in my earlier example of juggling.

Once a person recognizes the problem, the remedy is not hard to find. When I urged you, early in this chapter, to bend your arm as if into a banana (which amounts to moving it under a different body map), I asked you to compare that movement with your usual one and notice how the two movements felt. You discovered that they felt different. That is to say, the information from the kinesthetic sense was available when you paid attention. But if a person does not attend, the information is easily ignored and might as well not exist. The situation is just like what we find with respect to other sense modalities. If you are engrossed in conversation, you may not notice a knock on the door. Not that the knock was inaudible or that sound waves didn't enter your ears; they did enter your ears and send signals to your brain, but you were otherwise occupied so you were not aware of the sound. Similarly with movement. The information is available, but only if we attend to it.

Attention is vital, but attention alone does not guarantee improvement of the body map. Suppose I ask you to pay attention to how your arm feels when you move it. You can do that easily; most people, if they choose, can attend to the sensation of their own movement. So, you move your arm attentively and you say, "Well, yes. I'm aware of it. That's how it feels to move my arm. What of it?" What you have done is to move your arm in your usual way, that is, according to your established body map, and the movement, unsurprisingly, feels like your ordinary movement. Merely turning attention to the body and its movement does not automatically produce accurate awareness of the quality of the movement. Indeed, it is sometimes astonishing how *in*accurate people's ideas about the quality of their movement can be. It is very easy for a person to direct attention to movement and still move according to habit, doing what feels familiar and normal but doing it attentively. If the habit is poor and leads to injury, the person will be mystified. I once talked to a pianist who insisted that neither she nor her students could possibly become injured because her technique and the technique she taught her students was so entirely "natural." In fact, she was very tense when she played and her technique included habits that could easily prove injurious. "Natural" for her had no objective meaning. It didn't mean, "Consistent with the freest movement permitted by the structure," it simply meant, "What I'm used to, what feels familiar, what comes easily." She had no independent standard by which to evaluate her habits and determine what movements would be effective and safe.

To evaluate or improve your body map, it is insufficient just to register awareness of movement that already seems normal. The question, after all, is whether the movement that already feels normal is the *best* movement, the one that will be easiest or freest, given your anatomical structure. To make that determination you need some information other than what is supplied just by attending to your ordinary movement–you need some independent understanding of what the movement ought to be.

Your habitual movement, the default movement that occurs without your conscious direction, is the movement directed by your body map. But habit is not immutable. With attention, a person can perform movements contrary to established habits. If you move attentively in the best way permitted by your structure that movement, too, will provide kinesthetic information. The structure itself and the movement at the various joints can become objects of awareness. Thus, you can learn to perceive your habitual movement and compare the sensation it offers with the sensation of movement grounded on perception of the actual structure. Consistent kinesthetic self-awareness coupled with accurate anatomical knowledge of desirable movements can direct new movements, which can become new habits. There is a process of reciprocal reinforcement between attention and awareness. The more one pays careful attention, the more inclusive one's awareness can become; conversely, the more acute one's awareness, the more it will direct attention in useful ways.

Summing up this part of our discussion, we conclude that improving one's body map requires three things. First, it requires information. One must know what the structure is and how it can move efficiently. Second, it requires attention. One must pay attention to kinesthetically supplied information about one's actual movement and relate it to the anatomical structure accurately understood and perceived, not merely to a fantasy image of the structure. Third, it requires awareness, which is the product of knowledge and attention. By paying attention in the light of knowledge, a person becomes aware of particular movements, the quality of the movements, and how one movement differs from other similar movements.

The three components complement and reinforce one another. Knowledge serves to focus attention in the right direction, attention in turn enhances awareness, and awareness permits one consistently to select the better movement. Exercising the three components leads to continually improving results. A person learning to draw will come to see more as a result of looking more carefully; likewise a person who begins to attend to the quality of movement and relates it to the anatomical structure will come to perceive increasingly subtle differences and achieve greater refinement and control. Not only can a performer who works this way avoid or recover from injury, he can also make significant, even startling, progress in performance.*

* There is a growing list of publications offering anatomical information specific to the needs of different performers. My previous book, *What Every Pianist Needs to Know about the Body*, is one, also *What Every Violinist Needs to Know about the Body*, by Jennifer Johnson, *Oboemotions: What Every Oboe Player Needs to Know about the Body*, by Stephen Caplan, *Body Mapping for Flutists*, by Lea Pearson, *What Every Dancer Needs to Know about the Body*, by Robin Gilmore, *The Structures and Movement of Breathing: A primer for Choirs and Choruses*, by Barbara Conable (all available from GIA Publications), *What Every Singer Needs to Know about the Body*, by Melissa Malde, MaryJean Allen, and Kurt-Alexander Zeller (Plural Publishing), and *What Every Trombonist Needs to Know about the Body*, by David Vining (Mountain Peak Music).

Although improving one's body map can lead to dramatic improvement in performance, it is vital to recognize that the converse is *not* true. Improving one's performance does not guarantee a corresponding improvement in the body map. That is: the artistic quality of a person's performance is not a reliable measure of the quality of the body map that guides it. Many fine musicians play beautifully but become injured, sometimes ending their careers. Their outstanding playing was achieved at a physical cost that their bodies could not sustain indefinitely.* This is tragic because it is unnecessary; with healthy movement a musician can play for a lifetime. On the other hand, there are many great performers who do move exceedingly well. Some twentieth-century musicians acknowledged to be exemplary in the quality of their movement were Wilhelm Furtwängler, Jascha Heifetz, Artur Rubinstein, and Claudio Arrau. Whether or in what ways they consciously attended to their body maps, I cannot say—sometimes good movement just seems to come instinctively—but Arrau, at least, was sufficiently aware of what was special about his movement that he could describe it and he could even use his awareness to help injured pianists.†

In our juggling example, a mismapping of the forearm led to tendonitis, which resolved when the map was corrected. This is exactly the way performers often use Body Mapping, especially if they are injured. They focus on individual parts, identify faulty habits, and make appropriate corrections in their movements to establish new habits and an improved body map. Now, successfully remapping various parts of the body may be enough to resolve an injury, but more is needed to reach a high level of performance. There is another step to be taken. The parts must be brought into a whole. Imagine a dancer whose self-representation was of a collection of parts, not a whole integrated body. She might not be injured, but she would be

* That is why the fact that a person plays well does not by itself guarantee that he will be a good teacher, or that his technical recommendations will be sound.

† Joseph Horowitz, *Conversations with Arrau* (New York: Knopf, 1982). See in particular the chapter on piano technique and the tribute to Arrau by Garrick Ohlsson.

unlikely to exhibit the grace and coherent movement of a great dancer. Likewise with our juggler. A juggler cannot juggle just with his arms; his entire body must be alert, attentive, coordinated. Or consider a pianist. Some pianists concentrate on their hands and fingers, and, indeed, there are piano teachers who explicitly identify the fingers, hands, and forearms as "the playing apparatus" and insist that attention to the playing apparatus alone will solve all problems. But concentrating on fingers, hands, and forearms to the exclusion of the rest of the body is a recipe for wooden playing and possible injury. Piano playing is not a function just of hands and arms but a function of the entire body. The *body* is the playing apparatus, not just some parts of it, and performers need to cultivate a sense of the whole. It is no accident that we speak of a *body* map instead of an arm map, a leg map, and so on; a performer must map himself as a whole composed of integrated parts.

The body map is part of "how we think of ourselves," part of our self-image, although it functions for the most part below the level of consciousness. Now, how we think of ourselves affects the way we move. A self-confident person moves differently from someone who is embarrassed, ashamed, or fearful, and we can often tell a lot about a person's self-image just by looking. The process also works in reverse: how we move can influence how we think of ourselves. In short, how we think of ourselves—our self-image—and how we think of our bodies are intimately connected and often amount to the same thing. This is not surprising; after all, we *are* our bodies, and when we move our bodies we are moving ourselves.

The conclusions reached in the last few paragraphs are more significant than they may seem at first. A performer directs the body to move in particular ways, which involves commands traveling from the brain to the body. At the same time, kinesthetic and other information travels from the body to the brain, where it serves to evaluate movement and guide future movement. Brain and body work together with signals traveling in both directions. This kind of cooperation of brain and body occurs in many living creatures, but in humans, whose brains are complex enough to portray bodily changes in the form of interconnected sensory maps, the sense of the body moving in response to commands from the brain yields a sense of conscious agency, an awareness of oneself as an individual. In short, the process I have sketched is the process by which we construct our very selves.

To be aware of one's self is to be aware of one's body, or is the result of being aware of one's body. The self is not a little person somehow trapped in the head, nor is it a ghost in a machine. It is an ongoing construction derived from activities in the body and in the brain and their interaction. The philosophical claim, common before the twentieth century, that thinking and consciousness could occur in a mind entirely independent of any body is no longer remotely plausible. On the contrary, thinking and consciousness are physiological functions of the brain interacting with the body, and awareness of ourselves as individuals is based on awareness of our bodies. This means, however, that in attending to themselves as integrated bodies acting in response to intention, performers are attending to the foundation of their own selfhood. They are, in a perfectly literal sense, constructing themselves as individuals. Performance is an activity of self-creation.

Scapino. Cap.ⁱ Zerbino

3 • *Motion II: The Brain*

The concept of the body map emerged as a pedagogical tool in the 1970s. One of the people centrally responsible for developing the concept and applying it to music teaching was William Conable, a cellist at The Ohio State University and also an Alexander teacher. Years later, he described the experience that led to the development of the idea of Body Mapping. He said a colleague asked him to observe a violin student who was having trouble with her bow arm. Observing her, he wondered what conception of one's anatomy might lead a person to move as she was moving. He asked her what she knew about the movement of the elbow, explained to her the true location of the joint and its movement, and she immediately was able to play more freely.* This is exactly like the situation I described in chapter 2, where we saw that a person's representation of the body, even if not consciously formulated, determines the movement. If the representation is false the person will try to move according to it, even if conscious understanding is accurate.

William and Barbara Conable systematically developed the idea of the body map and the teaching technique known as Body Mapping. Other teachers and musicians have also recognized the power of accurate anatomical information as

* Conable describes this occasion in a paper presented at the Third International Alexander Congress, Engelberg, Switzerland, August 1991. A revised version of the paper is available online at the website of Andover Educators, www.bodymap.org.

a teaching method. For example, Renée Fleming describes the practice of her teacher, Beverley Johnson:

> Beverley kept a battered copy of *Gray's Anatomy* close to her piano among the stacks of scores. She was forever pulling it out to explain something about the mechanism of the voice. "See that?" she would say, tapping on the page. She would show me a drawing of the pharynx and the larynx, the epiglottis and hard and soft palates, the breath cavities and the diaphragm.*

Fleming speaks of "trying to understand how my own body worked" (p. 41) during her student years, and throughout her book, *The Inner Voice*, she makes clear that she is vividly aware of the anatomical structures and the movements involved in singing. She is using what amounts to a Body Mapping approach, although she does not use that terminology.

The origins of Body Mapping were practical, not theoretical. Teachers embraced the concept because it offered an effective way to train movement. Nevertheless, by extraordinary coincidence, neurophysiological research almost immediately established that the body map is a physiological reality, an actual configuration in the brain. The brain contains maps, neural maps; in fact it contains not one but many maps, representing not just the state of the arms and legs and musculoskeletal system, but also internal conditions and mechanical properties of the body, visceral states, physiological processes, and many other things. Neurologists often use expressions like "internal representation" or "neural map" rather than the expression "body map," and some authorities believe that "internal representation" will eventually become the standard term. Nevertheless, I shall continue to use "body map" to refer to the representation that governs movement, since it lends itself to the practical and pedagogical issues that are my concern in this chapter and the next. The concept of the body map is an example of a conjecture adopted for practical reasons that subsequently received scientific verification.

* *The Inner Voice* (New York: Viking, 2004), p. 39.

In this case, the scientific facts were established entirely independently; researchers did not purposely set out to show that teaching based on the body map had a neurological foundation. Instead, their work led to the discovery of neural maps, which we now recognize as the physiological basis of the pedagogical approach known as Body Mapping.

That the body map is a physical reality may not seem especially important to performers, even those who embrace Body Mapping as an effective teaching strategy. It works, isn't that enough? In fact, it is profoundly important for performers to recognize the physical reality of the body map because it changes the way we practice, teach, and perform, and makes those activities more effective. Indeed, appreciating the reality of the body map gives us better insight into what we are really doing when we practice, teach, and perform. To see why this is so, we need to consider how the brain works. We do not need to examine the neurophysiological details; indeed, at the cellular and molecular levels the facts are staggeringly complex and not yet fully understood. But we do need a schematic understanding of how interconnections among neurons in the brain lead to the formation of neural circuits or maps. We need to understand that such things as acquiring a skill, learning new repertoire, or changing a habit are—or at least they involve—physical changes in the brain. Some of what I present may be new to performers, and some has been discovered only within the last thirty years. But though recent, it is firmly established; nothing I describe here is controversial.

The operations of the brain are carried out by nerve cells or *neurons*. According to some estimates, there are approximately 100 billion neurons in the brain, which receive and send signals to and from the body and one another. Each neuron consists of a central body and numerous threadlike extensions. The extensions are of two kinds: there is an output fiber, the *axon*, that sends signals to other neurons, and there are numerous input fibers, *dendrites*, that receive signals from other neurons. The tip of the axon meets a dendrite of another neuron at a junction called a *synapse*. When a neuron becomes active, or "fires," it sends an electrical signal down the axon to the synapse, which may trigger the release of a chemical neurotransmitter. The neurotransmitter acts on the dendrite of the other neuron, which may cause that neuron to become active and send a signal of its own. Synapses can be strong or weak; the strength of the synapse determines whether or not a signal will be transmitted to the next neuron. A group of neurons linked by strong synaptic connections constitutes a "network" or "circuit." Local circuits are organized into larger groups and systems: the brain is a hierarchical organization of systems.

The circuits and groups of circuits have particular functions. Circuits with related functions may be located together in a distinct region of the brain, but this is not always the case. Some functions involve interconnections between cells in different regions. Our interest in this book is with motor control, which T. Richard Nichols, a neurophysiologist at the Georgia Institute of Technology, describes as

> a very distributed system, with hierarchical organization through the brain, brainstem, and spinal cord. The notion of hierarchy is very important here. There are subsystems that regulate specific aspects of motor function, and each subsystem has maps associated.*

Neurophysiologists have made immense progress in identifying exactly which regions of the brain perform different functions, and already their discoveries are beginning to have therapeutic value for people suffering from epilepsy, trigeminal neuralgia, and other conditions. The identification of the regions of the brain responsible for particular activities is often called "mapping" the brain or the mind. This is a legitimate use of the word "mapping," which I mention to distinguish it from the body map as discussed in this book and from Body Mapping as a pedagogical approach. The body map we are interested in is a functional concept. To be sure, it is also an anatomical structure (or structures) and it does have a loca-

* Personal communication. Quoted with permission.

tion (or locations) in the brain and nervous system, but we are not concerned with cerebral topography or the details of the neurophysiological operations by virtue of which the body map does what it does. Our focus is on the way the body map functions as a representation or set of instructions, and on the power of a Body Mapping approach for training movement and developing a skill. It is essential for us to recognize that our thoughts and actions are grounded in and carried out by anatomical structures in our brains, but not to ascertain exactly where our body maps are situated in our heads. We also need to appreciate that from a functional point of view, three sectors of the brain are involved in each of its activities. These sectors, too, do have physical locations, but once again, it is their functional separation, not their locations, that concerns us here.*

First, there is the "input sector," which receives signals from the body and the world. There are many kinds of signals—supplied through vision, hearing, taste, or other sense modalities, as well as chemical signals from the body.

Second, there is the "output sector," which issues commands to the body. These commands initiate voluntary or involuntary movement, as well as bodily functions like heartbeat and breathing.

Third, there is an "intermediate sector" between the input and output sectors, which reflects the fact that the input and output sectors of the brain do not generally communicate with one another directly. That is, a signal received in the input sector does not immediately cause a command to be issued by the output sector; their relationship is not simply that of cause and effect or stimulus and response.

Sometimes, to be sure, the relation between input and output is comparatively direct, as when the brain senses an elevated level of carbon dioxide in the blood (input) and responds

* T. Richard Nichols has written an illuminating essay on the scientific basis of Body Mapping. The essay is available on my website, www.pianomap.com/Nichols.html.

by causing faster breathing and heart rate (output), or when contact with a hot surface sends a signal to the central nervous system (input), which issues a motor command (output) to pull away. But at other times the relation between input and output is more complex. Consider, for example, the knowledge and experience presupposed if, on a rainy and mostly cloudy day, I notice the sun on my right and turn to the left to look for a rainbow. Between the input (a signal from my eye) and the output (a motor command to turn my head) a series of intermediate steps must occur, which may include recollection of facts about how rainbows are formed, inference about where to look for a rainbow in relation to the sun, and other things.

When a signal from the world or the body arrives in the input sector of the brain, it sets up a pattern of activity among neurons, a neural representation, which can become the basis of an image. The intermediate structures between the input and output sectors generate and manipulate images, interpret them, form concepts, make plans and decisions. All our knowledge and experience is stored here, in the structures intermediate between the input and output sectors. What we call "thinking" is a processing of images.

Knowledge and experience are not stored as fully formed images in the brain. The brain is not like a library where books wait on the shelves until someone takes them out again, or a museum storage room where pictures sit until someone chooses to look at them. Books and pictures are unchanged in storage; they are still books and pictures whether anyone is looking at them or not. But knowledge and experience are not stored that way in our brains. Instead they are stored in neural circuits, the networks of synaptic connections described earlier. Surrounded as we are today by computers, we have become accustomed to the idea that information, including pictures and recorded sound, can be stored digitally. But when we store a photo on our hard drive, what we actually store is not the image but a set of instructions for creating the image. When we call up the photo, the instructions are activated and an image appears on the computer screen, created according to those instructions. Similarly, we do not store images in our brains; we store instructions for constructing images.*

Following Antonio Damasio, a neurophysiologist at the University of Southern California's Brain and Creativity Institute, I shall refer to such sets of instructions as "dispositions" or "dispositional representations." They are neural circuits that contain "the firing patterns which trigger the momentary reconstruction of an approximate representation" of an object.† The word "dispositional" serves to make clear that we are dealing not with actual images but with instructions for constructing images. Moreover, most of these patterns are not innate in our brains; they are generated – acquired – in the course of our lives. These dispositional images are examples of what Damasio calls "acquired dispositional neural patterns."

* This example is not intended to suggest that the brain is in other respects like a computer: the brain does not work serially or digitally the way a computer does.

† *Descartes' Error*, (New York: G. P. Putnam's Sons, 1994), HarperCollins paperback edition, p. 102.

Schematically, the process of perception, memory, and recall is this: When I see an object (or perceive something by means of another sense), there is a "mapped activation" in the sensory cortices (the "input sector") that constitutes an actual image. This mapped activation (actual image) may give rise to a disposition (dispositional image), that is, a neural pattern elsewhere in the brain (in the "intermediate sector") containing directions for reconstructing the image. This is what happens when we learn or remember: neural circuits are established that contain instructions for reconstructing what we have learned or remembered. Thinking, the processing of images, relies on the information contained in dispositional representations to construct images that are used to direct movement, and for reasoning, planning, and other activities of life. A memory image comes from reconstructing a pattern or map in the sensory cortices, and this reconstruction, a "mapped activation," is triggered by dispositional representations elsewhere in the brain.

There are other kinds of dispositions besides the ones that generate memory images. In particular, there are dispositions that govern movements. In the case of memory, a sensory signal generates a mapped activation in the sensory cortices (actual image), which can generate a dispositional representation elsewhere in the brain. When that dispositional representation is activated, it generates another mapped activation in the sensory cortices (memory image), similar to the earlier one. Likewise, a physical movement corresponds to a mapped activation in motor cortices, and that mapped activation can give rise to a dispositional representation elsewhere in the brain. Activation of that dispositional image brings about renewed mapped activity in the motor cortices, leading to a physical movement like the original one.

There are yet other dispositional representations besides the ones that store imageable knowledge and bodily movements; in particular, there are dispositional representations that prescribe the ways we operate on those images. Damasio offers a fuller description:

> Hidden behind those images [e.g., memory images, of which we are conscious], never or rarely knowable by us, there are indeed numerous processes that guide the generation and deployment of those images in space and time. Those processes utilize rules and strategies embodied in dispositional representations. They are *essential* for our thinking, but are not a *content* of our thought.*

To see how this may work, we can offer an analogy with language. The dispositional representations embodying rules and strategies that guide the deployment of images are analogous to the rules of grammar by which we organize words into sentences. Paraphrasing the formulation quoted above, we can say that the rules of grammar are not ordinarily what our sentences are about; the rules are *essential* for our conversation, but they are not its *content*. I speak grammatically (most of the time), but I am not normally aware of the rules of grammar when I speak. Speaking grammatically is something I do because I have dispositional representations in my brain containing "rules and strategies" that organize my words in the manner we call "grammatical." To say that I have a habit of speaking grammatically simply amounts to saying that my brain contains the dispositional representations that organize my words into grammatical sentences. Of course, I *can* think about grammar if I wish. But notice that the dispositional representations—i.e., the neural circuits in my brain—that organize my sentences are still not the content of my thinking even when the rules of grammar are what I am thinking about.

Bodily movements and internal images of bodily movements are likewise the result of dispositional representations, and as with images, it seems that besides the movements themselves and the images of movements, there are rules and strategies governing their occurrence. Nichols offers an example:

> There is a strategy for dealing with postural disturbances that is not conscious and probably takes place in the spinal

* *Descartes' Error*, p. 108.

> cord and lower brain stem that involves a representation of the mechanical properties and structure of the body, through which sensory information about the current state of the body is channeled and processed. So the 'strategy' may well be encoded in the form of neural connections.*

In view of this, we can modify the statement by Damasio quoted two paragraphs back, adapting it to make it apply specifically to movement. It would then go this way:

> Hidden behind our movements, never or rarely knowable by us, there are numerous processes that guide the generation and deployment of those movements. These processes utilize rules and strategies embodied in dispositional representations. They are essential for our movement, but are not what we are aware of when we move.

These dispositional representations guiding the generation and deployment of movement constitute what I have up to now called the body map.

The dispositional representations we are discussing, the "rules and strategies," are encoded hierarchically at various levels of the central nervous system. There is not just a single center where rules are established, or a single "strategy center;" a physical activity may be governed by dispositions at two or more levels. In walking, for example, the detailed instructions to the muscles come from circuits in the spinal cord. They are modified, however, by signals from the periphery, brain stem, and brain to adapt to different situations, such as the contour of the terrain. Therefore, rules are established on at least two levels.†

In chapter 2, I characterized the body map as a "representation in the brain used to govern movement." We can now specify more exactly what the body map is. The phrase "representation that governs movement" has the drawback that it might lead us to suppose that we have a representation or

* Personal communication. Quoted with permission.

† This example also was supplied by Richard Nichols.

image of a movement, and we produce a movement corresponding to the image. But that cannot be what happens. For one thing, it is impossible to say what "corresponding to the image" could mean, since it presupposes a point of view from which the two could be compared. The representation used to govern movement cannot be an *image* of a movement, instead it is the set of instructions that, when activated, produce a movement. Thus, when we talk of the body map as a "representation," we turn out to be talking about a *dispositional* representation. Therefore, adapting and reorganizing Damasio's formulation, we can say that the body map consists of *rules and strategies embodied in dispositional representations that guide the generation and deployment of bodily movements.* Many of these dispositional representations are not innate; they are acquired. The body map, therefore, is the set of (mostly) acquired dispositional neural patterns that relate to bodily movement.

Acquiring a Body Map

The dispositional representations we have been discussing are local circuits in the brain, networks of neurons connected by strengthened synapses. They are structural parts of the brain, each with a particular configuration and location. Some networks are genetically determined – those regulating basic mechanisms of survival like heartbeat, breathing, or homeostasis. Some bodily movements – reflex movements, for example – may also be innate in the sense that we are born with the necessary neural connections already established. In addition, some combinations of muscles (synergies) that are used for many different activities may be present at birth. Some movement patterns, like walking, based on innate "building blocks" may be learned more quickly than highly skilled movements like musical performance. But although we start life with some circuitry in place, most voluntary movement must be learned. We must develop neural patterns in our brains to direct voluntary movement, which amounts to developing a body map.

The neurological details of this development are endlessly complicated, but for our discussion it will be sufficient to identify two kinds of process that appear to be centrally involved. The first is what David J. Buller, professor of philosophy at Northern Illinois University, refers to as "proliferate-and-prune."* This expression refers to the early production of many more neural connections than will eventually make up the brain and the subsequent reduction of those connections. For example, each muscle fiber in an adult is innervated by just one neuron, but this is not true early on. Instead, there is an initial huge proliferation of "extra" connections, which retract or atrophy in the course of development, leaving just one neuron to control each muscle fiber. This process of winnowing, which occurs in many brain systems, seems to involve competition and selection among the neurons and is thus analogous to the evolutionary process of selection (although, unlike in evolutionary change, selection of one neuron instead of another is clearly not based on different levels of reproductive success). This process of pruning extra cells and connections leaves networks of neurons with strong synaptic connections, which carry out various cognitive, motor, and other functions.

Another process is vital as well, however, namely the input from the body and the environment. Random firings of neurons may trigger bodily movements, but those movements in turn send messages back to the brain that are essential for developing motor control. Input from the body and the environment is necessary; visual and auditory stimuli, for example, are required for proper development of sight and hearing. Like these and other cognitive and sensory capabilities, the body map develops through an interaction of the brain with the body and the environment. The design of the body map is thus partly shaped by experience: I have the particular body map I have partly because of the way I have moved in the past. I was not born with my present body map, or, indeed,

* *Adapting Minds: Evolutionary Psychology and the Persistent Quest for Human Nature* (Cambridge, Massachusetts: MIT Press, 2005), pp. 197–99.

with much of any body map at all. My repertoire of voluntary movements as an infant was very small, and so was the set of dispositions directing my movements. In time, through the interaction of brain and body with each other and with my surroundings, a network of strengthened synapses developed that enabled me to replicate the movements I was performing, which amounts to saying that I had a set of dispositions relating to movement: a body map. Babies spend much of their waking time in precisely this way. They move their arms and legs and bodies randomly at first; then they coordinate eye and hand movements; eventually, they crawl and walk. They are actively creating a body map, establishing a set of dispositions. We commonly speak of this as "learning." We say that babies "learn" to move their arms and crawl and walk. We also use the word "knowing," as when we say that the baby now "knows how" to walk. Analogously, we may say of stroke victims that they have "forgotten" how to walk or talk.

Notice, however, that such knowing is different from the sort of knowing that includes the possibility of conscious recollection. I might know how to walk and yet be unable to explain how I do it or teach it to someone else, whereas no one would accept my claim to know who was the first president of the United States if I couldn't name the person. The difference between the kind of knowing embodied in the body map and the knowing that allows for conscious recollection is like what philosophers describe as the difference between "knowing how" and "knowing that." The difference can also be described as a difference between "implicit" and "explicit" learning; the two kinds of learning appear to have different neural mechanisms. Although the body map is learned in the sense we have described, it is not consciously acquired. Establishing a body map is an example of the sort of learning that we share with creatures that are not conscious. In this regard it is like the learning that occurs in less complex organisms; the epoch-making work of Eric Kandel on learning and memory used the sea slug *aplysia,* a creature of rudimentary neural capacity, to discover some of the fundamental neurological bases of memory.

In introducing the concept of the body map in chapter 2, I claimed that in order to direct movement, the brain must contain information about the body—information about the structure, size, and function of the various parts—and I characterized the body map as the representation in the brain that governs movement. Subsequent discussion has shown that the body map is better described as a disposition, a pattern of connections that, when activated, brings about movement of a certain kind. The body map is more like a set of instructions than it is like a picture or representation. We must now consider how viewing the body map as a set of dispositions relates to the earlier claim that it contains information. Clearly, the body map is not a mental picture or conscious image. But it does depend on the structure and possible movements of the body. That is, my disposition "how to move my arm" does not *represent* my arm or its structure, but it *relies* on my arm having a particular structure; in that sense my structure is built into my disposition "how to move my arm." Suppose that as an infant I try to clap my hands. Sometimes, at first, I miss. Then, gradually, I learn not to miss. I repeat the successful attempts and in time my hands always meet when I set out to clap them together. We could say that my brain has learned how long my arms are, or that my body map takes account of the length of my arms. Saying that my body map "represents" my arms as having a particular length amounts to saying that movements based on arms of that length have been successful, have been repeated, and a disposition has been established to move my arms as if they were that length.

The body map as a habit or disposition is not on the same logical level as individual bodily movements. It is not an individual bodily movement; it is what we earlier called the "rules and strategies that guide individual movement." It *underlies* everything I do with my arm, every individual movement, but not any one particular movement rather than another. The body map can direct the sort of activity that led to its original formation and thus it becomes a guide or template for future activity. A creature with a body map will characteristically move in the manner directed by its body map. Exactly which rules and strategies become incorporated into the body map can vary from person to person and in the same person at different times. There are similarities, of course; most people's maps contain the dispositions that can direct their arms to perform everyday movements like picking up a coffee cup and their arm movements are broadly similar, reflecting the fact that they share the same anatomical structure. Nevertheless, the manner of performing even everyday movements can vary among people. Running offers a good example of this. Watch a group of runners from behind and you quickly see that no two look just alike; each has a characteristic style of running.

As the collection of dispositions that underlie voluntary movement, the body map permits us to have other goals and purposes than mere physical movement. Ordinarily, when I engage in an activity that involves moving my arm, it is not the arm movement itself that I am mainly conscious of; the arm movement is not what I'd name if someone asked, "What are you doing?" Instead, I would state the goal or purpose of my action. My body map would still be functioning, but behind the scenes. As an example, suppose I'm standing at the sink, dipping my hands in and out of soapy water, picking kitchen objects up and putting them down again. You ask, "What are you doing?" and I reply, "I'm washing dishes." That's true, I'm washing dishes, but I am also moving my arms, reaching for things, picking them up and putting them down. However, I'm not attending to the moving of my arms, I'm attending to the goal of my activity, namely, washing dishes. I look for hardened bits of dirt, make sure the dishes are clean and rinsed before putting them in the rack, and I can do that–attend to the state of the dishes without attending consciously to the movements of my arms–because I have dispositions in my brain that work automatically, without my conscious direction, to move my arms. I don't need to direct my arms consciously, I just think of my task, namely to get the dishes clean, and my arms move on their own, as it were. The dispositions that direct my arm movements, which we have labeled the rules and strategies, are neural patterns that exist and can fire even when I'm not consciously attending to the movements they direct.

An established body map can serve as the foundation for other, specialized movements. A person learning to play the piano ordinarily comes to the first lesson already equipped with a body map that enables him to move his arms. He then learns and repeats the particular movements used in piano playing, and in time establishes dispositional representations in his brain to direct those movements. We could say that he has mapped the movements of piano playing, or that the basic map of the arm has been modified–expanded to include the movements of piano playing.* That such a thing can happen–that we can establish a set of dispositions (moving our arms) and then refine them, adding an additional layer of specialized

* Saying that the map has been expanded is the literal truth. Neurologists have shown that when people devote a lot of time to specialized activities such as piano playing, a larger part of the brain is devoted to those activities than in individuals who do not engage in them.

dispositions (playing the piano) on top of them—is a remarkable and wonderful capacity of our brains, the basis for much of human education and culture. Other species can learn, but human potential in this regard vastly surpasses that of any other species.

I pointed out that the map of the arm informs all the activities in which the arm is used. Let us develop this point. Consider several activities that all involve moving my arm: playing the piano, combing my hair, and washing dishes. The basic use of my arm is common to all three. If "A" represents the basic use of my arm, then I could represent the three specific activities by "A + P" for playing the piano, "A + C" for combing my hair, and "A + D" for washing dishes.* The quality of the "A" component will affect all three activities. If the basic use of my arm includes a thumb-oriented manner of rotating my forearm,† then, since all the activities mentioned require rotation of the forearm, I will use a thumb-oriented rotation in all of them, not just one. Whether this constitutes a problem or not depends on what activities I engage in. If I use forearm rotation only to comb my hair in the morning I will probably not suffer, but if I take up piano playing and play for hours every day, thumb orientation becomes dangerous. If I eventually develop tendonitis from thumb-oriented piano playing, it is likely to affect other activities as well.

In daily life we don't just move in general, we perform specific movements aimed at specific tasks and we direct our

* These examples, "A + P," "A + C," suggest what neurologists call "synergies." On this model, an activity like playing the piano would consist of a sequence of muscle synergies, some laid down early in development and easy to learn, and others that take longer to learn.

† "Thumb orientation" refers to a habit of rotating the forearm in a tense manner. It is a principal cause of injury for musicians and anyone else (computer users, for example) whose activity requires frequent forearm rotation or is performed with the forearm in a pronated position. The habit of ulnar deviation that some pianists call "twisting" and recognize as a cause of injury is generally a symptom of an underlying habit of thumb orientation. I offer a fuller description of thumb orientation in *What Every Pianist Needs to Know about the Body*, pp. 80–86 and 108–9.

attention to the specific tasks. Thus, when we engage in an activity "A + X" where "A" is the part of the movement that is directed (usually without our being aware of it) by the body map and "X" is what is special to that activity, the "X" component is what we would normally single out in describing what we are doing. "X" is what we would answer to the question "What are you doing?" even though what is really happening is "A + X." We can conclude from this that the "A" component, the portion guided by the body map, which several activities may have in common, is essential for any of those activities to occur at all and it influences their quality, yet it is the part of any activity which we are least likely to mention and least likely to have in our awareness when we describe what we are doing.

Most voluntary activities are like washing dishes in that they involve a variety of movements and we are ordinarily aware of some of those movements but not others. But the movements of which we are not aware, and which we therefore do not consciously intend, are necessary for the movements of which we are aware, and do intend. I may not be aware of my upper arm, but it must move in order for me to wash dishes or play the piano. What directs the part of the activity that I am not aware of is habit, which is to say the body map: the dispositional representations that generate movements like those that have happened before.*

As a neural network, the body map is not an object of conscious awareness; we cannot be directly conscious of the neural networks in our brains. The reason we cannot is that we have no perceptual mechanism to ground such awareness. We have no sense receptors that represent to us our nerves or the circuitry of our brains, the way we have sense receptors to represent sounds and colors. But, although we cannot be directly aware of our body map, we can discover its contents. We do this in several ways, but mainly by observing its effects,

* Not everything we call a "habit" is appropriately thought of as part of the body map. A habit of smoking is not, although how I use my hands to hold a cigarette or strike a match is. The habits that reflect or reveal my body map relate not to *what* we do (e.g., smoke) but to *how* we do things–how we physically carry them out.

that is, by examining the movements it directs. Although in activities like washing dishes or playing the piano I may not ordinarily attend to the movements of my upper arms that are directed by my body map, I *can* become aware of those movements if I choose. I can decide to become aware of what my upper arms are doing. In short, I can *pay attention.* I do have sense receptors to gather information about my movement; I have a kinesthetic sense.* Thus, I can be aware of the effects of my body map, namely the movements it directs, and in that way I can know the contents of my body map, even though I cannot know *it* directly. Moreover, when I attend to the way my arms move, I can, if I wish, choose *not* to move my arms the way I ordinarily do. Individual movements are subject to my will. I can use bizarre arm movements as a joke, I can imitate a monkey or Aunt Agatha's funny way of washing dishes, or whatever. In other words, I can *override* the directions of my body map. The dispositions embedded in my brain direct my habitual, unattended movement. They provide the default movement. If I'm not paying particular attention to my movement, the default pattern is the one that operates. But I am perfectly able to move my arm in a different way if I pay attention. I can choose individual actions *and* the manner of performing them. This means that I have a choice, and the consequence of this is that I can modify my body map.

Anyone who attends for the first time to habitual movements that have been previously overlooked may be surprised, even shocked, by what he discovers. Suppose someone complains to me about my affected way of drinking coffee. According to this person I extend my little finger in an exaggerated effeminate manner, like Albin in *La cage aux folles.* Naturally, my first inclination is to protest, "No way!" So, to prove it, the

* Notice that the kinesthetic sense, introduced in chapter 2, represents not only the movement of the body but also whatever instruments we are using. A flutist's kinesthetic sense represents the movements of "arm + flute," not just "arm." The representation thus is of the mechanical environment in which movement occurs, including the tools or instruments that are used.

person holds up a mirror, I lift my cup as usual, see my little finger reaching stupidly out to the side, and exclaim in horror, "I didn't know I looked like *that!*" In exactly the same way, performers watching a video of themselves often perceive habits of which they had been completely unaware. Confronted by the evidence of the mirror, I will probably say, like Albin, "It just *does* that." And that *is* how it feels; my finger seems to act on its own. But that isn't what is really happening. My *finger* doesn't do it; *I* do it, though not deliberately. This is a vital point, because assuming responsibility for one's movement in such a situation confers the power to change it.

Many people do not understand this. How often do we hear people say things like, "My bad back is killing me" instead of "My back hurts because I chronically stand out of balance"? So long as I think my finger moves independently of any conscious direction from me, I will continue to hold my coffee cup in an affected manner. Once I understand that I have the power to move my finger some other way I can form a new habit and cultivate a different manner of drinking coffee – start to drink coffee, as Georges urges Albin, *en homme*. In the process I will have to be vigilantly attentive, consistently directing a new movement until a new disposition is established in my brain. Until then, the old movement will reassert itself whenever my attention strays.

I have spoken of neural patterns being established in our brains, but it is vital to emphasize that our brains are not fixed, once and for all, at birth or at any other time. They change. Synaptic strength can be affected by repetition. If a particular synapse is activated frequently it may be strengthened or reinforced; thus, frequent activation of a particular set of synapses creates a pattern of reinforcement among them such that the activation of one is likely to activate others according to the pattern that has been reinforced in the past. Conversely, if a synapse is not activated, it may become weaker. Synaptic strength can also be affected by other factors – attention, for example. In this way established circuits are modified by later experience; they change throughout our lives in response to our activity. Who we are and who we become depends a lot on what we do. Neurologists describe this as "plasticity of the brain" and it is far more pervasive and persistent than researchers recognized until very recently. In the words of David J. Buller:

> The concept of neural plasticity refers . . . to *the brain's* ability to remake itself in response to changing environmental demands.
>
> Neural plasticity isn't confined to what we mark off as the process of development from infancy to adulthood. Our brains are changing all the time, quite rapidly and profoundly . . . not only do our brains continue to grow (at least in some places), but they continually reorganize themselves in response to environmental demands.*

In the end, the circuitry of each person's brain is unique to that person. No two people are outwardly identical, and their uniqueness extends inward, to the detailed structures of their brains.

Plasticity of the brain implies that established patterns, including the body map, can change in the course of a lifetime. Indeed, it is vital that they do so in order to adjust to changes that occur in the body and the world. For example, the length of my arm has not been constant throughout my life. When I was a child my arm was much shorter than it is today. As I grew and my arm became longer, movements based on a shorter arm became less successful, and movements based on a longer arm became more successful. Consequently the movements based on the longer arm were repeated, those based on the shorter arm were progressively abandoned, and a new disposition, based on a longer arm, was established. This amounts to a change in my body map. My body map changed to take account of my altered size.

The body map can change throughout a person's life, but there is no guarantee that such changes will always be improve-

* *Adapting Minds*, p. 137. Italics in original.

ments. The body map is simply the set of dispositions—habits—that have been formed in the course of development and growth, and people can develop bad habits as well as good ones. Sometimes a person's body map is inaccurate, meaning that it directs movement as if the structure were different from what it really is, and therefore it does not make the most efficient use of the person's actual structure. This can come about in various ways. Suppose, for example, that as a child I am told to "stand up straight," and the concept of "standing up straight" that is urged on me is the one embodied in the posture myths ("chest out, shoulders back, etc.") that infect our culture. Suppose also that I am obedient, eager to please, and enjoy being complimented on the straightness of my posture. So I deliberately stand according to the posture myths and eventually I have established a disposition to stand that way. That is, standing that way has become the way I stand ordinarily, even when I'm not particularly attending to how I'm standing.

Now, this amounts to a habit of back orientation (since the posture myths demand that we throw our weight back of where it would balance easily) and standing that way is not efficient from an anatomical point of view. But of course, I don't know that. Someone who understood the anatomy of standing in balance might observe me and say, "You've mismapped your spine. You think it's further back in your body than it really is." And it is true that I stand *as if* I thought the spine further back than it really is. Nevertheless, although I could be said to have "mismapped my spine" in the way just described, the mismapping was not the result of conscious misrepresentation or misunderstanding of my anatomy. Someone *could* develop an inaccurate body map as a result of conscious misunderstanding, but saying "you've mismapped your spine" doesn't assume anything one way or the other about a person's knowledge or understanding; it simply means that you have a disposition, a habit, to move in a way that stresses your spine unnecessarily. In itself, a mismapping is not a false understanding, it is a faulty set of instructions in the brain. It may, however, be accompanied or brought about by false understanding. In either case, acquiring accurate information can be helpful, even decisive, in changing it.

That the body map can differ from a person's intellectual understanding of the body is possible because the dispositional image that moves the arm or directs standing is different, situated in a different part of the brain, from the cognitive image that constitutes a person's knowledge of anatomy. The dispositional image and the cognitive image can disagree because, as anatomically separate neurological patterns, they do not necessarily communicate with each other. Therefore, I could know that the weight-bearing part of the spine is closer to the center of my torso than to the surface of my back, but nevertheless continue to throw my weight backward. Similarly, taking the example from chapter 2, I might know that my forearm cannot bend into a banana, but still move with the tension associated with trying to bend it into a banana. I wouldn't consciously think, "Oh, I'm throwing my weight back of balance," or, "There I go again, pulling my forearm into a banana." I probably wouldn't think anything one way or the other unless I experienced problems connected with standing or moving my arm, when I would say something like, "I can't stand for long periods without pain; I guess I have a bad back," or, "It really hurts to bend my forearm." Back orientation and banana-shaping forearm movements would have become normal. It wouldn't occur to me that there could be another way. It is only when I learn to pay attention and consciously compare an accurate intellectual understanding with my kinesthetically perceived movement that I can say something like, "There I go again, trying to pull my forearm into a banana." When I can do that I am in a position, if I wish, to change my body map, thereby establishing a new habit.

I can change my body map, but not directly, the way I choose an individual movement. The body map is a disposition in my brain, a neural pattern, and neural patterns in my brain are not directly subject to my will. But neural patterns are established in part by repetition of individual movements,

which *can* be consciously attended to and controlled. If I consistently choose a particular sort of movement, then that sort of movement can become established as a disposition. In this indirect way I can influence the dispositions in my brain, which amounts to changing my body map.* This is, in fact, the way babies build their body maps; they attend to a movement – e.g., clapping their hands – and feel satisfaction and reinforcement when they succeed in clapping their hands together, and after a while they can clap their hands at will. Their brains have

* Our physical habits, governed by our body maps, are strikingly like the moral virtues as described by Aristotle in Books II through V of the *Nichomachean Ethics*. According to Aristotle, a moral virtue like generosity is not acquired by direct choice; one doesn't simply decide, once and for all, to be a generous person. Moral virtues are acquired by acting. One becomes a generous person by performing generous actions. A generous person is one who is disposed to act generously because of the way he has acted in the past, just as a person who has a habit of balanced posture has it because of the way he has used his body in the past. It is tempting to speculate that from a neurophysiological point of view, moral virtues and physical habits may be very similar.

developed the circuitry to direct hand clapping accurately. If I move repeatedly in a certain way and establish a new habit, I'm doing the same thing that a baby does when acquiring its body map. But *attentive* movement is more effective than mere repetition, and movement consciously guided by accurate anatomical information is more effective still. Sometimes, indeed, information alone can trigger a change, as in the case of the violin student who had mismapped her elbow.

Some people take a long time to establish new habits whereas some can make changes immediately and have them stick. I suspect that those who change their movement immediately and never revert to old habits do not really make an instant change in the neural circuits that constitute their body map—what really changes is the quality and consistency of their awareness in directing individual movements and the change in neural circuits follows afterwards. On the other hand, we know that neural circuits *can* change abruptly, so perhaps some people do instantly and permanently change their body maps in response to new information or instruction. In practice, as we teach and perform, we find that although each individual is different, most people require a period of time in which to cultivate attention and awareness before a new body map is established.

Two paragraphs back I used the example of a baby learning to clap its hands. I described the baby's activity as a process of trial and error, with positive reinforcement in the form of satisfaction when the hand clapping is successful. This model of human action has been called a "sensory-motor" model, and it has dominated people's thinking on these subjects until quite recently. It is true that repetition such as I described will strengthen the appropriate neural connections, which is certainly part of what happens in acquiring or refining a physical skill, whether a rudimentary skill such as hand clapping or a refined skill such as piano playing or juggling. But recent discoveries in neurology have seriously undermined, and perhaps disproved outright, the sensory-motor model as the fundamental account of how we learn.

Mirror Neurons

In the early 1990s, a group of neuroscientists working in Parma, Italy, made a series of extraordinary observations. They were conducting a series of experiments on macaque monkeys, whose brains are smaller than human brains but sufficiently similar to be illuminating for human neurophysiology. The particular region of the monkey's brain that was the object of study was a portion of the premotor cortex, the area that controls physical action. Unsurprisingly, the motor cells in that region were active when the monkeys performed various movements and grasping exercises. But the investigators discovered, to their astonishment, that neurons associated with physical movement were also activated when the monkey was *not* performing an action. It was sufficient for the monkey merely to *observe* an action without actually performing it. The cells involved in this vicarious action have become known as "mirror neurons" and they are altering our understanding of human action, learning, and interpersonal relations.*

It appears that, thanks to the activity of mirror neurons, we recognize actions by simulating them internally. Moreover, the mirror neurons respond not only to an action but to the context in which it occurs, which enables us to recognize the intention or purpose behind the action as well as the action itself. Thus, I know the intentions of other people not as the conclusion of an inference, but by perceiving their actions in context, and this perception relies on mirror neurons. Moreover, the internal simulation of action enables me to *imitate* the actions of others. This last point is vitally important because it means that imitative behavior is, as it were, hardwired. We are by nature imitative beings. Because of this, we do not so much learn *to imitate* as we learn *by imitating*. This conclusion is supported by neurology, but just a little reflection is enough

* An account of the discovery of mirror neurons and their implications for science and society is *Mirroring People* (New York: Farrar, Straus and Giroux, 2008) by Marco Iacoboni, a neuroscientist at UCLA and one of the leaders in the investigation of mirror neurons.

to confirm it in our experience. Consider the baby mentioned above who is learning to clap its hands. I described that process previously as a matter of trial and error reinforced by satisfaction when it is successful and I claimed that repetition was important in establishing the neural patterns that direct hand clapping. There is truth in that, but anyone who has spent time with a baby knows that it is not the whole story, or the most important part of the story. The baby learns to clap its hands, first of all, by *imitating*. We *teach* the baby to clap, by playing "pat-a-cake," for example. Babies love to imitate adults, just as adults love to imitate babies, and the interpersonal back and forth of imitation is the real foundation of learning. Thus, the "sensory-motor" model mentioned above is replaced by an "ideomotor" model, based on the activity of mirror neurons, which takes intention to be primary in action and learning.

Imitation, which formerly was regarded as a common occurrence among many species of animal and relegated to a low rung on the ladder of intelligent behavior, is now regarded as "a rare ability that is fundamentally linked to characteristically human forms of intelligence, in particular language, culture, and the ability to understand other minds."* These conclusions make clear why demonstration, followed of course, by imitation, is such a fundamental and effective pedagogical tool. It has limits, as mentioned in chapter 3, but it is grounded firmly in the nature of our brains and the way we are constructed for learning. The discovery of mirror neurons and their importance for interpersonal relations also has implications for the relation between performer and audience, which I shall discuss in chapter 6.

* Quoted by Iacoboni, *Mirroring People*, p. 43.

Razullo.
Cucurucu.

4 • *Motion III: Practicing*

The way the body map influences movement, the way it arises in the brain, and the way experience alters it, have implications for practicing and rehearsing. To perform is to move, and to practice is to learn and perfect the movements that will constitute the performance. Dancers and actors know this because they communicate by means of movement itself, but many musicians are less keenly aware than are actors and dancers that when they practice, they are training movement. Because a movement approach may seem less familiar to musicians than it does to actors and dancers, I shall discuss practicing mostly from the perspective of musicians, pianists in particular. I choose pianists because as a pianist myself I am better acquainted with the practice habits of pianists than I am with those of other musicians, or of actors and dancers. However, my focus on pianists as a source of examples should not obscure the importance of these topics for other kinds of performers. The ideas I shall present are vital for all performers.

The French word for "practice" is *répéter,* "to repeat," and repetition is what many musicians appear to think practicing consists of, whether or not they know French. They talk of getting the notes "in their fingers," which they do by repeating them many times, assuming, apparently, that repetition will give security. If a passage is insecure or unreliable they say they need more practice, but they rarely mean that they should do anything different from what they've done before. They mean that they need to do whatever they've already been doing, but more of it. So they repeat the passage over and over. But all too often they attend to the notes they are playing rather than the movements that produce the notes and the passage remains insecure. They rarely attribute slow or unsatisfactory progress to faulty practice habits, and if they notice that progress is slow are likely to conclude, "I need to practice more," rather than, "I need to practice differently," although the second conclusion is often the correct one.

Artistic performance is a complex activity involving vision, kinesthesia, touch, and hearing interacting with one another. It also involves emotional and expressive feedback, which is not another sense modality but does need to be carefully mapped in relation to the sense modalities. Practicing should be as complex as the activity it prepares, with a constant interplay of intention and feedback. Many musicians, particularly when practicing, skip or curtail the feedback/judgment/appraisal part of the process, and notice only whether they play the correct notes. They repeat a passage without taking time to think how they propose to modify it, and the passage sounds much the same at the end of the practice session as it did at the beginning. If you listen from the next room to someone practicing, you rarely hear moments of silence that suggest thinking. I once read a story about the legendary British pianist Myra Hess; she was a house guest somewhere and went into the music room to practice. Her hostess in the next room heard very little actual playing, and was puzzled. At the end of an hour Myra Hess emerged and said, "I've just had the most lovely practice." I suspect that in fact she made better use of an hour than many pianists do.

Technical exercises, the cornerstone of some pianists' technical training, encourage a habit of paying more attention to the notes than to the movements that produce the notes. Many people acknowledge that possibility, but nevertheless persist in hours of technical exercises because they believe—or their teachers believe—that repeating a prescribed series of notes, if only they do it sufficiently many times, will create a skill. Indeed, C. L. Hanon, the nineteenth-century French pedagogue whose piano exercises are more widely used than any others, makes exactly that claim in his preface. He asserts that playing his exercises every day will confer marvelous skill:

> This entire volume can be played through in an hour; and if, after it has been thoroughly mastered, it be repeated daily for a time, difficulties will disappear as if by enchantment . . . we offer this work as giving the key to all mechanical difficulties.*

But Hanon's claim is false, despite its uncritical acceptance by generations of pianists and teachers. It is also incoherent. He talks of benefits that will accrue if one plays through the volume *after* having mastered it. Apparently one must master it first, before one can repeat it daily—but how does one do that? And if one does, somehow, have the skill to play it, then why bother? The exercises have no musical interest whatever. Hanon's program, by his own account, appears to be either impossible or unnecessary.

It is not the notes we play today that enable us to play tomorrow. What enables us to play tomorrow is the dispositional patterns established in our brains by the movements we use to play the notes. To be sure, repeating notes may establish patterns in the brain, but whether those patterns can serve as the foundation of a skill that will meet the demands of the literature without risk of injury will depend on the quality of the movements used to establish the patterns. Repeating notes using inefficient, tense, or awkward movements does not produce a skill, it merely ensures that next time the person plays, the movements will again be inefficient, tense, and awkward. I do not claim that technical exercises *cannot* be used intelligently, but repeating them mechanically, as students often do to comply with their teachers' instructions ("Play these exercises for twenty minutes every day without fail! Understand?") is likely in the long run to do more harm than good.

Such attention as pianists and teachers do give to movement is often confined to such recommendations as "Curl the fingers for a crisper sound," or "Use a wrist movement to play

* *The Virtuoso Pianist* (New York: G. Schirmer, Inc: 1900), preface.

staccato octaves." Sometimes suggestions like these produce a better result, sometimes not, but as commonly administered they are methodologically inadequate. First, the *piano* doesn't know whether my fingers are curled or not. All *it* responds to is how fast and for how long the key is depressed. Second, and more important, telling someone to curl his fingers or snap his wrist focuses attention on the fingers or the wrist. But we do not play just with the fingers or wrists; we play with the entire body. What we do with the fingers and wrists must be understood and experienced in relation to the rest of the body. That is because when we concentrate attention on just one part, the parts that we exclude from our awareness are likely to become tense and immobile. This not only creates the possibility of fatigue or pain, it also means that the movements of the parts one is concentrating on will be less efficient than they could be, since efficient use of a part depends on appropriate interaction with other parts, and ultimately on support from the whole body. Thus, if I concentrate on hands and fingers alone and my upper arms are tense, not only do I risk fatigue or pain in my upper arms, but the movement of my hands and fingers will be compromised and potentially injurious as well.

There is a further point. Suppose that I have dutifully focused on hands and fingers without much attention to my upper arms and torso, and that my upper arms and torso are tense, though I'm not aware of that, or if I am, I do not know that the tension is an inevitable consequence of the movements I've been working into my hands and fingers. In other words, the only movements I know to accomplish a particular pianistic task are movements that involve tension in my arms and torso. If someone observes that I am tense and says to me – or if I say to myself – "Relax!" I cannot possibly comply, because the only way I know how to play is inherently tense. This situation is extremely common, yet teachers constantly tell students to relax. They might as well tell them to fly. The way to play without tension is to learn movements that do not involve tension. Trying to relax while repeating movements that are inherently tense is certain to prove futile. As the great teacher Edna Golandsky said once in a lecture, "In an efficient technique there is nothing to relax *from*."

We need to develop a better understanding of what goes on when we practice intelligently. I believe we can do this by exploring the way voluntary movement is the result of a body map governing that movement. The conclusions we shall reach are intrinsically interesting, and they give practical insight into practicing. Indeed, they can completely transform a person's practicing and performing.

Golandsky also said, "The brain teaches the hand to play the piano." Her idea was that practicing should be guided by a clear understanding of the physical movements of piano playing. What she said is true and important, but there is an equally important complementary point, namely that influence goes in the other direction as well, not just from brain to body but from body to brain. We need to consider not only the way the brain directs movement, but also the messages that, by moving, we are sending to our brains. When we practice intelligently, the conscious mind examines the demands of the passage or composition and discovers a set of movements by which the body can meet those demands with ease and comfort, without risk of tension or fatigue. Then, with full kinesthetic attention and awareness to verify that those are the movements actually being used, the brain guides the hand and the body, moment to moment, in executing the movements. Attentive repetition of those movements establishes patterns in the brain that can direct future movements. Thus, the brain finds solutions, and at the same time movement trains the brain to guide future movement. Someone who practices intelligently repeats solutions, not just notes, and future playing is grounded in those solutions.

Performing is intentional bodily movement. But intention alone does not generate movement. The brain has to know how to move the arm before it can direct a movement that fulfills an intention. That is, carrying out a bodily movement depends on there being a representation in the brain—a body map—that can guide the movement of the body. Since the body map can be thought of as a cluster of dispositions, we can say that an individual voluntary movement is the joint product of intention and disposition: it results from an intention occurring in the context of dispositions that can bring about the intended movement.

Although dispositions are necessary for intentional action, we may not be consciously aware of them, either at the moment of acting or at any other time. Indeed, they ordinarily are *not* objects of conscious awareness. We are usually aware of the goal or purpose of our activity, but we often do not pay explicit attention to the bodily movements involved in that activity, let alone the underlying dispositions that direct those movements. We think of our actions as "drinking coffee," "riding a bike," or "playing the piano," descriptions that name the activity or state its purpose but do not refer explicitly to bodily movement. Indeed, we are so accustomed to *not* thinking of the bodily movements involved in our actions that it can seem odd when someone does call attention to them. Describing an action by naming the bodily movement, which is the part of the activity brought about by dispositions, often counts as a joke or a picturesque expression, as when someone refers to drinking cocktails as "bending an elbow." We can see from this that what we are generally aware of under descriptions like "drinking coffee" or "playing the piano" is just the top of the iceberg. The underneath of the iceberg is a hierarchical layering of dispositions, all of them necessary for the movement that constitutes the conscious activity, but usually outside our awareness.

The hierarchical arrangement of dispositions means that one set of dispositions can serve as a foundation for other dispositions that refine or elaborate the first ones. The capacity of established dispositions to function without conscious direction frees us to turn our attention to the precise requirements of particular tasks and underlies the development of higher levels of skill. At the same time, however, our capacity to establish a hierarchy of dispositions that can function without conscious attention sets the stage for two sorts of problems. The first problem arises when dispositions are inappropriate, that is, not well suited as foundations for the skills we try to build on them. The second arises when established dispositions lead to mindless activity.

Inappropriate Dispositions

Let us examine the conclusions of the last few pages in relation to piano playing. Clearly, before I can even begin to play the piano, some basic abilities must be present. In the first place, obviously, I must be able to move my arms, and the fact that this ability is rarely lacking in beginning piano students and therefore is taken for granted does not make it any less necessary. Assuming that I know how to move my arms, which amounts to assuming that I have the relevant set of established dispositions, I can rely on those "moving my arm" dispositions to function automatically. This frees me to focus on more specialized tasks, like playing a B-flat major scale. I don't have to think about moving my arm, that just happens, and I can pay attention instead to the specialized task: "B-flat, C, D, E-flat . . .". After a certain amount of time and repetition, that activity sets up another disposition, namely "B-flat major scale," that can operate without conscious direction, freeing me to turn my conscious mind to nuances or to other more complicated tasks. Thus, in the eighth measure of Mozart's Sonata in B-flat, K. 333, which contains a B-flat major scale, I no longer have to think "B-flat, C, D, E-flat," I just play the scale, thinking, if I think anything, "Oh, B-flat major." Instead of the notes I can attend to the tempo, the dynamic level, or the tone quality. As one skill becomes established as a set of dispositions I build on it to achieve further improvement.

Some components of voluntary movement, though available in principle to consciousness, are less easily noticed than others. That is because dispositions have different ranges of application. Some are general and others are specific. An example will make this clear. Consider once more the eighth measure of Mozart's Sonata in B-flat and assume, as seems likely, that it is unique in the sense that no other measure in the entire piano literature consists of that precise series of notes. If so, then when a pianist learns the sonata, some of the dispositions established will apply to that measure alone. They will be activated only when playing that measure.

But measure 8 contains a B-flat major scale, and B-flat major scales occur in many different works for piano. Therefore, the disposition "B-flat major scale," which is activated in measure 8, is also activated in other situations. We can therefore say that the disposition "B-flat major scale" has more general application than the dispositions that are activated exclusively in measure 8. Now, "B-flat major scale" is in turn a particular application of a still broader set of dispositions, those corresponding to "scale playing."* Scale playing, in turn, rests on other dispositions with even broader application, like "how to move my arm."

The dispositions unique to measure 8 and those for scale playing are activated only in playing the piano. But many dispositions used in piano playing underlie other activities as well. Piano playing thus relies on a combination of highly specialized dispositions and very general ones. Whether the specialized or the general dispositions are more important is moot; both are necessary. Nevertheless, if one of the general dispositions is poor – that is, if it generates a poor quality of movement and a correspondingly imperfect result – its consequences will be more pervasive and potentially more serious than those of a flawed specialized disposition.

Imagine a pianist in whom the dispositions specific to measure 8 of K. 333, activated nowhere else, are poor. Assume they generate awkward movements, turning her measure 8 into a shambles. It is uneven, inaccurate, and sloppy. Nevertheless, by hypothesis, those dispositions are never activated except in that one measure. Therefore, though measure 8 may be abysmal, the rest of the sonata, and the rest of her playing, could be excellent.

* Some teachers, and I am one of them, regard playing different scales as an adaptation of a single skill. All scales have the same fingering; one scale differs from another only in which finger begins the scale and in the in-and-out movements of the arm as it accommodates different combinations of white and black keys

Now, although flaws in the disposition "measure 8, Mozart K. 333" would affect that measure only, flaws in the disposition "B-flat major scale" would have wider consequences. If a flaw in the disposition "B-flat major scale" causes that scale to be uneven, then the pianist will play an uneven scale not just in measure 8, but wherever in the literature a B-flat major scale occurs. A flaw in dispositions of still wider application will have correspondingly wider consequences. If a pianist pronates the forearm in a manner that involves excess tension, then, since everything at the piano is done with the forearm pronated, every note of every composition she plays will be played with excess tension. This may undermine the quality of everything she plays. This does happen. Tension in the manner of forearm pronation ("thumb orientation") is one of the most common causes of injury among pianists.

Although the dispositions of wide application are important because they underlie so many different activities, they are also the ones of which we are least likely to be conscious. There are two reasons for this. One is that they are so general. Take the example of forearm rotation. Forearm rotation may seem to be more a matter of "how I move my arm" than of "how I play the piano" since it occurs in many activities of daily life, not just in piano playing. It is like a constant that, because it is present everywhere, ceases to be noticed at all, or like a bad smell that seems to disappear once we are accustomed to it. The second reason for being unaware of the broadest dispositions is that people ordinarily devote the most of their attention to specifics: specific movements, specific pieces, specific technical situations and problems, rather than to the underlying habits. Pianists may spend hours practicing the B-flat scale or the unique demands of a single measure of music, but few of them, unless they are injured, consciously practice pronating their forearms. This is sometimes unfortunate, because if the broader dispositions are poor, improving them can make a bigger difference to the person's playing than concentrating on specifics. In addition, it is often the key to recovering from injury.

Established dispositions functioning without conscious attention underlie what we can call our "default movements." These are the movements that occur in the absence of a conscious choice about how to move. Suppose I am concentrating on my fingers as I repeat the notes of a particular passage, and suppose further that somewhere in the passage an arm movement is required to move my hand across the keyboard to the next note. By hypothesis, I am not attending to my arm. Nevertheless, my brain will supply an arm movement. It will do so automatically, with no conscious decision from me, in the same way that it automatically supplies the arm movements that lift a coffee cup or the adjustments that keep me in balance when I ride a bicycle. But the movement my brain supplies will be based on established dispositions, habits formed in the past, perhaps in activities other than piano playing. There is no guarantee that movements supplied that way will be the best for this particular passage. Nevertheless, since they *are* my habits, they will feel normal to me. If the passage is unsuccessful it may not occur to me to examine my arm movement. I may say, "This is an awkward passage" instead of, "This passage feels awkward because my arm isn't adjusting properly." So I may simply play the passage over and over, hoping that repeated attention to my fingers will confer security.

Dispositions that become established and subsequently function without the person's being aware of them might seem to be entirely outside the person's power to control, but that, fortunately, is not the case. Although the dispositions that move one's arm *can* function without conscious awareness, they *need* not work that way. Their effects, even if ordinarily overlooked, are *available* to consciousness. In this they differ from dispositions whose effects are not available to consciousness at all. For example, I cannot be directly aware of the pH level of my blood or the dispositions by which my brain controls it, because my brain does not generate images of my pH level or the neural patterns that regulate it. Arm movements are not like that. I do have sensory systems to convey information about my arm movement to my brain, and images of

that movement are produced in my brain. If I'm not aware of my arm movement, it's because I'm not paying attention, not because I couldn't perceive it if I wanted to.

Many pianists, if asked, will admit that they are not aware of their arms and bodies as they play; their awareness includes only their fingers and hands, and, perhaps, part of their forearms. Their arms and bodies move, of course, but by habit only, sometimes in ways that jeopardize the results they are trying to achieve. Not only does such playing carry the risk of injury, it undermines the expressive quality of the performance because inattention to the movement of the whole body virtually guarantees that the player will be unaware of the emotional effect of the playing. Occasionally, performers come to appreciate what they are overlooking if asked this question: "If your audience could see only the parts of your body that you are aware of, what would they see?" In order to establish effective, healthy patterns in the brain, intelligent practicing requires attention to the underlying dispositions—the bottom of the iceberg. This is not the same as just repeating notes. Practicing that takes advantage of how the brain works consists of discovering a movement that will get the desired result with freedom and ease and without risk of injury, and then repeating that movement. Repeating the movement does entail repeating notes, of course, but it is the movement, not the notes, that trains the brain to direct future movements.

Many musicians confront an obstacle when they try to apply this approach to their own practicing because they do not know which movements are biomechanically advantageous and which are dangerous. Vital though this information is, it is almost never part of a musician's training, nor is it included in most music education programs. For example, many pianists do not know what "thumb-oriented movement" refers to, or that it is probably the most prevalent single cause of pianists' injuries.* Even those who know, intellectually, what thumb orientation is, are often unable to recognize it when they see it in themselves or their students. Worse still, many movements that are firmly established in traditional pedagogy are actually harmful if performed with the frequency demanded in piano playing. Some accepted methods of imparting skills – teaching octave playing, for example – often do not produce the desired skill and may actually injure students who try to follow them.

A pianist who becomes injured by technical exercises is similar to a person who becomes back-oriented as a result of instruction. Just as the posture myths, if followed consistently, can lead to dreadful back problems, many accepted bits of piano pedagogy are dangerous to one's health. Many teachers cannot explain from a movement perspective how to play their instrument safely and expressively, any more than most people can explain to someone else how to sit or stand in balance without tension. The large number of musicians who suffer from stress-related injuries proves that these are serious problems, and addressing them will require a profound change in the way music is taught. I hope that the information I have offered in *What Every Pianist Needs to Know about the Body*, together with

* On thumb orientation, see 73n.

the conceptual framework offered in this book, will contribute to bringing about that change.*

Mindless Playing

That an established disposition can be activated without conscious direction is a source of power, since it creates a foundation for higher levels of accomplishment, but it also presents a danger. The danger is that if a person has established a disposition by repeating a set of movements, he can then execute those movements without full attention, or, indeed, entirely automatically. The disposition produces the movements on its own, as it were. I expect that every pianist has at some time had the experience, when playing a piece whose notes have been learned, of being distracted but continuing to play. In this condition, it is possible to play an entire page of music, or even more, with no awareness, in the moment, of playing, and no recollection afterward of having done it. I shall call this *mindless playing.*

One can practice mindlessly also. Mindless practicing can produce habits—any repeated activity has the potential to create dispositions—but habits established by mindless repetition are mere movements; the person is, literally, just "going through the motions," and motions are all he is imprinting on his brain. Some common ways of practicing encourage mindlessness. In particular, an approach that relies on technical exercises or numerous repetitions of scales and arpeggios can easily become a mindless routine. Some pedagogues in the nineteenth century actually endorsed purely mechanical practicing, urging students to read a book while their hands played scales and arpeggios. But the more a person plays or practices without full attention, the more mindlessness itself becomes a habit and the more difficulty the person encounters when trying to be absolutely attentive. After all, attention, too, must be trained. It

* Books with anatomical information for other kinds of performers are listed in the footnote on page 52.

is worth asking oneself, "Am I attending at every moment?" or, "If my attention wanders do I stop practicing, take a break, and resume later?" or, "Can I play through this piece or passage with absolutely full attention at each moment?" Mindless playing and practicing are bad for a person's performance, but not necessarily injurious. Someone might have healthy habits of movement and still play mindlessly, repeating the notes entirely mechanically.* Such a person would not be physically injured, since the movements, by hypothesis, are healthy ones, but the quality of the playing would suffer.

Mindlessness can be complete, when someone plays with attention entirely elsewhere, or it can be partial, when someone attends to only one aspect of the playing. An example of partial mindlessness would be when a pianist attends just to the correctness of the notes or the technical difficulties of the notes while ignoring other aspects of the music, such as the emotional or expressive content. She may justify this by saying that one must master the notes first, before considering the expression. Indeed, some teachers encourage this. They regard learning and practicing the notes as something separate from addressing interpretive issues; expression, they seem to think, can be added later.

But they are wrong about that. Artistic performance, though it *is* movement, is not *just* movement; it includes emotion and communication, which means that it requires a coordination of circuits across different parts of the brain, those that control bodily movement *and* those dedicated to emotional response and communication. These different parts of the brain are capable of operating independently, to some extent, but the goal of artistic performance is to have them operate together. Therefore, the goal of practicing must be to create dispositional images whose activation will involve

* This is like a point attributed to Dorothy Taubman, a Brooklyn piano teacher who made immense contributions to our understanding of efficient piano technique. According to my teacher, Robert Durso, she complained that some students did not practice intelligently even after learning an efficient technique. Their practicing, she said, amounted to "drill, but with better movement."

not just bodily movement but the emotional and communicative elements of the work as well, and to incorporate those elements into the movements that constitute the performance. If someone practices without attending to the quality of the sound, the sound is likely to be poor. If someone practices without attending to the emotional content of the music, the playing will be inexpressive. Someone who practices in these ways cannot shift suddenly in performance and insert expression or improved quality of sound. The piano responds to movement, not to intentions that have not been mapped as movement. If someone has made habits out of movements that produce inexpressive sounds, merely thinking of a different result at the time of performance is unlikely to produce appropriate changes in the movement. Intention cannot bring about action if the appropriate dispositions are not already present.

The point I am making – that attending to the expressive content of the work is a vital part of preparation, including the part of preparation that some people consider to be merely technical – is extremely important, and worth expanding a bit. Antonio Damasio argues at length in *Descartes' Error* – indeed, it is a principal thesis of the book – that emotion and reason, though people often think of them as separate, are intimately connected. Reduced capacity for emotional response, as from an injury to the portion of the brain responsible for emotions, may result in impaired capacity to reason, which can lead to irrational behavior.

My point is similar, but more obvious. Practicing is a process of discovering and training the movements to be used in performance; we can think of it as reasoning about movement. Now, the ultimate goal of practicing is to discover and perfect movements that will deliver the notes *and* convey the emotional content of the work. That means that an emotional response to the work must be cultivated in order to determine what movements to use. If a musician does not absorb the expressive content of the work and appraise the sounds he actually produces from that point of view, then he can't possibly evaluate the effectiveness of the movements he is using to convey that content. An essential part of the feedback loop is missing. On the other hand, if the musician learns the music with attention to the expressive content and the movements that convey it and later refines or modifies his interpretation, he has the framework in which he can do that. The cultivation of an emotional response in this context is an example of the cognitive use of emotion that I introduced in chapter 1 and will explore further in chapter 5. Without that use of emotion it is easy to deceive oneself about the quality of the result and to believe, falsely, that the desired result is the one actually achieved.

A pianist who tries to "add the expression" after having learned the notes has a difficult assignment. If the playing is inexpressive, she will need different movements to get a different result, but different movements will go counter to the dispositions already established. What usually happens is that the pianist thinks of expressive effects and imagines that they are emerging from the piano, whereas in fact the playing sounds the same, thanks to the established dispositions. This occurs very often; a common teaching situation furnishes an example. A student plays, and the teacher says something like, "It sounds too flat. You need to differentiate between loud and soft." The student protests, "But I'm *doing* that." And she sincerely believes she is doing it. In fact, she is really just "hearing" her intention. A frequent reply from the teacher is, "Well you need to do more. You need to *exaggerate*." Now, it is true that new, unaccustomed movements may feel at first like exaggerations, but the teacher's suggestion does not address the real problem. The real problem was in the learning.

Damasio points out that a facial expression triggered by emotion is different from an expression that is "put on" voluntarily. He gives the example, with photographs, of an artificial "smile of politeness" and compares it with a genuine smile.* They are subtly different. It turns out that different muscles are activated in the two cases, and some of the muscles activated in a genuine smile are not under voluntary control. A performer

* *Descartes' Error*, p. 141.

who practices without consistent attention to the expressive content of the work, and then tries to "add back" the expression later, is like a person putting on an artificial smile.

Mindless, mechanical practicing not only produces mindless, mechanical performance, it also produces insecure and unreliable performance. It is indeed possible, through repeated activity, for the mindless practicer to establish habits – dispositions that deliver the notes – and then, with the notes "in her fingers," she may imagine that she has done her job of preparation. What has really happened is that her hands and fingers have acquired motor habits that can work more or less automatically provided she doesn't pay close attention to exactly what she is doing. What she thinks she knows – that is, what her fingers can do automatically at home, where she is under no pressure and nothing is at stake – becomes insecure, unreliable, and foreign-seeming at the lesson or in performance. This is so common that music stores sell novelty buttons: "It was better at home." But it *wasn't* better at home. The student thought it was better because conditions at home didn't call attention to the insecurity.

This situation, of encountering insecurity when performing something the performer thought had been thoroughly learned, is worth examining more closely. The experience of a pianist is something like this: She is playing, and then, perhaps because of an approaching difficult passage or because something goes slightly wrong, she realizes that she is not fully in control. Her hands continue to play by habit, but her mind is left behind and she doesn't know how to bring her hands under intentional control. At that moment she feels helpless. So she hopes or prays, desperately and usually in vain, that her hands will find their way safely to the end of the passage or the composition. That is, she hopes – though she doesn't think of it this way – that the dispositions established in her brain by all those hours of practicing will function automatically and carry her through. But trying consciously to allow your arms and hands to move automatically – i.e., unconsciously – sets up a conflict. The feeling is of being disconnected from what one is doing. In fact, it is the simultaneous recognition of two things: 1) that she is trusting to habit alone, and 2) that she doesn't actually know, in the instant, what she is doing or how to bring the playing under intentional control. When this occurs in performance, the result usually is disaster. Sometimes this sort of situation is called a lapse of memory. She appears to forget, and it's true that it can feel like forgetting. But it may not really be forgetting. She may know the music very well, both intellectually and on a motor level. The real point is that the link between intention and movement has been broken, or worse, never established in the first place.

A person who has had this kind of experience more than a few times is likely to approach performance fearfully. He fears that he will "lose it," but thinks losing it or not is in the hands of fate. In fact, his is the kind of performance anxiety that comes from insufficient preparation, but it doesn't occur to him that it comes from insufficient preparation. People can't imagine how they could be insufficiently prepared when they've repeated a work hundreds or thousands of times. The truth is that their concept of preparation is flawed. The goal of practicing is not – or should not be – to establish motor habits that can function automatically. Instead, as I sometimes insist to students, "You don't want it to be *automatic*, you want it to be *reliable*." "Automatic," in fact, is *un*reliable in performance. The performer who practices the notes apart from the intention that will guide them in performance will *inevitably* approach performance fearfully. Sensing that his performance is unreliable, he may repeat the work over and over in the desperate hope that a few more repetitions of what has already been repeated thousands of times will finally yield security.

A Better Approach

A more useful concept of practicing emerges when we return to the basic insight that performing is voluntary movement, and voluntary movement is what happens when an intention occurs in the context of dispositions that enable and direct a physical movement that realizes the intention. Voluntary movement thus has two components, intentions and dispositions, and to train voluntary movement a person must consciously train *both* components, not just one. Moreover, the two must be practiced *together.* When learning a passage or a composition a person must consciously direct movements that play the notes *and* meet the expressive elements of the music. The expressive elements must be worked out in detail; it is not enough just to think of the general features of the work, not enough just to say to oneself "this is a sad piece" and expect the result to improve. One must examine the particular character of each moment and every note: what quality of sound to produce in the first chords and the bodily movement that produces that quality, what quality of sound is needed in the second measure and the movement needed to get it, and so on to the end. A pianist must not just intend the notes but also a tempo and a dynamic and a type of sound, and must intend these things physically, feeling them in the body so that intention takes the form not of a mere wish but is a conscious directing of bodily movement.

A performer who works this way knows with perfect clarity what he wants to accomplish, he knows what he needs to do in terms of movement to achieve it, and he knows how to intend the movement. If he misses a note or makes a mistake he can quickly recover, because he knows at each instant exactly where he is and where he is going. There is no panic ("What do I do now?"), no trusting to luck ("I hope my fingers can make it to the end of this section"), no sudden sense of detachment or disconnection from one's movement. It is important from the outset to intend movements in relation to musical results, because this generates different movements from the movements that would merely play the notes. After all, someone who plays expressively must, *ipso facto,* move differently from someone who plays inexpressively, otherwise the two would sound identical. Someone who proceeds as I am urging will establish dispositions that can not only play the notes, but can play them in a chosen manner, the relation of movement to the expressive result having been firmly established.

When the proper dispositions have been established, then, because of the hierarchy of dispositions discussed earlier, they can serve as the foundation for other dispositions and they can operate without conscious direction. At that point, but not before, the performer is free to intend *the music*. He is able to listen for the results he wants and rely on dispositions to supply the movement. At the same time, he is able at any moment to turn his attention to the movement if that seems necessary or desirable. He knows how to direct the particular movements needed throughout the piece, and if he misses a note or a chord he can quickly recover. Notice that awareness of movement is not the only element involved; harmonic, structural, and rhythmic awareness are also important. But awareness of physical movement is essential to avoid stumbling in the first place and also to enable recovery; no amount of harmonic awareness will prevent stumbling if the movement is wrong.*

These conclusions illuminate what is missing from the preparation of the pianist who has practiced the notes countless times and can play them automatically in unthreatening surroundings but is insecure when performing. She isn't accustomed to applying the mental focus and attention needed to perform reliably. When she tries to focus on what she is doing, she may find that she doesn't really *know* what she is doing, or more precisely, she knows what she *wants* but not what she needs to *think*, in the moment, to achieve it. The proper intention cannot just be turned on in a moment. It, too, requires practice.

I have focused on piano playing in this discussion, but the conclusions reached are entirely general, and apply – or can be easily adapted – to all sorts of performers, whether musicians other than pianists, or dancers or actors. It is not enough for an actor merely to know the emotion to be communicated in a scene, because that knowledge alone does not guarantee communication. He must also know the movements and the

* The points in the last two sentences of the paragraph were made in a personal communication by British pianist Paul Roberts.

vocal inflections (also achieved by bodily movement) that will convey the emotion, and the movements must be trained in relation to intention and emotional awareness. Similarly with other sorts of performers.

In describing performance as intentional bodily movement I am using the word "intentional" and the corresponding verb "to intend" in a particular sense. In ordinary conversation, "intend" can simply mean "on purpose" ("Did you intend to insult him?"). Moreover, a person can form an intention separately from the action that fulfills the intention ("I intend to go to the bank tomorrow") and without determining the means ("I intend to go but haven't decided whether to walk or take the bus"). But it is no good for the performer merely to form an intention of this kind; it is not enough to think or say, "I intend to play very beautifully tonight." That is doubtless a laudable intention, but it is not *performing*. In performance, intention must govern the particular movements, moment to moment, that realize the intention and constitute the performance; the intention in performance is "the thought that guides and accompanies action."* Notice, by contrast, that practicing, unlike performing, *does* involve the forming of intentions apart from the actions that fulfill them. When practicing, a person formulates definite intentions and then, through attentive experimentation, discovers movements that realize those intentions.

What I mean by the "proper intention" is worth some additional illustration. Suppose you have a pie plate full nearly to the brim with water. It is on your kitchen counter, and you wish to move it across the room to the opposite counter. But how will you accomplish that? Obviously, you can't just casually pick up a pie plate full of water without risking a spill. You will have to be attentive. Indeed, in imagining this example, you may find, as I do, that the greater the detail in which you imagine the operation, the harder it is to imagine not spilling a drop, since pie plates full of water are tricky to manipulate and

* I take this formulation from Stuart Hampshire, *Thought and Action*.

prone to spilling. In any event, imagine that you carefully pick up the plate, being sure not to tilt it or move abruptly. Then, as you walk across the room with it, you move very smoothly, attending closely to each step. When you reach the opposite counter you set the plate down gently, with no abrupt movements. Notice that the delicacy of the maneuver forces you to be aware of the movements throughout your body – arms, legs, and torso – that affect the outcome. In short, the task requires uninterrupted attention, moment-to-moment direction of each movement in the context of a heightened awareness of the entire body, as well as ongoing appraisal and adjustment. These are the characteristics of what I shall call "fully intentional" activity, and it is indispensable for reliable artistic performance.

The delicacy of maneuvering a pie plate full of water forces attention to the entire body. But what if attention didn't expand to include the body? Imagine trying to move the pie plate while concentrating just on your hands and fingers, with no awareness of your arms, torso, or legs. It is hard to imagine succeeding at the task in that mental state. Nevertheless, that – or its analogue – is the condition in which many people practice. They repeat notes with only partial awareness of how they do it, without knowing the role of the rest of the body, which leads to insecurity in performance. Intelligent practicing must be fully intentional, just like performance.

Kinesthetic, visual, tactile, and auditory images must be linked. When this is done, the dispositional image connected with a particular piece or passage is a complex image in which sound and movement are mapped together. Then the intending of a certain musical result occurs in the context of dispositions that can get that result. If there are no previously established dispositions to control the descent of the keys to produce a singing tone or a pianissimo or an emotional nuance, then intending those results will be ineffective because it becomes a case of trying to intend something one doesn't know how to do.

The example of the pie plate illuminates this point. Walking across the room with a pie plate full of water without spilling a drop is difficult. It is not a task one has to perform often, but suppose you decide, for some reason, that it is a skill you wish to acquire. So, you practice, going back and forth across the kitchen with pie plates full of water, and most likely the floor is soon covered with puddles. You mop up the water and decide to pursue a different strategy. The new strategy will consist of simplifying the task for practice purposes: you now practice with an empty pie plate. Clearly, you will have no trouble moving the empty plate, so you do it over and over, making your movements very smooth and fluid. Under these conditions you can easily convince yourself that you are mastering the delicate skill of pie-plate manipulation.

But you are setting yourself up for disappointment. As soon as you actually fill the plate with water, you will find that what seemed easy is suddenly hard again, and you'll have to get out the mop. The reason is that in the name of practicing a certain task, you've actually substituted a *different* task. Moving an empty pie plate simply does not test or train the skills needed to move a pie plate full to the brim with water. It does not force heightened whole-body awareness. A successful strategy would train the skills you will actually need to carry out the task, not substitute some other skills whose mastery only gives you a false sense of security. This is the conclusion I have been urging with regard to performance: the skills needed in actual performance must be conscientiously trained beforehand. They cannot be added at the last moment, like icing to a cake or water to a pie plate.

I have described how practicing with the proper attention helps to establish dispositions that confer security in performance, but attention has another, surprising power as well: when we act with full attention *we have more time.* This seems like a paradoxical claim, but some performers and teachers have recognized it, at least in a practical way. A teacher of mine often said such things as, "Remember, there is time actually to *play* every note," or, "*Finish* each note before going to the next." Such suggestions puzzled me. How, in a rapid passage, could one possibly follow them? Nevertheless, I found, to my surprise, that when I tried to play according to those instructions, things actually did improve. I found that even in a fast piece or a rapid passage I could develop a sense of being on top of every note, and I came to believe that even though a piece might have a rapid tempo as measured on a metronome, and might sound fast to a listener, if it felt fast *to me* it was out of control (another of my teacher's precepts). Puzzling as such points may seem, they are borne out by recent experimental investigations of time perception. Things take longer—we have more time—when we pay close attention. David Eagleman, a prominent researcher on time perception at Baylor College of Medicine, says, "Time is this rubbery thing. It stretches out when you really turn your brain resources on, and when you say, 'Oh, I got this, everything is as expected,' it shrinks up,"* and he concludes, as summarized by Burkhard Bilger, "The more detailed the memory, the longer the moment seems to last."†

Practicing and Performing

Failure to practice the skills needed in performance creates a gap between practicing and performing: the two become different activities. That, in fact, is how many performers think of them. They consider performance to be essentially different from practicing or rehearsing, an alien activity for which no amount of preparation ever seems to be sufficient. That attitude turns performing into an impossible assignment and makes a mystery of the fact that there are people who learn to do it. It may be tempting simply to acknowledge the mystery and say, "Well, some people are just born performers and that's all that can be said." Many people seem content to leave it at that, but in fact it is a cop-out. The kind of preparation I am advocating bridges the gap between practicing and performance. Narrow-

* Quoted by Burkhard Bilger in a profile of David Eagleman, *The New Yorker,* April 5, 2011, pp. 60–62.

† *Ibid,* p. 60.

ing the gap and, ideally, eliminating it is essential for successful performance. Recognizing this, some teachers try strategies like urging their students that the only difference between practicing and performing is that in performance one plays the composition through without stopping, and wears nicer clothes. But that is helpful only if the focused intention required in performance is also part of the preparation.

When practicing does include the intention required in performance, the difference between performing and practicing becomes largely a difference in description. If I am playing Chopin, I could describe my activity as "playing the Fourth Ballade" or as "moving my arms to play a certain series of keys with a certain quality of sound." When I think of myself as "playing the Fourth Ballade," I am in performance mode; when I think of myself as "moving my arms to play a certain series of keys with a certain quality of sound," I am in practice mode. Thinking of the activity under that description may lead me to recognize things I previously hadn't noticed that affect the quality of my playing. I can then make appropriate changes and cultivate the intention that will deliver the result I want and carry me through in performance. When I switch to performance mode, I intend the music. But the intention to play the music now occurs in the context of dispositions that not only play the notes but also control the expressive result. I can play securely and am free to focus on the musical result, even to make musical choices while performing, because my practicing included everything required.

I am not suggesting that the performer who prepares in the way I have advocated will always approach performance with complete self-confidence, without a trace of nervousness or performance anxiety. On the contrary, many superb performers are doubtful or apprehensive before a performance, despite years of successful performing. Vladimir Horowitz claimed once in an interview that he was always terrified of walking out on stage, but his fear vanished the moment he was at the piano. He always knew then, he said, exactly what he had to do. This brings us to the important point that there are several kinds of performance anxiety. One of them, the sort Horowitz appears to have suffered from, disappears when the performance begins. From that moment, the performer is fully engaged in the intentional voluntary action that is his performance. Along with some other writers, I shall refer to this kind of anxiety as "butterflies." The symptoms can be severe. People can, literally, worry themselves sick, although not many performers go to such extremes. The best, most thorough preparation will not necessarily prevent a person's experiencing butterflies. The remedy is to begin the performance. Why an accomplished performer should feel nervous is not entirely clear; nevertheless, very few performers, even with years of experience, approach a performance with no apprehension whatever. Perhaps the apprehension stems from reluctance to undertake the kind of self-exposure that performance necessarily entails. Or perhaps it is a sort of acknowledgement that performance is inevitably uncertain. Every performance – like every human action – is in doubt until it actually occurs.

Another sort of performance anxiety is the result of insufficient preparation, or of the wrong kind of preparation. This is the sort I have been addressing, and I contend that insufficient preparation and the wrong kind of preparation are far more common than many performers know or acknowledge. One reason is that skill in performing is not the same as skill at one's particular instrument or medium. Skill in piano playing, to pursue the example we have been using, does not guarantee the ability to perform successfully. Some people are superb pianists, in the sense that they can negotiate the most difficult and demanding passages with ease, but are poor performers. The reverse can be true as well. Some pianists are better at performing than they are (from a technical point of view) at playing the piano. If I am a capable pianist but a poor performer – which describes a vast number of people who play very well alone but perform poorly – then additional practicing of my piano skills will not solve my problem. Performing, too, is a skill, and *it* is the skill I need to cultivate. Attending to mental focus and intention in the manner I have described

will help me to make progress in this direction. Notice, however, that although cultivating mental focus and attention will make me better, it will not necessarily turn me into a great performer. Performance on the highest level is a complex activity, and it requires many skills that do not always occur together. Obviously, a great pianist must have technical skill adequate for the repertoire he chooses, and he must have the skill of focused intention we have discussed. But in addition he needs musical insight and understanding. He needs the skill of communicating with an audience, along with other skills and abilities, including, some people insist, an ironclad digestion. All of these are separate attributes, in the sense that a person can have one of them but not another. On rare occasions, they all come together at the highest level in a single individual. When they do, we have a Vladimir Horowitz or an Artur Rubinstein. I do not pretend that everyone can attain that level, but I do claim that we can make progress. If I understand clearly what skills I need and know how to cultivate them, I can improve. I am a better pianist and performer now than I was last year; next year

I expect to be better still. I will not be Horowitz or Rubinstein, but I will be closer to being the best I can be.

Intention

I have described intention as the conscious direction of bodily movement, and I have insisted that it must be trained if a performer is to achieve security. That makes intention sound like a skill, a mental skill, we might say, to be cultivated along with the necessary technical or physical skills. That is true. Focused intention *is* a skill. But it is more than just a practical advantage, something that improves the quality of performance. It is a *conceptual* requirement. Without it we wouldn't simply have a poor or insecure performance, we would have no performance at all. To see this, suppose that you are attending a piano recital and suddenly realize that the sounds you hear are not made by the piano in front of you. The pianist is depressing the keys, but this is a silent piano and her movements cause no sound. Instead, the sounds come from a CD player concealed in the piano. Clearly, we would deny that she is performing the music. Moving one's body to depress the keys is not sufficient to perform a piece of piano music; the depression of the keys must actually create the sounds we hear.

But even if the pianist's movements do cause the sounds, that is not yet sufficient. For the pianist may depress the keys and produce sounds in the regular way, but what if she is drugged or hypnotized or in a trance, with no awareness or possibility of recollecting what she is doing? What if she is like the heroine of *La Sonnambula* and is really asleep? Or, more likely, what if she is not drugged or in a trance or asleep, but is merely inattentive? Through diligent practice she has trained her hands to play the notes, then a distracting thought crosses her mind and holds her attention, and she continues to play the notes automatically even though her mind is elsewhere. Suppose that she is thinking about her dinner and how hungry she is. Clearly, in that moment she is not playing intentionally; her playing is a case of the mindless playing we have already encountered. Since she is not aware of herself playing at all, she cannot be aware of the particular result she is getting, nor can she be intending it. It is plausible to say that even though she may not have missed any notes, she was not truly in control; she was not directing what she was doing, nor did she choose to play as she did; her playing was just the result of habit, a conditioned response rather than an intentional action. In all the cases we have considered, the pianist appears to be performing, but she is not really performing, because in none of them do the sounds result from intentional action.

At this point we should call attention to two features of intentional actions. The first is that when an action is intentional, the person who does it knows that he did it. He may not have formulated his intention in words; he may have difficulty finding the right words to describe his exact intention; he may even have acted spontaneously and say something like, "It just seemed the right thing to do at the moment." Nevertheless, he knows that he did it, and the question, "Why did you do that?" is not out of place. Conversely, if a person does not know that he did something, then it was not an intentional action of his.

The second feature of intentional action is that the intentionality of an action depends on a description. It may be intentional under one description and not under another. If someone crosses a field but does not know that crossing the field is an act of trespass, we would say that he crossed the field intentionally, but he did not intentionally trespass. Thus, it is possible for someone to act intentionally and to know what he is doing under one description, while under another description the action is not intentional and he does not know what he is doing.

These two features of intentional action help us to better formulate the requirement that performance be intentional. At a performance, we assume, first, that the performer knows what he is doing. We assume that it always makes sense to ask a performer, "Why did you do that?" or, "Why did you do it that way?" and this assumption takes for granted that the performer knows that he did that and can say something about what his intention was. We assume this about every part of the performance, even the smallest details. If we ask a pianist, "Why did you make a ritard there?" we expect her to have an answer. Similarly if we ask a dancer, "Why did you smile and look away from your partner at that moment in the dance?" or an actor, "Why did you deliver that speech so slowly?" If the performer replies, "Gee, did I do that? I didn't know I did," we conclude that, with respect to that particular detail, the performance was imperfectly intentional, which would count as a flaw. We assume, second, that the activity of performing is the description under which the action is intentional. In the case of the distracted pianist mentioned above, she *is* playing the Fourth Ballade, but if she is actually preoccupied with thoughts of food, she does not *know* that she is playing the Fourth Ballade; what she knows herself to be doing (her true answer to the question, "What are you doing?") is thinking about food. That is, her action is not intentional under the description "playing the Fourth Ballade," so we conclude that although she appears to be performing, she is not really performing.

The requirement that performance be intentional action must not be taken so strictly as to imply that the slightest lapse from full intentionality will undermine the entire performance. Real life is not so tidy. Unintentional and unexpected things do happen even in fine performances. The pianist misses a note or a chord, the dancer misses a step, or, less obviously, a passage simply doesn't come out as intended even though we in the audience do not know that. Such lapses may be disastrous, or they may be inconsequential. A momentary distraction from which the performer immediately recovers is insignificant, but a loss of attention that leaves the performer uncertain where he is, or unable to proceed, will ruin the performance. What we should conclude is that the determination to remain consistently focused, likewise the intention and the ability immediately to recover focus if it is momentarily lost—these are themselves intentional skills that must be cultivated. They amount to a sort of second-order intentionality, as if the performer were to say, "I am determined to remain consistently focused, but *also* determined, should a distraction arise, to immediately recover and regain my focus," or, "I can't guarantee that nothing untoward will happen, but I can guard against it by having a 'plan B' in reserve, namely my trained ability to return to myself." The importance of this point is hard to overstate. No one is entirely immune from occasional intruding thoughts, and there can always be distracting noises or disturbances in the hall that could unnerve a performer. One cannot prevent such things, but one can learn to deal with them. First-rate performers recover their focus without the audience perceiving any interruption or uncertainty. Performers who cultivate this skill will deliver fine performances despite occasional departures from full intentionality.

Inspiration

There are occasions when everything falls into place. The performance goes smoothly, even effortlessly. Difficulties or passages that were troublesome in rehearsal are suddenly secure. Performers may describe such occasions with comments like, "It seemed I could do nothing wrong," or, "It felt as if the music just flowed through me," or, "I must have been inspired." I shall say that on such occasions performers have *a sense of being one with the work*.

The concept of inspiration, which people sometimes invoke in connection with outstanding performances, is worth examining because it can mean different things. If someone says that a person's performance was "inspired" that may simply mean that it was unusually good. If someone says he is "inspired" by Stephen Hough's piano playing, that may mean that he admires Stephen Hough's playing to the point of wishing to emulate it. Such uses of "inspiration" are harmless. But sometimes when people speak of inspiration being necessary for a good performance, they are thinking of inspiration in an etymologically literal sense, as a receiving of some power or force from outside themselves – becoming "in-spirited" by a divine or spiritual source that enables them to perform well.

It turns out that many performers, even if they do not use the word "inspiration," think that their performance depends on some such force or power. When the force is with them, the performance is a success; when it isn't, the performance fails. Performers with this sort of belief will therefore worry about what they need to do to make sure that the force is with them – an uncertain undertaking, since the force or power they rely on is, by hypothesis, outside themselves and not under their control.

Whether they know it or not, performers who think this way are relying on an old and extremely influential philosophical theory of art, according to which artists are empowered by spirits, or forces, or deities. An early articulation of this view is in Plato's *Ion*. Ion is a rhapsode, someone who recites Homeric poems, and is therefore a performing artist. In the dialogue, Socrates offers a series of arguments by which he gets Ion to agree that his ability to produce an effect on his audience does not derive from any skill or knowledge that he himself possesses. Instead, Socrates claims that when Ion recites he is carried out of himself. He is inspired, and not in his right mind. His power is not his own; it comes from the muse, or the gods, or Homer speaking through him. Socrates says:

> All good poets, epic as well as lyric, compose their beautiful poems not by art but because they are inspired and possessed.

And he continues:

> There is no invention in [the poet] until he has been inspired and is out of his senses and the mind is no longer in him: when he has not attained to this state, he is powerless and unable to utter his oracles . . . not by art does the poet sing but by power divine.*

Socrates offers no arguments for this view. He merely presents it as his theory, and the arguments by which he gets Ion to apply it to himself are specious and entirely unpersuasive.

* Plato, *Ion*, 533–34.

Nevertheless, the theory itself—that artists are possessed by, or are conduits for, some power or force outside themselves—has been immensely influential ever since the time of Plato. I shall call it the "Socratic theory," and it is still very much with us. Performers who say, when things go well, "I don't know where it came from; the music just seemed to flow through me," or "I was suddenly inspired" may not think that they are invoking Socrates, but all too often they actually do imagine that their successful performance was due to a spiritual power, or a force, or a god—something outside themselves—and they are therefore subscribing to the Socratic theory.

Despite its historical prestige, the Socratic theory is entirely implausible. We can see it as an attempt to explain artistic creation. Now, artistic creation is admittedly a profoundly mysterious thing. Exactly how artists arrive at their ideas and insights, how they arrive at the astonishing skill some of them possess, is puzzling, just as it is puzzling how mathematicians come to their theorems. But we do not solve the puzzle by denying the artist his agency. To explain a poet's creation by saying, "Well, *he* didn't really do it, he was out of his mind the whole time and a spirit put the words in his mouth," does not explain anything. Instead of seriously examining the question it merely substitutes a ludicrous myth. If we cannot explain artistic creation we are better off describing it as Jane Austen describes Mrs. Musgrove's surprising recollection, in *Persuasion,* that Captain Wentworth had been her son's commanding officer, calling it simply "one of those extraordinary bursts of mind which do sometimes occur."*

Many great artists have accepted some form of the Socratic theory. Any number of composers, writers, and painters through the centuries have believed not only that their art served a higher purpose—religious, moral, or whatever—but that their very ability to create their work came from outside themselves, from God, or the angels, or a spiritual force, or something. Some artists holding such beliefs have produced great masterpieces.

* *Persuasion,* chapter 6.

Now, if an artist produces masterpieces, the truth or falsity of his beliefs about the source of his power does not matter much. He could believe something utterly bizarre—that his brush was actually guided not by his hand but by fluctuations in the earth's magnetic field—but if the work were good we could overlook his peculiar beliefs. We might even maintain that his beliefs, though peculiar, were helpful to him.

In the case of performers we could similarly put up with the Socratic theory if it were useful. If it offered a reliable way for performers to improve their performances, we could accept it as a practical tool without concerning ourselves about its literal truth or falsity. But it does not, and performers who buy into it are making a very bad bargain. A believer in the theory may say after a disappointing performance, "I didn't abandon myself sufficiently to the music," or, "I wasn't receiving the right vibes," or, "Tonight just wasn't my night," or perhaps, "I didn't pray enough." But none of those feeble explanations will enable a better performance next time. The theory makes a mockery of preparation. What is the point of practicing or rehearsing, if the result is in any case outside one's power? Trusting to luck or the gods or the spirit world is notoriously ineffective.

Even performers who believe in the influence of outside powers will admit, when pressed, that their belief has not helped them consistently to achieve more satisfying performances. On the contrary, their belief assures that they will always be disappointed. If a performance goes badly they will be disappointed by the failed performance even if they attribute the failure to an outside power, but if the performance goes well they will also feel inadequate, because *they* didn't do it. How, after all, can one feel good about a performance or take credit for it if it was not one's own doing? Belief that performance depends on something outside oneself is therefore likely to undermine a performer's self esteem, which is yet another strike against it, because having a favorable opinion of oneself and one's capabilities is absolutely essential for a performer.

The Socratic theory of inspiration is a dead end. Those who subscribe to it, in whichever of its numerous formulations, are adopting a view that makes their task impossible. The only solution is to abandon the theory. In fact, performers who abandon it often experience a huge sense of relief. They are, as it were, "off the hook" and can turn to more productive ways of improving their performance. They may not immediately become great performers, but at least they can take matters into their own hands and make progress, and *that* is liberating. Performers should strive for the awareness: "I am doing this," not the feeling: "this is happening to me." Instead of a sense of being possessed, a sense of themselves as conscious agents is what they should aim at.

I can think of just one situation in which an appeal to luck or chance or the gods is other than harmful. A well-prepared performer might say, before walking on stage, "Wish me luck," or, "From here on, it's in the lap of the gods," or something. But he is not trusting to luck or the gods in lieu of preparing. I take his remark simply to be a recognition, an acknowledgement of the uncertainty that is part of *any* performance. As a human action, a performance is not predetermined. It is contingent until it actually occurs.

We began this discussion of inspiration by considering the experience of a successful performance. We have seen that some descriptions of that experience – "the music just flowed through me" – can lead to a form of the Socratic theory, but I also offered an alternative formula, "feeling one with the work," which has the advantage that it does not suggest the Socratic theory. I propose now to examine that feeling, with no further reference to Socrates. I believe we can say something useful about what the feeling is and the conditions that make it possible. It does not come from outside oneself, or from nowhere, nor is it a spontaneous generation, as Aristotle supposed mice to be (and even mice, Aristotle thought, didn't come from *nothing* – they were generated, he surmised, from dust). If feeling one with the work were entirely a matter of chance, how would we explain why some performers achieve it more consistently than others? It is not plausible that they are merely enjoying a lucky streak. I believe that by examining the experience of feeling one with the work in relation to some of the concepts developed earlier in this chapter, we can arrive at an understanding that will be interesting in itself and also of practical use to performers as they work to improve their performances. To approach this topic we must revisit the concept of action.

Let us distinguish two sorts of action, which I shall call *indirect* and *direct* action. An indirect action is something I do, but I do it by doing something else, something that has the thing I am setting out to do as its effect. As an example, suppose I am a golfer setting out to get the ball into the cup. I can't simply put the ball into the cup. The rules of golf require that I do something else, namely, hit the ball with my club in order to cause it to roll into the cup. Sinking the putt is an action of mine, but I do it indirectly, by doing something else that causes it to happen. A direct action, by contrast, is an action such that there is no other action of mine that causes it, nothing else I do to bring it about. An example is raising my arm. When I wish to raise my arm I just do it – I don't do anything else first to make it move. Now, saying that I raise my arm directly does not mean that there are no causes of my arm going up. There are causes; my brain sends a neural message to appropriate muscles, which activates them, and the muscular contraction causes my arm to go up. But those causes are not things I *do;* they occur in my body but are not actions of mine. *I* just raise my arm; my brain, outside my awareness, takes care of the rest.

Although the conceptual distinction between direct and indirect action is clear, which individual actions fall in one category or the other is not always obvious, nor is it fixed. I claimed above that raising my arm is a direct action. Ordinarily, I think that is true, but under some circumstances it could be an indirect action. For example, I occasionally wake up at night in a position that has caused my arm to go completely asleep. In that condition I cannot raise my arm directly as I normally do. I have to pick it up with the other arm to move it. I can raise it, but only indirectly. (Fortunately, I have never yet awakened with *both* arms completely asleep.) We also saw above that if I raise my arm directly, the cause of its going up—let us take it to be the contraction of my bicep—is not an action of mine. But that contraction *could* be an action, the bicep being a voluntary muscle. Suppose I am working out with dumbbells and, following my coach's instructions, I focus on tensing my bicep. In that case, what I'm doing is tensing my bicep. Tensing my bicep brings about the going up of my arm, but as an effect, not as what I'm consciously doing. I may be raising my arm, but I am doing so indirectly.

It is clear from this that whether an action is direct or indirect depends on the representation that directs the action, which is like saying that it depends on how our brain is mapping the action. If I raise my arm, that could be a direct action on one occasion and an indirect action on another, depending on how I think of it, where "how I think of it" refers to my intent and the way I represent the action to myself. Two movements could look identical to an observer and yet one could be direct and the other indirect, because an observer cannot always tell what the body map is that guides a particular movement. Let us now apply these distinctions to performance.

Suppose I decide to learn Chopin's Fourth Ballade. The Fourth Ballade is a very difficult composition. Many pianists consider it to be one of the most difficult in the piano literature. I am not likely, therefore, to be able simply to sit down and play it. I will have to learn it. If I follow my own advice and adopt the approach to practicing advocated in this chapter, I will learn it by attending carefully to the movements that will send my fingers to the proper keys. I will examine the demands of the piece and discover movements that can meet those demands. They must be movements that will in the end enable me to play the piece as fast as I think it should go, even though I may repeat them slowly at first. They must not lead to tension or fatigue. In short, they should be healthy movements based on an accurate and adequate body map. Having discovered what movements will enable me to play the piece, I then repeat those movements. Now, when I practice this way I am, in fact, playing the Fourth Ballade. But I am playing it indirectly. What I am doing directly is repeating certain movements, movements that have the Fourth Ballade as their effect. The movements occur simultaneously with the ballade, but since I'm still in practice mode and focused on the movements—that is, moving a certain way is how I represent my activity to myself—it is clear that what I am doing *directly* is repeating the movements and what I doing *indirectly* is playing the ballade, just as when I work out at the gym I directly tense my muscle and indirectly raise my arm, even though the two occur at the same time. An actor developing a character goes through a similar process. The actor considers the personality of the character he is creating and decides how that character should move, how the character would stand, what the character's habitual gestures and vocal inflections would be. He then carefully practices those movements. He is enacting the character, but indirectly.

In time, through repetition and attention, the movements that will play the Fourth Ballade become habits—dispositions in my brain. That is, the movements have been stored as dispositions that can function even without my consciously calling on them. That can be a danger, since as we saw earlier it makes mindless playing possible. But it need not lead to mindless playing. Instead it can lead to greater achievement, because when I have established the appropriate dispositions, playing the Fourth Ballade becomes something I can do directly. I no longer have to think of executing movements in order to play the ballade. Instead I can think of playing the ballade, and my brain will produce the necessary movements without my consciously having to think of them.

Let us suppose that the movements I have imprinted in my brain are adequate not only to the technical demands but also to the musical requirements of the piece. The Fourth Ballade is very difficult, but under the supposition we are adopting, playing it will be easy. By that I mean that negotiating the notes, complicated though they are, will no longer be a problem for me. A difficulty, after all, ceases to be a difficulty once it has been mastered, which, by hypothesis, is the case here. Indeed, playing *must* be easy in the sense I have specified, because no one could reliably perform anything if the technical demands of the work were still an obstacle. Leopold Godowsky reportedly made a similar point. Godowsky was one of the great piano technicians of the twentieth century. His arrangements of the Chopin études are more difficult than the originals, and many pianists regard his original compositions as unplayable. It happens that my childhood piano teacher, Jessie Siegel, was acquainted with Godowsky in the 1930s in New York. She told me that he once said to her, "Nothing is hard any more." Other pianists may have to struggle with Godowsky's compositions, but for him they were easy. From this I conclude that when we speak of a technically difficult piece, we really mean a piece that is demanding to *learn*, one that requires highly developed skills. Acquiring a skill may be a lengthy business, but having acquired it, one can exercise it at will.

Claiming that playing the Fourth Ballade will be easy after I have imprinted adequate movements in my brain is not the same as pretending that I will always play it flawlessly, or that every performance will be as good as every other, nor should what I have said be taken to imply that performing is easy or automatic. The movements may be available, but consistent focus, attention, and intention are as necessary as ever. Performance is demanding and exhausting, even though carrying out the necessary movements may have become something I can do because I now have the skill. What my claim really means is that I have reached a place where I can play the music directly. I can intend the music. I no longer move my arms or play notes *in order* to play the music. My arms do move, but moving my arms is not what I'm doing consciously; my brain takes care of that part, just as it supplies the necessary muscular contractions that cause my arm to go up when I raise my arm. Saying that moving my arms is not what I am consciously doing does not mean that I'm unaware of the movement. I can be aware of the movement, just as when I raise my arm directly I am aware of my arm going up. When I move my arm directly there is no separation in my experience between my intention and the going up of my arm. It isn't merely that they occur together; in my experience they are the same event. Similarly in performance. What I do is the music. I am one with the music. An actor who has mastered his character, including the gestures and movements and vocal inflections, is in the same situation. He no longer thinks of moving in order to create the character; what he directly does is enact the character, and the movements, imprinted in his brain, occur. The character and the physical movements of producing the character are indistinguishable in his awareness.

When a performer reaches the condition I have described, not only are there no further steps to be gone through, it is also the case that the skill is available, within limits, to respond in the moment to different intentions. If I decide in the middle of a performance to do something differently, I can do it. But that description already suggests too great a separation. I don't (or I needn't) *decide* first and then *do* afterwards. Deciding and doing are the same action, once the appropriate dispositions are established. The separation between me and what I am doing evaporates; I am the music, I am the character. For the duration of the performance I become the work I am performing.

I said earlier that in practicing a person repeats movements, thereby establishing neural patterns in the brain, which become dispositional images that guide future movements. What I am describing now – the experience of being one with the work, is the same thing, but from a different point of view. The earlier discussion offered a description from the outside – the account a neurologist might give (but without the neurological detail). It took the perspective of an observer, a scientist explaining how neural patterns can become established in the brain and can be the basis of future movement. Let us call this a *third-person* perspective. We are now considering the same sequence of events, but from a different perspective, that of the person in whose body the events occur. We are describing the events according to how they feel, what they are like to the person who has them. We can call this a *first-person* perspective. From a first-person perspective I am not aware of establishing neural patterns in my brain when I practice, even though I know that from a third-person perspective, that's what occurs, and I can take advantage of that knowledge to make my practicing more effective. What I am aware of in the first person is how it feels—a hard passage that, after careful practice, becomes effortless, such that I no longer have to do anything else to make it happen. I just intend the result and the notes are there. The feeling is of being one with the music.

The reality described from the two perspectives is the same—a series of events in the brain—but the two descriptions use words with different meanings, and there would be no way, from the descriptions, to know that they refer to the same thing or to derive one from the other. How could one possibly guess, from looking through a scanner at a neural network in someone's head that *to the person* that network was the recollection of a favorite melody? And how could I know, when I recall a favorite melody, that what gives me that experience is a sequence of neural events occurring in my brain? The relation between the two perspectives is a mystery of philosophy and also of neurophysiology.

I conclude this chapter by offering to performers three recommendations that summarize the practical application of the issues discussed in this chapter.

1) *Always* be awake kinesthetically; that is, be attentive to movement throughout your body and to the way your movement contributes to the effect at which you are aiming. This means attending and feeling very carefully.

2) *Never* repeat anything mindlessly—that is, without forming a new intention.

3) *Never* practice or rehearse without attention to the expressive or emotional content of the work.

For most performers, scrupulously following those three recommendations will make practicing and rehearsing more effective and bring about a transformation in performance. Although the recommendations were derived in this chapter from a discussion of piano playing, they are entirely general and apply to all performers, whether musicians, actors, or dancers.

Franca Trippa.
Fritellino.

5 • *Emotion*

I asserted in chapter 1 that performers use emotion and feeling cognitively in preparing and presenting a work of performing art, and audience members use emotion and feeling cognitively in apprehending the work. I shall explore that contention more fully in this chapter, but first I shall consider a more familiar view whose inadequacy will show the need for a different approach. Let us agree that many works of performing art have an emotional or expressive content that the performer makes – or tries to make – available to the audience. How does the performer do that? Many people have claimed – or assumed – that the performer actually experiences the emotion and communicates it to the audience through the performance. An actor, for example, experiences an emotion of fear and his performance communicates or expresses his fear. This theory has been argued back and forth for centuries and has had as many attackers as defenders, the attackers insisting, correctly, that it simply isn't true that an actor must actually be afraid in order for his performance to communicate fear. Nevertheless, many people assume that feelings and emotions experienced by the performer are *somehow* relevant to the performance. That is to say, they assume that the nature and quality of the performance depend at least partly on the nature and quality of the emotion the performer is feeling in the moment. I believe that this is an unacceptable position. Nevertheless, a lot of teaching relies on it, so I shall discuss it in the context of a teaching situation.

Suppose a piano student plays inexpressively and her teacher, hoping to stimulate a more expressive result, says,

"Remember, this is a very sad piece," or, "Think of being in love," or, "Think of a beautiful sunset." Instructions like these are the stock in trade of many teachers, but they can be taken in several ways. One way to understand them is that the teacher accepts the view that art in general, and piano playing in particular, are an outward manifestation of something internal and that their quality depends on the nature of the inner experience. She therefore offers the student an image intended to stimulate a suitable inner state, namely certain emotions or feelings, which, she thinks, will cause the playing to improve. Since the teacher is using images or fantasies to evoke feelings in the student, I shall call this an "image-based" or "fantasy" approach. Sometimes, fantasy works. The teacher says, "Think of a lovely sunset," and the student plays better. But often it doesn't work, and when the teacher says, "Think of a lovely sunset," the student plays as badly as ever. The teacher may then resort to a different fantasy, or a smörgasbord of fantasies, trying one suggestion after another until she finds one that works: "Think of a rainbow," "Think of a dove," "Think of flowing water." If the student finally plays better, the teacher can ask, "What did I say that made the difference?" and add a new fantasy to her bag of pedagogical tricks.

A large repertoire of fantasies may have a greater probability of success than a small one, but the approach is still unreliable. It is *inherently* unreliable, for three reasons. The first is that fantasies mean different things to different people. A cellist friend of mine described a teenage student who was learning Saint-Saëns's "The Swan" and getting an ugly, aggressive sound. My friend urged her to "think of a swan floating on a pond," whereupon the sound became even worse. It turned out that the student had once been attacked by a swan. Clearly, the fantasy of a swan meant something different to her from what it meant to the teacher. The second reason the approach is unreliable is that when it works, neither the teacher nor the student knows why it works, and when it fails they do not know why it fails. Suppose a teacher says, "Think of a beautiful sunset." The student plays, and the result is poor. The approach we are discussing assumes that the reason for failure is that the student isn't feeling the proper emotion in relation to a beautiful sunset, or isn't responding to it in the right way; that is, the student doesn't have the appropriate emotion, and therefore the playing is inexpressive. If the student could feel differently, she would play differently. But that is only one possibility.

A second possibility is that the student does have the proper emotion, but the emotion does not cause the playing to change. After all, there is nothing in the image to indicate the means of actually achieving a better result. "Think of a beautiful sunset" contains no clue about what to do, how to move differently. If a student plays better after getting that advice, she may not know what she did, how she changed her movement, although she must, necessarily, have changed her movement if the result was different. Because she doesn't know what she did, she may not be able to reproduce the improvement, let alone teach it to others whose responses to mental images of sunsets may be different from hers. In such a case, the student does not need to be told what to *feel* but what to *do*. It is true that if the improved playing was indeed the result of the student's being in a certain mental state, she could doubtless reproduce the improvement by putting herself again in that mental state. There are, in fact, "methods" of performance, acting in particular, that rely on the performer's managing to adopt a particular mental state. But they do not always work.

The third reason for failure of the approach is this: suppose a student does have certain feelings and does move in a way to give them expression, but the result is poor because the feelings, though accurately conveyed, are trivial or silly or inappropriate. This is the situation with the student attacked by a swan. She regards swans as vicious, dangerous creatures and her ugly, aggressive sound does convey her feelings about swans. The problem isn't that she can't convey her feelings, but that those feelings are inappropriate to the music. But this undermines the whole approach, because in saying that certain feelings are inappropriate to the music it appeals to knowledge about how the piece should sound that is independent of the performer's feelings, which means that just expressing one's feelings *can't* be a reliable foundation for a good performance.

How do we know that an aggressive sound is inappropriate here? The answer is actually quite obvious: we *listen*. That is, someone plays the music – or we play it ourselves – observing such directions concerning tempo, dynamics, and tone quality as are in the score, and we listen to the result. We inquire, "Does the tempo seem right? Should it go a little slower? Should there be a slight crescendo here? A ritard? We try the music a little slower, we try a crescendo, and we consider the effect. We adopt some changes, reject others, and our appraisal of the result leads gradually to a satisfying interpretation. We are *using* our musical responses, that is to say our feelings, to reveal the music to ourselves. This is a case of using feelings cognitively: our feelings enable us to reach an understanding of the work.

Let us return to our teaching situation. Up to now we have supposed that when a teacher offers a fantasy – "Think of being in love" – the intent is that the student will experience certain feelings and her feelings will cause her playing to improve. But a second way to understand the situation is this: the teacher is offering a concept, a description, or a definition, and asking the student to produce a result that fits the concept, description, or definition. On the first alternative, if a student fails to play better after being told, "Think of being in love," the failure would be attributed to an absence of the appropriate feeling. She plays badly because she is not experiencing a feeling of love. On the second alternative, a failed performance does not come from lack of feeling, it comes either from lack of knowledge or lack of competence. That is, the student might not understand the concept, description, or definition and thus be unable to produce a result that fits. That would be lack of knowledge. She plays badly because she does not know what love is. On the other hand, she might understand the concept but not know how to match her playing to it. That would be lack of competence, and she would need to be shown what to do, how to alter her movement to get a better result.

These different ways of understanding the fantasy approach are not always distinguished, and sometimes they are not distinguishable. Take the case of the student attacked by a swan. She may, in the moment of playing, have been experiencing fear of swans, which caused the sounds to emerge as they did. On the other hand, her playing may have been influenced by her conception of swans: she thinks of swans as aggressive, vicious creatures, and without actually experiencing fear, she produced sounds to match that description. We couldn't tell just from listening which of these explanations was correct.

In the last paragraph I offered an interpretation of the fantasy approach according to which it does not prescribe feelings that the performer should have, but offers a description or definition. Descriptions and definitions can be useful. A musician may be set on the right track by being told that a piece of music should sound "like a march," or "is a waltz." For example, I think it is helpful to recognize that Chopin's G-Major Nocturne is a barcarolle, although the word does not appear in the score. Some works have descriptive titles, as in the piano music of Debussy and Ravel where we encounter titles like *Feux d'artifice* (Fireworks) and *Jeux d'eau* (Fountains). Such titles may help a pianist decide what character the music should have. Similarly, a description of what Lear is feeling at a particular moment in the play may help an actor as he works out an interpretation. But descriptions are starting points only. They do not really take us very far. The reason is that descriptions are general whereas each artwork is unique, and the more complex the work, the less satisfactory a description is likely to be. I would be at a loss to describe the special character of the opening measures of Chopin's Fourth Ballade. The more I play it and the more carefully I shape the phrases and reflect on the music, the more vivid, unique, and significant it seems, and the more irrelevant any verbal description—but this has brought us back to the cognitive use of emotion and feeling to uncover the nature of the work.

I shall not explore the fantasy approach further. I consider both forms of it to be unacceptable models of feelings and emotions as they occur in actual artistic performance. When I play the piano I do not aim to express myself or give vent to some preexistent emotion, or try to match my playing to an external model or description. My goal is to present the work in a way that, when apprehended by my audience, will seem to them convincing and enable them to experience the work. Not all presentations of a work do that. One pianist may play the Fourth Ballade in a way that makes it boring, another in a way that makes it emotionally compelling. Now, the difference between the instance that is emotionally compelling and the one that is boring is a difference of interpretation. Consequently, the question of how to present the work so as to make possible a satisfying experience for the audience amounts to the question of how to develop a suitable interpretation.

Developing an Interpretation

The performer begins by studying the score, or the script, or the choreography. Some scores and scripts have extensive instructions about the manner in which the work should be performed. Others have very little. Nevertheless, however carefully the composer, playwright, or choreographer notates the work, the instructions are necessarily general rather than specific and the performer must choose among possibilities. For example, the score of the Fourth Ballade specifies that the piece begin with three octave Gs, played *piano*, that the tempo be *andante con moto*, that the pedal be used, and that there be a slight crescendo beginning in the first measure and extending to the middle of the second measure. Those directions may seem precise, but they leave a host of questions for the pianist to answer. Exactly how fast is *andante con moto? Andante* indicates a range of tempi, not any precise one, so the pianist must choose a single tempo within that range. How soft is *piano?* How large, and how gradual should the crescendo be? What tone quality should be used for the three octave Gs? Should the upper note or the lower note stand out, or should they be equal? Similar questions arise throughout the piece. At every moment there are various ways of complying with Chopin's instructions. A pianist may not consciously formulate all these questions, but her playing will necessarily incorporate answers to all of them, whether she consciously chooses or not. In saying that, I am recapitulating the conclusions reached in chapter 1 that every instance of a work of performing is under some interpretation, and the instructions in the score or script are only a starting point in deciding what interpretation to adopt.

The same is true of suggestions performers receive from sources other than the composer or playwright. An actor receives suggestions and advice from directors, from other actors, from coaches, and friends. Likewise, a musician considers historical performance practice, suggestions from colleagues, critics, and teachers. All these things are helpful—essential even—in preparation, but they still leave alternatives open and in the end, the performer himself must decide just how he wants the work to emerge and assume responsibility for making it emerge that way. The interpretation that a performer works out in this manner is a conception of the work as a complex structure of interrelated sounds or movements that he believes will embody the work in a powerful way, and it rests concretely on possibilities of response that the performer discovers in the details of the work itself.

The word "interpretation" is often used in other ways, which I mention only to distinguish them from the kind of interpretation I am discussing. Someone may "interpret" Shakespeare as a world historical figure, or as an exemplar of the Elizabethan spirit, or as part of the unfolding self-realization of Western consciousness. Someone may say that Chopin's music "captures the heart of the romantic spirit" or "embodies Chopin's Polish patriotism." Such theories are legitimate and sometimes fascinating. They constitute one kind of interpretation, but not the kind I am discussing. They are interpretations from the outside, from the point of view of historians, literary critics, or philosophers. They may be helpful in steering a performer toward a particular view of the work, but they are not the same as the intricate web of individual details that an actor who plays Lear or a pianist playing the Fourth Ballade must make the basis of a performance.

At this point we must distinguish direct apprehension from knowledge based on words or concepts. When I ask, "What is that?" and someone tells me, "It is a rose," the knowledge I gain is a case of fitting the object in front of me under an appropriate name or concept. This kind of classification is different from direct apprehension, in which one simply confronts an object. The approaches to developing an interpretation that we considered earlier – the fantasy approach and its variants – are like knowledge based on words or concepts. They offer advice that is general in the sense that there could be many ways of complying with it and they rest, inevitably, on concepts, words, or fantasies, which are heuristic tools. The most they can do is point a direction. But actual performance does not work through concepts, words, or descriptions, nor does it rest on images communicable separately from the performance. It works through direct apprehension. It is not by *describing* Lear that an actor gives the audience the character, any more than it is by *talking* about the Fourth Ballade that a pianist presents that sublime work. The performer presents the thing itself, not a description, and the audience apprehends it directly.

Now, direct apprehension *cannot* be derived from words or description. This is one of the fundamental principles of empiricist philosophy. Hume, for example, invokes it at the beginning of his *Treatise of Human Nature,* where he introduces the distinction between impressions and ideas. Impressions, for Hume, are like what I am calling direct apprehension and ideas are like what I am calling words, concepts or descriptions. Hume insists that ideas are derived from impressions, not the other way round. To give someone an idea of orange or scarlet, he says, "I present the objects, or in other words, convey to him these impressions; but proceed not so absurdly, as to endeavor to produce the impression by exciting the ideas."* A performer, similarly, communicates the work by setting the

* Book I, Part I, Section I.

work itself, not a description, before the audience. But *his own* experience of the work can no more be derived from words or concepts than can that of the audience. He must arrive at an experience of the work by setting it before *himself.*

This means that the performer must examine the work in a direct and personal way, using the feelings and emotions he discovers in himself as a means of perceiving the work. In the course of learning a work of music, I produce sounds with particular qualities, which I appraise as attentively as I can. Is that sound beautiful or harsh, loud or soft? What is its emotional quality? The emotional quality of a sound depends partly on what went before and what follows after. A C-major chord feels different as the tonic of the key of C major from the way it feels as the dominant of F, and different again from the way it feels as the relative major of A minor. What emotional quality does C-major harmony have in this measure? What quality do I want it to have? How is the emotion different from that of the A minor harmony used later with the same melody? I listen and scrutinize the feelings that the sounds evoke. I consider the intrinsic qualities of the sounds and I consider them insofar as, taken together, they constitute a work of music. I cannot know before studying the score what feelings will or should emerge, because every work is unique. I must learn the emotion of a piece from the music and then, by examining my responses and refining my movement, find ways to make my experience more nuanced, more coincident with the emotions that the score seems to demand. In the end, the whole composition is mapped as a complex of interrelated emotions as well as a complex of sounds. I am using emotion and feeling cognitively to discover the nature of the work.

An actor likewise develops an interpretation by studying the play, relying first on his own human experience and his own responses. At a certain point in the play, an actor playing Lear is called upon to say, "O! I have ta'en too little care of this" (III, ii, 32). The actor must ask himself, what does Lear mean by "this"? What is his emotion here and what emotion should the line evoke? Is it merely a casual remark, or is it a significant moment in the transformation Lear undergoes in the course of the play? The actor must answer such questions in order to decide how to deliver the line. So he studies the play. In time he arrives at a grasp of Lear at each moment. He develops a map of Lear's emotions and the emotions his speeches and actions should generate in the audience. This is exactly analogous to the dancer mapping a series of movements with attention to their emotional effect or to the musician mapping a composition as a complex of interrelated sounds. A performer may be able to describe what he does and what he intends, or he may not, but inability to describe an interpretation in words does not imply that the interpretation or the performance is poor. It is easy to imagine an actor who knows exactly how he intends to play Lear but cannot *say* what he intends. The only way he can communicate his conception is by *doing* it.

The process we are describing requires that the performer be receptive to whatever the work may offer. He must learn from the work, not impose a scheme worked out ahead of time. He must "open himself" to the work and examine, reflect on, and experience its particular emotional qualities. It is tempting to appropriate Lear's admonition and say to the performer "expose thyself to *feel*" (III, iv, 34). Insisting that performers must be receptive in this way to the emotional import of the work is important because some performers neglect it. Some musicians never ask themselves what the particular emotion of a work or a passage should be. That may be because they approach interpretation through descriptions – a version of the fantasy approach – instead of through direct apprehension. But all a description can do is specify that the music, or the action, be of a certain kind. That is not enough for a pianist preparing the Fourth Ballade or an actor portraying King Lear. Performance does not merely offer a description or an image of the work, nor does it offer the work just as an example of something of a certain kind, it offers the work as a unique object to be apprehended directly. The pianist must intend a series of specific sounds that will constitute an instance. The dancer must intend a specific series of movements. The instance that

emerges may be of a certain kind, and it may satisfy a description, but it will also be unique, and it will inevitably have an expressive or emotional quality of its own. *That* must be the focus of the pianist's intention. Similarly, an actor must intend a series of particular actions and speeches that will constitute the character as undergoing certain feelings and emotions. Instead of, "Think of a swan," the proper admonition to a student is: "*Listen!*" The student must experience the sounds and examine their emotional effect. She will then learn accurately to apprehend the quality of the sounds she produces and hear them as they relate to each other within the work. She will use her feelings to illuminate the work in her mind and understanding and she will discover how she wishes to present it to her audience. She will learn to use her feelings and emotions cognitively.

When I examine the emotional import of a work of music in the manner just described, I am assuming the role of a listener. I listen to the sound and appraise its emotional and aesthetic qualities. But if I am playing the piano I not only hear sounds, I also cause the sounds that I hear. I have the experience of sound as a listener, but I simultaneously have the experience of being the cause of what I'm hearing. I therefore occupy two positions at once, that of a listener and that of an agent. Since the two perspectives are distinct, I can consider them separately. As a listener I am aware, if I am properly attentive, of the emotional impact of the music. I can consider whether the tempo is right or the sounds appropriately expressive; in short, I hear and judge the quality of the music. For me as an agent, the experience includes the kinesthetic awareness of moving my body to play the piano. I can examine my movement and judge *its* quality, whether tense or free, stiff or fluid. But although the two roles are distinct, they are also intimately related. For one thing, they occur simultaneously, which I shall describe by saying that I can map them onto one another. In addition, one is the cause of the other, which means that each can provide feedback for the other. If as a listener I do not like what I hear, I can as an agent alter what I hear by changing my movement. Conversely, if the movement feels stiff or awkward, the sound is probably less good than it could be. By improving the movement I am likely to discover a better sound. I appraise the musical result, the cause of that result, and the two in relation to one another.

Similar accounts can be given for dancing and acting. A dancer learns, perhaps with the help of a coach and a mirror, to evaluate the visual effect of her movement. She develops a feeling for what it looks like and what it should look like, and relates that to the kinesthetic awareness of herself executing the movements. A pirouette by the White Swan in *Swan Lake* ought not to look like a pirouette by the Black Swan. The two have opposite motives, feelings, and desires. A single ballerina ordinarily performs both roles, but she must change more than just her costume if she is adequately to portray them both. Having considered those things in her role as audience, she must then, in her role as agent, find movements that embody the White Swan, and other movements for the Black Swan, movements that will transform a series of *fouettées,* which could look like a mere floor exercise, into an episode of bravura seduction and a climactic moment in the ballet. An actor likewise evaluates his activity by relating the feelings brought about by his activity to the feeling of himself physically engaged in that activity.

Each step of this process necessarily occurs in the context of an interpretation, an intention as to just how the work should go. When I appraise the sound, I judge whether it embodies my interpretation, but I also appraise the interpretation. If I realize my intention, I must consider whether I am satisfied with that intention. Perhaps there is a better way to do it. I reflect on such questions and the process enables me to identify other possibilities, additional subtleties that could be incorporated in this or future performances, and I alter my intentions accordingly. Thus, the interpretation evolves through an interaction between actuality and possibility, which in turn reveals further possibilities. All of this relies on feeling and emotion, since I am appraising what I do by scrutinizing the feelings I discover in myself in response to what I do. I am using my emotions and feelings cognitively, both to judge the adequacy of my performance and to reveal the nature of the work.

We use emotions cognitively in more situations than perhaps we realize, as Nelson Goodman argued in *Languages of Art*, and to understand other things than artworks. A few pages back I adapted an admonition of Lear's, where he says, "Expose thyself to feel," but I quoted only the beginning of his sentence. The full sentence is:

> *Expose thyself to feel what wretches feel,*
> *That thou mayst shake the superflux to them,*
> *And show the heavens more just.* *

We can plausibly see this as a case of emotions used cognitively: Lear appears to be saying that by *feeling* injustice someone may come to *understand* what justice is. If that is indeed Lear's point, then I think he is right. Indeed, I am inclined to

* III, iv, 34–36.

go further and say that the cognitive use of emotions should be more widespread than it is in today's world. For example, if terrorists truly apprehended, on an emotional level, the horror of their activity, would they continue to perpetrate their ghastly crimes? And surely, if some politicians truly felt the hardships confronting large numbers of people, they would do more to meet the needs and promote the well-being of ordinary citizens, instead of merely acknowledging those problems verbally while advocating policies that serve the interests of a small minority.

Until recently, the very idea that there could be a cognitive use of emotion would have seemed absurd. Philosophers have insisted for centuries that reason and emotion should be scrupulously separated. They have warned against any intrusion of emotion into the realm of reason and intellect, praised men who live according to reason, and condemned or pitied those led by emotion or passion. The life of reason, presumably untainted by the infection of base feeling, has been their ideal. To such philosophers, Goodman's proposing a cognitive use of emotion would seem utterly indefensible, if not incoherent.

His proposal is more plausible today than perhaps it seemed when he made it, partly because some philosophers have subsequently defended the rationality of emotion, but also, and more important, because recent neurological discoveries support the connection of reason and emotion. The portions of the brain responsible for reasoning and decision-making are newer, from an evolutionary point of view, than those concerned with biological regulation and emotion. But these newer portions did not arise independently, they arose by developing out of and within the older structures, as is typical of evolutionary change, and they remain rooted in those evolutionarily older structures. In his book, *Descartes' Error*, Antonio Damasio explains how damage to the older regions of the brain, those concerned with regulation and emotion, whether through accident or disease, impairs a person's ability to reason and make decisions. Efficient reasoning and decision-making are not independent of emotion; on the contrary, they depend on it. Traditional philosophers are right, of course, that emotion may affect a person's reasoning, and in some situations undermine it. But it does not follow that reasoning can or should be separated from emotion altogether. Improper use of emotion may impair reasoning, but proper use may enhance it.

One might assume that a performer's arriving at an interpretation, which amounts to having a precise intention concerning the instance he is producing, is sufficient to ensure that the performance will embody that intention. In fact it is not, and if a performer assumes that it is sufficient, he is in danger of performing without much awareness of the results he actually gets. Vividly aware of the effect he intends, he may fail to see the gap between intention and achievement. This is an easy trap to fall into, because listening to one's own playing and hearing it accurately, as a musician must do, gauging the effect one's movement will have on an observer, as a dancer must do, monitoring the effect of one's physical movements and vocal inflections, as an actor must do – these are demanding skills. It is easy to deceive oneself about the effect and quality of one's work. I suspect that this explains a lot of flat, expressionless performing, and also the dismay that performers often feel when they hear recordings or watch videos of themselves.

The enterprise I have described is sufficiently complex and demanding to seem impossible. How can anyone do all that? And how can anyone do all those things *simultaneously?* The short answer is that we do it with our brains. The longer answer is that we *learn* to do it. Through experience and practice and by training attention and awareness, we can learn to do very complex things. By attending to the results of his actions, appraising his intentions and developing awareness of nuances of execution, the performer is training his brain. The more one pays scrupulous attention, the more one can discover, and each new level of discernment can be a platform for subsequent refinement of awareness and sensitivity. Performers can grow and improve throughout their careers.

I have used the example of a pianist attending to two kinds of feeling, kinesthetic and auditory. But this description implies a separation between the two categories of feeling, and, consequently, a division of attention. It suggests that the performer must be constantly attending to two things at once. Now, deliberately attending to distinct categories of feeling, shifting attention back and forth and perceiving their relationship, does describe what the pianist does in practicing, and it can occur, sometimes, in performance as well. But performers can move beyond it. The division of attention can be overcome.

We know from chapter 3 that motor skills and habits become hierarchically ordered, and once a certain pattern of movement has been established in the body map it is available without having to be consciously called up. This applies to a pianist performing the Fourth Ballade. She has learned the Fourth Ballade, which is to say she has established the movements of playing the piece in her body map. The movements are then available and can occur "on their own" in the sense that she no longer has to intend them as movements; she can intend the music and her body map supplies the movements.* This needn't mean that she is unaware of the movements. She may be aware of them, or some of them, but she no longer has to direct them consciously as movements. If I have properly prepared a performance, the relations of sound and movement have been united in a complex map – a map of the Fourth Ballade – and what I do is to intend the music. What previously seemed a divided activity of comparing different kinds of feelings has become unified. I am aware of myself as an agent, an active being, and what I am doing is the music. This is another approach to what I described in chapter 4 as the experience of being one with the work.

When I play the piano, my experience of the sounds occurs in me alone, but the sounds from the piano are available to my

* Notice that although I may intend the music and not consciously intend the movements, this is not the same thing as playing mindlessly. I *am* intending, even though what I intend is just the "tip of the iceberg," namely the music, and thanks to the hierarchical nesting of habits and skills in the brain, the movements occur. Mindless playing is what occurs when my thoughts are elsewhere entirely, and movement occurs that is mere movement, mere habit, not directed in the moment by intention.

listeners as well as to me. I rely on physiological similarities between me and my listeners to assure that the sounds I produce will generate an experience of hearing in their bodies similar to what they produce in my body. I also assume, because of other similarities between them and me – shared social experience, cultural background, interests, and preferences – that their appraisal of that experience of hearing will also be similar, that they will judge the sounds to be expressive, beautiful, or appropriate, and they will recognize those qualities as belonging to the work. That is to say, they will use their feelings and emotions cognitively to grasp the nature of the work set before them. It is in this way that performers communicate with their audiences.

The performer's communication with the audience is not like imparting information, not like what happens in language when I communicate some fact or observation to someone else. If I say, "Washington crossed the Delaware" to someone who does not know that historical fact, then (assuming that the person hears my words and understands the language) the result of my utterance is that a particular content – Washington's having crossed the Delaware – is communicated to him. Moreover, the content that he has received is the same content that I was thinking of. But that is not what happens in performance. Works of performing art are not communicated through symbols; they come to life as experience. I cannot give you my experience, but I can engage in a series of actions that enable you to have an experience of your own. The situation in performance is analogous to what we would have if I communicated Washington's crossing of the Delaware to you not by saying, "Washington crossed the Delaware" but by setting Washington's actual crossing of the Delaware in front of you, enabling you to see it for yourself. Obviously, since Washington's crossing the Delaware occurred long ago, it is impossible actually to observe it; it is no longer available to be observed directly. But works of performing art, by being given instances, *are* available to be apprehended directly. When I play the piano, I give you the actual work. Likewise an actor communicates

Lear's feelings and actions not through descriptions but by setting Lear directly before the audience. Shakespeare created Lear four hundred years ago, but the Lear that an actor presents is before us now.

When I play a Chopin ballade, the sounds I produce are an instance of an artwork, and they are related among themselves as prescribed by the score. The feelings stimulated by those sounds, which taken together constitute my experience of the ballade, are related among themselves as the sounds are related, that is, in the manner demanded by the score, and thus those feelings constitute an experience that has the formal properties of the ballade. The ballade, therefore, has not only been embodied in an instance that is a series of sounds, *it has been instantiated in me as experience.* Since the sounds I produce are available to others, they reach the ears of my listeners, where they give rise to feelings, and the relationships among the sounds will be reflected in the relationships among those feelings. In this way, the ballade is instantiated as experience in my listeners also. Thus, I do not merely set the work before my audience, as I would do with Washington crossing the Delaware, if I could set that event before them. Instead, I give them the work as experience; it is instantiated in their very selves.

Self-Creation and Self-Exposure

Who I am—my personal identity, my sense of self—develops over the course of my life. I am a body with certain physical characteristics, a certain genetic endowment, and a sufficiently complex brain and nervous system to have conscious thoughts, form memories and plans, acquire skills, and learn. From infancy my body has grown and changed and accumulated a continually growing fund of experience. My sense of myself is the first-person awareness of a particular body interacting with persons and objects in the world and responding to intentions and desires that are also first-person experiences. At each moment in my life, events occur that constitute the experience of that moment. They leave their mark on me and partly determine who I am at that moment and who I subsequently become. The things I do and the things that happen to me contribute to my developing self. My self is a network of experiences centered in my body in the ongoing course of my life. It is the result of a lifelong process of creation.

Many of the events that contribute to the development of my self have little apparent connection with each other. They are related by the fact of occurring in the same body—mine—but not in any other way. For example, suppose I am sitting absorbed in a book. The phone rings. I did not expect the phone to ring just then, and there was no way I could have predicted it from my activity of reading. There is no causal relationship between my reading and the phone ringing. Afterward, however, the two are part of my life history, and are linked by being experiences of mine. They are both part of the ongoing process that defines me, and I may come to think of them as related, but in the moment they are not connected. Now, if I mark off a short period of my life at random, a stretch of ten minutes, let us say, it is likely to contain some experiences and actions like those in this example, experiences and actions that have no particular connection with each other except that they occur in the same body in the same stretch of time. Some of them will be consequences or anticipations of actions and events in other portions of my life. Some of them will seem unrelated to others. The random ten-minute stretch is part of my self, part of me, but it is not self-contained or intrinsically coherent. It is not composed of parts that in their own nature are related to one another.

By contrast, let us now imagine a stretch of time that *was* self-contained, one whose components *did* bear relations to one another such that the entire stretch of time seemed intrinsically coherent. That is what happens when I experience a work of music or dance or drama. A network of feelings and emotions occurs within me over a stretch of time, and that network has the formal characteristics of a work of performing art. Those feelings are an instance, in experience, of a work of performing art, a sonata let us say, and since they are also part of the ongoing course of experience that over time defines my self, they are part of me. But if we confine attention just to the stretch of time under consideration, we can say that during that period, the feelings *are* me, they are what I am then being or experiencing, and they are also an artwork, a sonata in this case.

Let me put this point slightly differently. I am imagining a stretch of time such that the experiential events contained in it are related among themselves so as to constitute an instance of an artwork. The stretch of time is just a short portion of the longer stretch of time that makes up my life, but it is marked off from the rest of my life by the fact that within it there is an interrelation of feelings that makes them, taken together, an artwork. It is a piece of myself, but it is a whole in itself as well. The notion that a portion of oneself can be regarded as an artwork may sound odd. It does not occur – or at any rate, I believe it is rare – in theoretical discussions of artistic performance, but although it may have escaped philosophers, it has not escaped poets. T. S. Eliot writes:

> *you are the music*
> *While the music lasts.* *

The experiences that shape me, during the stretch of time under consideration, into an artwork have another feature in common. If I am performing, then those experiences are not just things that happen to me, they are my actions; they are things I *do*. They are the events that serve to define me, in that stretch of time, and they are part of the ongoing series of events that create me, through my life, as the person I am. So we can say that during that stretch of time I not only *am* the music, but also, because the events that define me in that stretch of time are my own doing, I *create myself as* the artwork. It is not common to say that a musician creates himself as a sonata, but the situation is exactly like what occurs in other performing arts, where such claims are more familiar. Most people, I

* *Four Quartets*

think, would not balk at the suggestion that an actor makes himself into Lear; indeed, that he *is* Lear, while the play lasts. Nevertheless, many people who would accept that description might suppose that it was purely metaphorical, whereas I am claiming that there is a sense in which we should take it literally.

The idea of an actor being King Lear for the duration of the play may seem plausible because we assume it to be a case of something we are familiar with in our daily experience. We all have had the experience of role-playing and imitating other people. Perhaps the actor being King Lear is doing much the same thing, but more thoroughly. But despite its apparent similarity, creating a role is not simply a more developed or more skillful exercise of the role-playing and imitation with which we amuse ourselves in daily life. It is more of a piece with the musical example than it is with everyday amusements. The play-acting of daily life is mere imitation; one is playing a part, always conscious that it is a pretense. The actor who offers himself as King Lear, isn't *imitating* Lear, he is *being* Lear. He is engaged in the same sort of activity as the musician who makes himself into a sonata. "You are the music while the music lasts," is exactly parallel to "You are King Lear while the play lasts," or "You are Giselle while the ballet lasts." Once again, the point has not eluded poets. William Butler Yeats asks,

*How can we know the dancer from the dance?**

And my answer is, "We can't." For the duration of the performance, they are the same.

The actor who is Lear is not being or pretending to be another person, which would be impossible; he is being Lear, who is not a person but a creation of Shakespeare's. To see the difference, consider that in life, who I am in a particular stretch of time is partly a result of events and experiences that occurred outside that stretch of time. I can choose to focus on a particular part of my life and isolate it in my mind from the rest, but my existence is not actually confined to that time. I

* "Among School Children."

did exist at other times as well, and events occurring in those other times may influence the events that occur within the time I'm considering. In short, there is a reality outside the stretch of time I'm contemplating, and I could investigate that reality if I wished.

A work of performing art is different. The *only* reality is what is offered in the work. A character in a play has no life or existence other than what is given in the script, similarly for the theme of a symphony or a role in a ballet. Obviously, plays do often include references to events that are supposed to happen offstage or before the play begins; Oedipus's killing of his father is supposed to have happened years before the events presented in the play, and his blinding occurs offstage, not before our eyes. We know of those events, however, through descriptions that *are* part of the play. In real life, by contrast, people's lives continue even when we are not in their presence, whether or not we have them described to us. If I ask a friend whom I've neither seen nor heard about for a long time, "What have you been doing since I last saw you?" I know there's an answer. He's been doing *something*, although I don't know what it is.

But it makes no sense to ask what a character in a play is doing apart from what is presented or described on stage. He exists only as created by the playwright. Portions of the play in which he doesn't appear either onstage or in a description are portions in which he hasn't been given any being at all. Asking what he is doing in *those* periods is like asking what the first theme of a sonata is doing while the second theme is being played. This point is marvelously illuminated, in reverse, by Tom Stoppard in *Rosencrantz and Guildenstern Are Dead*. Imagining what Rosencrantz and Guildenstern might be doing between the scenes Shakespeare wrote for them, Stoppard shows that they are then in a kind of existential limbo; they have no reality then because Shakespeare didn't give them any.

In performance I offer an instance of an artwork, and that instance is simultaneously part of me. Consequently, performance involves revealing or exposing oneself, which for most people does not come easily. Of course, the portion of myself that I convey to my audience in performance is not the self of my daily life, it is a separately definable portion that assumes the form of an artwork, which might seem to mitigate any sense of exposure I might feel in offering it to others. On the contrary, the sense of exposure in performance is more acute than what we normally reveal in daily life, for three reasons.

The first is that in daily life I reveal only bits of myself at a time. Most of myself is hidden at any given moment. Moreover, I can choose to reveal my thoughts and feelings or not, and I can balance what is revealed against what is unrevealed. If I am impassive, reserved, or aloof in an encounter with others, I can console myself with the thought that my inner self is sensitive, open, and compassionate. But I can't do that with the self I offer in performance. *That* self *has* no inner life, no other occasions in which parts of it that are not present in the performance can be expressed or revealed. There are no such parts. What I reveal in performance is *all there is* of it. That is why performing can seem so intimately revealing, as if one's entire being at that moment were on the line, out there for all to see. Someone whose performance is insensitive or inexpressive is revealing himself, for that moment, to be inexpressive or insensitive. That is to say, the performance exhibits a self, which is simultaneously the artwork, and that self is insensitive and inexpressive. It is irrelevant that the performer may possess other qualities that emerge in other parts of his life, or that he may have in mind a more compelling interpretation than the one he succeeds in conveying. In the moment of performing, what the performance offers is all there is.

The second reason why the self-exposure involved in performance can seem threatening is that when I perform the Fourth Ballade I am offering a piece of myself. But the Fourth Ballade is a complex and difficult work. By the time I have studied it to the point of being able to perform it, I have invested a lot in it. I have practiced, I have reflected on each measure of the piece, tried to enhance my response to it and deepen my perception. Consequently it is not a trivial part of me, it is an especially significant part. I feel that a lot of myself is tied up in it, and this feeling is justified. Many performers have said that learning and performing works on the level of the Fourth Ballade or *King Lear* changes their lives forever. Offering those works to an audience is not like revealing a casual feeling or thought, it is like baring one's soul.

The third reason, related to the second but not quite the same, is that offering oneself as Lear or as the Fourth Ballade invites comparison of oneself with the work. How, the performer may ask, can I measure up to such a work? In presenting myself as Lear, may I not simply be exposing my own inadequacy, my own shortcomings? Few performers, I suspect, are free from such worries. They may never overcome their doubts entirely, but it is essential that they learn to set them aside during the actual performance if they are to do their best work. I shall have more to say in chapter 6 about the self-exposure involved in performance.

We can illuminate the topics we have been discussing in a different way. In the Rijksmuseum in Amsterdam is a famous self-portrait by Rembrandt in which he depicts himself as Saint Paul. It is easy to recognize that the individual in the picture is Rembrandt because he looks much as Rembrandt does in other self-portraits from the same period. But what makes this individual Saint Paul? It can't be that we can perceive a resemblance to Saint Paul; no one knows what Saint Paul looked like, and in any case, he certainly did not look exactly like Rembrandt. The individual in the picture is wearing a yellow turban and carrying a sword. The sword is in shadow and only partly visible, but it identifies the figure as Saint Paul, the champion of the early church. That is to say, we recognize this individual as Saint Paul not by what he looks like but by his surroundings, his accessories, what art historians call his *attributes*. In the artistic tradition of which Rembrandt is a part, *any* figure with the proper attributes is Saint Paul, just as any figure with a beatific attitude and riddled with arrows is Saint Sebastian and any woman accompanied by a wheel, or part of a wheel, is Saint Catherine. Let us suppose, therefore, that a yellow turban and a sword identify an individual as Saint Paul.* Anyone familiar with that tradition, seeing a picture of such an individual, would say, "That's Saint Paul," no matter what the facial features of the individual in the picture. So Rembrandt's self-portrait shows Rembrandt and it also shows Saint Paul; it is Rembrandt *as* Saint Paul.

That it is the attributes, not the facial features, that count in this tradition is amusingly shown in a painting by an unidentified French artist in the Musée Carnavalet in Paris depicting Saint Geneviève, patron saint of the City of Paris. She is recognizable by her attributes, which are a lighted taper, a book, an angel whispering to her, and a group of fleeing Huns in the background (her prayers are supposed to have saved Paris from attack by Attila the Hun in 451 A.D.). What is remarkable about the picture is that a later artist has painted a wheel under her feet, changing her from Saint Geneviève into Saint Catherine. Who she is, apparently, has nothing to do with her looks, and everything to do with the objects around her. Whether we should say that the later artist made her into Saint Catherine, or that he attempted unsuccessfully to make her into Saint Catherine, or that he made her into *both* Saint Catherine and Saint Geneviève is not clear.

Returning to Rembrandt's self-portrait, suppose, now, that another seventeenth-century Dutch painter, Frans Hals, decides to paint himself as Saint Paul. In his picture he also wears a yellow turban and carries a sword, and so his picture, too, is a picture of Saint Paul. But it is Frans Hals as Saint Paul, not Rembrandt as Saint Paul. Other painters could likewise depict themselves as Saint Paul. We could have Vermeer as Saint Paul, ter Borch as Saint Paul, de Hooch as Saint Paul, and so on. The pictures would not look very much alike, since each of the painters had different facial features and they

* The traditional attributes of Saint Paul are a sword and a book. Rembrandt depicts a sword, although it is almost completely obscured in shadow, but no book. The yellow turban has no art historical significance that I know (although it does offer a connotation of the East or Middle East), but since it is the most arresting feature of the picture I treat it in this discussion as an attribute of Saint Paul.

would probably be shown in different poses, with different surroundings, and rendered by different painterly technique. Nevertheless, all the pictures would be Saint Paul pictures. All the individuals in the picture gallery I have imagined would be Saint Paul, not because of what they look like but because of their props. Thus, each painter continues to be himself, but counts simultaneously as another person because of the attributes depicted with him. This is exactly analogous to what happens in the performing arts. In performing art, however, it is not the surroundings or attributes that transform the performer into another being, it is action, what the performer does.

If Renée Fleming appears as the Marschallin in *Der Rosenkavalier*, the person on stage is, obviously, Renée Fleming. She is Renée Fleming because that's the person she happens to be. But she is also the Marschallin, and what makes her the Marschallin is not who she *is* but what she *does*. Being the Marschallin consists of singing certain music expressive of various emotional and dramatic situations; in short, doing the things demanded by the score and the libretto of *Der Rosenkavalier*. Anyone who does those things is the Marschallin; if two sopranos do those things, both of them are the Marschallin. Nevertheless, since Renée Fleming simultaneously remains herself, her Marschallin will be different from that of another soprano, say Elizabeth Schwartzkopf. This Marschallin is Renée Fleming, that one is Elizabeth Schwartzkopf, just as this Saint Paul is Rembrandt and that one is Frans Hals.

What makes two individuals count as Saint Paul is the same for each: the turban and sword. Similarly, what two sopranos do to be the Marschallin is the same for each: they sing the music that defines the Marschallin. Moreover, there is nothing *else* to do in order to be the Marschallin. No arias to sing other than those in the score, no actions to perform other than those in the libretto; the Marschallin has no other reality, no other life beyond what is laid down in the score and the libretto. When Renée Fleming performs in *Der Rosenkavalier* we confront an instance of the Marschallin, a creation of Richard Strauss and Hugo von Hofmannsthal, but that instance consists of sounds and movements sung and performed by Renée Fleming. She does them. Thus she gives us an instance of the Marschallin and she also gives us herself; she is still herself even while being the Marschallin. Now, the sounds she makes and the actions she executes in a given performance occur on that occasion only. She therefore gives us an individual Marschallin, a Marschallin that occurs only once. If she performs in *Der Rosenkavalier* next week, she will produce different individual sounds, execute different individual movements, to make *another* Marschallin. Tonight's Marschallin and next week's Marschallin are both instances of a creation by Strauss and Hofmannsthal, but they are separate creations by Renée Fleming. Strauss and Hofmannsthal needed to write and compose *Der Rosenkavalier* just once, and after they did that, their work was finished. Renée Fleming must create a new Marschallin in every performance. Even if her conception of the role—her interpretation—remains the same from one performance to the next, each individual performance offers a unique Marschallin that occurs only once.

Rembrandt's painting is a Saint Paul picture, but when we look at it we feel that Rembrandt, not Saint Paul, is looking out at us from the canvas. Rembrandt is the compelling, living presence. We *know* that it is Saint Paul, but we *see* Rembrandt. That is because Rembrandt presents *himself* as Saint Paul. He uses his own face, his own features, but because of the props with which he surrounds himself, the picture counts as a Saint Paul. Renée Fleming does not present herself as the Marschallin in the same way. Instead, she *makes* an instance of the Marschallin, but she makes it out of herself. She moves her own body to carry out the actions required of the Marschallin, she sings with her own voice the music that defines the Marschallin. Her Marschallin will have her physical stature, her voice, her facial features. But even though she remains herself, she is not presenting herself the way Rembrandt is presenting himself, and even though her Marschallin has her physical characteristics, this is not a case of self-expression. She is presenting not herself but the Marschallin, a Marschallin that she makes out of herself. Ordinarily, we in the audience are perfectly aware of the situation. That is, we watch and listen to the Marschallin, but we are simultaneously aware that the person we see on stage being the Marschallin is Renée Fleming. This is not a bad thing; on the contrary it is something people seek out on purpose. Many people go to considerable lengths to see a particular performer in a particular role. Occasionally it happens that a performer hides himself in his character so completely that we see only the character and lose awareness of the performer. It is a remarkable achievement if a familiar actor makes himself unrecognizable as himself and appears only as his character. Nevertheless, it is still true that the actor who does that is both himself and his character; he makes his character out of himself.

Rembrandt depicts Saint Paul as a thoughtful, insightful, compassionate individual. Of course, he is simultaneously depicting *himself* with those qualities, and his ability to do that depends also on himself, that is, on his own life, experience, and skill. He may or may not possess all those qualities, but he must understand them well enough to be able to depict himself as having them. Similarly, Renée Fleming must understand the emotional state of the Marschallin when, for example, she willingly but regretfully gives Octavian over to Sophie. Renée Fleming may or may not have had similar experiences in her own life, but she must understand and convey the feelings she attributes to the Marschallin and create her Marschallin as someone having those feelings. Some of that she may derive from her own life, but much of it she learns from studying the music. The Marschallin's feelings, after all, are evoked by the music. Studying the play, listening to the music, contemplating the movements demanded in the dance—these things are vital for performers: the *work* teaches the performers what it is about. As Renée Fleming puts it, "Much of the information I need to create a role comes from the music."* Studying a work, a performer encounters feelings she might never other-

* *The Inner Voice*, p. 198.

wise experience; she may end up with an emotional range far exceeding that of other people. For some performers, and for some roles, *most* of the feelings communicated in performance are learned from the work, not from personal experience. Few actresses, I imagine, derive from their own lives the feelings they express as Lady Macbeth. Arriving in this manner at an understanding of a role is another example of the cognitive use of emotion and feeling.

Renée Fleming describes this situation, and also refers to the sense of exposure we discussed a few pages back, in the following passage:

> The role that breaks my heart is the one that expresses loneliness. It's very easy to become the Marschallin while I'm singing her. Forget about the inevitability of the end of her affair with Octavian: it's her isolation, her crisis of time and beauty, aging and losing her sense of self-worth, that are so crushing, and that are fairly universal concerns for women. When she looks at the clock and asks it to stop, I can identify with her predicament, for I'm no less affected by that clock than she. The chances are slim that I'll die of tuberculosis or be strangled to death by my husband, so while those sorts of dramatic roles can be exhilarating to play, they don't lead me to look into the mirror of my own life. But playing out the Marschallin's grief, her fears, and finally, her heartbreaking dignity – those are the moments I feel most exposed. There are nights when it can be hard to admit those fears to myself, much less to a crowd of strangers, and on those nights it can be equally hard to leave her sadness behind at the end of the performance.*

That Rembrandt makes his instance of Saint Paul out of himself is true in one sense; he dresses himself up as Saint Paul, making of himself an instance of Saint Paul. But the masquerading as Saint Paul, the making of himself into Saint Paul, is not his artwork. His artwork is the *painting*, something made

* *The Inner Voice*, p. 196.

out of paint and canvas that depicts him dressed up as Saint Paul. When we contemplate Rembrandt's artwork we are looking at a painting, we are not in the presence of Rembrandt *actually being* Saint Paul. That, however, is what we *do* contemplate in a performance. Renée Fleming makes her instance of the Marschallin out of herself, and we are present to her actually being the Marschallin. The unique Marschallin that she is on a given evening, as I shall argue in chapter 7, is her artwork.*

Let us approach this point in a different way. Suppose a painter paints a rose, using a particular shade of red pigment. Suppose that he then paints a carnation, using the same shade of red pigment. The two pictures will show different flowers, but the flowers will be the same color. That is, the same red is revealed in each flower; the flowers are *made out of* the same color. Painters use paint as an artistic medium; performers use themselves.† There is, however, a difference between the two cases. When we say that a painter makes different flowers out of the same color, what we mean, of course, is that he uses the same color to make *pictures* of two different flowers. The flower he makes out of red paint is not an actual flower, it is a representation of a flower. But when performers make them-

* Philosophical footnote (to be skipped if you prefer): Actors and opera singers are sometimes said to "portray" or to "imitate" or to "represent" their characters. But these are treacherous terms that can be used both in extensional and intensional senses. Now, Renée Fleming does not represent the Marschallin in an extensional sense—there is no actual Marschallin whom she represents—nor does she represent the Marschallin in an intensional sense—she does not give us a Marschallin-representation, as Goodman would express the intensional sense. Similarly with "portray," "imitate," and their ilk. Instead, the relation of Renée Fleming's Marschallin to the creation of Strauss and Hofmannsthal is that of an instance to the artwork it is an instance of. Her activity is thus more analogous to that of a naughty child who, during the period of her misbehaving, makes herself into an instance of naughtiness than it is to representation, imitation, and the others. It is also analogous to that of the pianist we met earlier who is the music while the music lasts, or the dancer who is Giselle for the duration of the ballet.

† It is not unusual to say that so-called "performance artists" are their own artistic medium. That is true, but it is equally true of performers who perform works by others.

selves into the work they are performing they do not give us a depiction or a representation; they give us the thing itself. Now, people often do speak of performers "enacting" or "portraying" or "representing" their characters, but such expressions do not make clear what is really happening. A representation or a portrayal is different from the object represented or portrayed. If the president sends the Secretary of State to confer with the leader of some foreign country, we may say that the secretary represents the president. The secretary *is* not the president, although she represents him. But if the *president* confers with a foreign head of state he does not *represent* the president; he *is* the president. In exactly the same way, Renée Fleming does not "represent" the Marschallin; she *is* the Marschallin. She is both herself and the Marschallin, just as Barack Obama, when he became president, still remained Barack Obama, and therefore was both himself and president. (The two cases differ, however, in that by being the Marschallin, Renée Fleming creates an artwork whereas Barack Obama, by being president, does not.)

Since Renée Fleming makes her instance of the Marschallin out of herself, her own life experience, including the experience she derives from the work, is part of what she uses to become the Marschallin; it is part of her artistic medium. That means, however, that she must be able and willing to reveal and communicate her own self, as she acknowledges in the passage quoted above. She is being the Marschallin, but she is being and revealing herself as well, and this, as I explain in the next chapter, requires love.

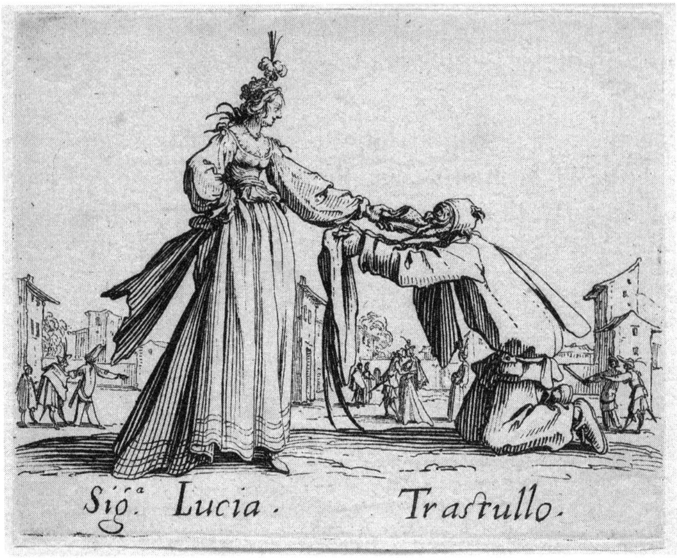
Sig.a Lucia. Trastullo.

6 • *Love*

Love, as related to performing, might refer to the performer's love of his art. We think of the musician inspired and sustained by love of music, the actor by love of the theatre, and so on. That is love in the sense of devotion or dedication to one's calling. It is obviously essential for performers, but it is not the topic I shall explore here. Love, as I shall discuss it, refers to an element of the performance itself, or, better, to a precondition of any performance that is more than perfunctory. It provides a context in which performances can rise to achieve their full potential. I shall discuss two sorts of love: 1) self-love, or self-esteem, and 2) loving relationships.

Self-Love

I have described how a performer uses feeling to guide performance. He listens to the sounds he makes and evaluates their quality, attends to the movements he executes and appraises their expressive effect, and modifies them as he perceives the need. He relies for this on his perceptions, feelings, and emotions. But in order to do this he must take his feelings seriously. He must acknowledge them as having the authority to provide a guide or standard in performance. This means, however, that he must take *himself* seriously. He must accept himself. He must think well enough of himself to trust his feelings. I regard this self-acceptance as a kind of self-love. It is supremely important, but it may not come easily. Some performers never achieve it; some are unaware of its necessity.

Therefore, I shall explore it further and describe some of the obstacles that stand in the way.

One obstacle is the culturally prevalent assumption that modesty, whether false or genuine, is in all circumstances a virtue. We are, it seems, not supposed to think well of ourselves, and we are especially not supposed to *say* that we do. Consequently, the self-love that I say is necessary for performance may seem to amount to presumption or conceitedness. Wanting to avoid the charge of conceitedness, performers may be afraid to rely on their own feelings or take them as providing insight into the works they perform. They may justify their reluctance by such self-deprecating comments as, "Who am *I* to say how Beethoven should be played?" But, diffident as some performers may feel about setting themselves up as authorities, they can't afford to be ambivalent. Anyone who gets up and performs Beethoven is saying through his action, "This is how Beethoven should be played." If in his conscious mind he simultaneously doubts his authority, his performance will suffer because it will rest on a sort of contradiction.

There is another point. By accepting his own feelings as his guide in performance, a performer is not necessarily claiming special superiority for his feelings as compared to someone else's; the allegation of conceitedness is misplaced. He relies on his feelings because they are *all he has* in the moment. If the feelings his performance brings about do not measure up to what he thinks the work ought to evoke, he cannot reject them on the spot. He still must rely on them, using them cognitively, for the current performance. Afterward, he can study the work, refine and deepen his response, and discover a way to realize that deeper conception in a future performance. There are performers who have performed particular works frequently over a period of many years and whose performances have steadily gained power, insight, and expressive depth. Recordings sometimes reveal this, when a performer has recorded a work more than once in the course of a career.

A different obstacle to the self-acceptance necessary for performance derives from the ambiguous position performers occupy in the artworld. Although they are referred to as artists, their status is precarious. They are in danger of being demoted from the aristocracy of artists and assigned a less prestigious role. We can see this in some of the ways they are described. They are sometimes labeled "interpretive" artists, as if to distinguish them from the "creative" artists whose works they perform, and they are said to "serve" the creators of those works—a formulation that explicitly imputes a subservient status. People who talk that way may not consciously intend to attribute an inferior artistic status to performers, even though their expressions have that implication, but such talk is not innocuous; it is harmful.

I shall address the artistic status of performers directly in chapter 7, but whatever conclusions we ultimately reach about their artistic status and the nature of their artworks, we can acknowledge here that as a practical matter, performers must *think of themselves* as artists. A performer must take himself and his activity seriously; he must give himself permission to engage wholeheartedly in an enterprise that involves discovering, exposing, and communicating his feelings, and indeed, his very self. That amounts, however, to saying that, as a practical necessity, he must assimilate, accept, and proclaim the self-image implied in "I am an artist." He must claim full stature as an artist and face the world from that position, while accepting artistic responsibility. Doing those things is a precondition for fine performance. Nevertheless, many performers doubt, at least at times, whether their work is truly creative and they wonder whether or in what sense they are artists in their own right.

If a performer thinks of himself merely as an interpreter who conveys the work of someone else without making any artistic contribution of his own, or if he thinks of himself as being subservient to the composer or the playwright or the choreographer, he may easily come to think that the artistic content of the performance comes exclusively from the composer or the playwright or the choreographer. That attitude toward his own activity will at the very least make it more difficult for him to achieve the self-confidence and self-acceptance required for expressive performance. Worse still, it may provide an excuse for neglecting that aspect of his work or blind him to its necessity.

Demeaning references to the artistic status of performers and diffidence on the part of performers themselves are two obstacles to the self-acceptance or self-love required for artistic performance, but there is another, more fundamental obstacle, namely the fear of self-exposure. Taking one's own feelings seriously as a guide in performance involves exposing those feelings. But our feelings are at the heart of our personal selves – they are essential to who we are – and, consequently, this kind of exposure feels especially intimate and revealing. The more successful one is at producing a sound that gives the proper intensity of feeling, the more one feels exposed and vulnerable. The more completely an actor communicates Lear or Willy Loman, the more he exposes himself, in that moment. This can be a frightening prospect.

A personal anecdote may illuminate this point. Some years ago, thinking it would help me overcome performance anxiety, I worked occasionally as a nude model for a life drawing class. I thought that if I could stand naked and motionless in front of a room full of strangers, then surely I could get up, clothed, and play the piano. The experience did help me with performance anxiety, but not in the way I expected. I discovered, first, that modeling was not difficult. I do not mean that it is easy to be a good model. What I mean is that bringing myself to do it at all – stand up naked before a bunch of strangers – was not hard. Once you persuade yourself that it's OK and decide to go through with it, it's no big deal.* Performing is not as easy as that. Performing demands exposing oneself in a far more profound and intimate way than merely disrobing; exposing one's skin is trivial compared with exposing one's feelings, one's inner self. The modeling experience made me understand the deeper kind of exposure that performing involves.

* Admittedly, this was before the days of cell phone cameras and compromising photos posted instantly on the Internet.

When I finally comprehended that and reconciled myself to it–which amounts, really, to understanding and accepting the conditions of performing–I could approach performing within that understanding, and nerves became less of an issue. I believe every performer who is sensitive to the emotional content of the work he is performing and tries seriously to communicate that content to the audience knows the sense of self-exposure and the attendant feeling of vulnerability I am describing. Renée Fleming mentions it in a passage quoted previously (p. 155), and Carlos Kalmar, music director of the Oregon Symphony, put it this way: "Sometimes you feel, especially in very expressive pieces–Gustav Mahler is one of those–that you are actually emotionally stripping naked in front of an audience."* I believe that acknowledging this is a precondition for authenticity in performance.

Not long ago, an actor friend of mine told a story about a director who refused to allow anyone to observe rehearsals. Having people watch while he was creating apparently made him feel exposed and vulnerable. It is easy to understand the director's feelings, but performers will not be very sympathetic. After all, they work in that space all the time. Doing your job as a director, composer, or playwright and then, when you've finished, setting your work before the world, is different from performing. Directors, composers, and playwrights may feel exposed, or doubt the quality of their work, or worry about its reception when it is performed, but they do not set the creative process itself before the audience, as a performer does. Performing, as I shall show more fully later, is also an activity of artistic creation, and precisely the kind of exposure and vulnerability that our director refused to allow is the daily bread of performers. They are exposed and vulnerable that way at every moment of every performance.

Performance involves self-exposure, but it is not self-expression. I shall not argue the point here, but I consider the view of performing as self-expression to be misleading and

* Unpublished interview, November 16, 2011.

potentially harmful, since it can lead to self-indulgent and idiosyncratic performance. Performers do not express feelings in the sense of merely exposing the feelings they happen to have at the moment; they experience feelings in response to a work as a way of understanding the work, and they try to create corresponding feelings in their audience (assuming appropriate cooperation from the audience). Of course, in one sense I necessarily express myself in everything I do, just because I am the one doing it; any action of mine bears the stamp of my personality. Because of that, when performing I inevitably rely on and expose feelings central to who I am. But it does not follow that self-expression, in that sense or any other, is the goal of my activity or what makes it significant. My performance includes self-creation and self-exposure, but in the end it isn't mainly about me. It is about the artwork I am creating.

The self provides the ground for the judgments and choices made in the course of performance; I test what I do, first and last, by appraising my feelings and putting them in the context of my autobiographical self, my accumulated first-person experience. I cultivate awareness and examine my response to what I do; if I don't like the response my action produces in me, I change what I do; if I do like it, I wonder whether I can improve it further. There is a constant interaction between the self and the product and the movement that generates the product. All this presumes a level of self-development in several directions, not only in the obvious sense of refining one's discriminatory powers but also in the direction of self-confidence and self-acceptance. I need to have the self-confidence to be willing to take my responses as a guide. I need to accept who I am and acknowledge that the better my performance becomes, the more it will reveal of my feelings and my self. Recognizing and accepting all this requires a special kind of courage. Somewhere in myself I must find that courage.

The depth of self-acceptance and the courage required can be considerable. The performer must use his entire self, or at any rate, his entire self must be available. There can be no holding back, nothing off limits or unavailable in principle. A famous director once said of an aspiring actor that he would not get anywhere until he acknowledged, at least to himself, that he was gay. I believe that what the director had in mind was that an actor must make his entire self available. Someone who keeps a part of himself in the closet may imagine that it makes no difference to his performance, but he is mistaken. My own experience bears this out. When I came out as a gay man, my piano playing improved dramatically. The improvement was apparent to everyone who heard me play, whether or not they knew the reason for it, which most of them did not. The sudden improvement surprised me. I had not expected coming out to make such a difference in a seemingly unrelated part of my life.

On reflection, I came to think of it as follows. I know that my orientation has been the same throughout my life. But although I've always been gay, I did not always confront it or acknowledge it. For years I had feelings and desires inconsistent with the straight person I took myself to be, but I dismissed them or explained them away with what I now regard as transparent bits of self-deception, rather than accepting my feelings and drawing the conclusion that was actually staring me in the face. Several of my friends told me later that they had recognized my orientation all along, although they said nothing since I appeared to be in denial. But it seems to me now that suppressing anything as central to who you are as your orientation can be done only by anesthetizing yourself emotionally, as it were. When, consciously or not, you suppress feelings you don't want to confront, you run the risk of suppressing a lot of other feelings as well, leaving yourself emotionally bereft. That, at any rate, was how my former life began to appear to me. When I finally came out, it was as if I had received permission to acknowledge who I was, which enabled me to experience and express other emotions as well. It was like becoming free to have an emotional life. One result was a dramatic improvement in my piano playing. I became more willing – and more able – to let my emotional response to the music inform my playing, and I realized that my previous attempts to play expressively had been superficial in comparison, as if I had applied expressive effects externally instead of having them derive from a genuine response within me.

This example has broader relevance than it may seem to have. Not everyone is gay, but everyone confronts emotionally charged issues from time to time. The death of a parent or friend, a child's illness, a divorce, a financial setback – such occurrences and their attendant emotions are part of life. The advice performers often get about such things is to ignore them. "Put that out of your mind. Don't let it affect your performance!" But that is very bad advice. Obviously, we don't want our performance to suffer, but we do not assure its quality by suppressing our feelings. If I have lost a parent, I must prepare for performance as someone who has lost a parent. I do not mean that I must have death constantly on my mind or wallow in sadness or self-pity, only that I cannot perform at my best if I am in denial or pretending not to have the feelings I have. Performers, like the rest of us, must assimilate life's vicissitudes, acknowledge them, and deal with them. Even misfortune, difficult though it may be to work through in the moment, can add to the fund of a performer's experience and become a source of power for future performances.

One of the most insightful things anyone said to me when I was coming out was this: "Each person you come out to gives you more space in the world." That is true, and it is an important idea for everyone, since everyone needs to have, and feel entitled to, a space in the world. This applies particularly to performers, whose space in the world is the theatre or concert hall. Claiming that space – playing *to* the audience – is vital, and I shall discuss it more fully later in this chapter. Here I am not explaining it or arguing for its necessity, but pointing out the self-acceptance and awareness that is a precondition for claiming one's space.

I have insisted throughout this book that we perform by moving our bodies, and nothing I am now saying about the importance of the self contradicts that position. I claimed, in discussing the body map, that "how we think of ourselves" makes a difference to the way we move. The focus of that discussion was the relation of the body map to bodily movement. But "how we think of ourselves" is not restricted to how we conceive the structure of our arms and legs. It also includes such things as self-esteem, confidence, insecurity, embarrassment – the things, in short, that make up our self-image. Those things affect the way we move, and if the body map is the representation that governs movement, as I have claimed that it is, then we should include the self-image, or what I shall call the "self map," in the body map. The self map is *part of* the body map. That the self map should be part of the body map may seem odd – even nonsensical – to people who accept the Cartesian view that the soul or thinking self is metaphysically prior to the body and could exist without it. Descartes surmised that he could be – or at least he claimed that there was no contradiction involved in supposing that he could be – the same person he was, with all the same experiences he had, even if he did not have a body at all and were only a mind or spirit.

But Descartes was wrong on this point. The skeptical solipsism he assumed as a starting point can be shown on philosophical grounds alone to be incoherent,* and the past forty years of progress in neurophysiology have removed the last shred of vestigial plausibility from the metaphysical dualism he so famously advocated. Clearly, we guide our movement partly by our self-image. This much even Descartes admitted as a fact, though his philosophy made it a mystery. In reality, the self develops as an elaboration of the awareness of the body. Descartes had it the wrong way around. I am a body, I am aware of myself first of all as a body with a location in the world, and from that awareness develops my awareness of myself as a thinking thing. Indeed, I am nothing more than a body: a body with bones and muscles and blood and a nervous system complex enough to form neural maps and the second-order neural maps – images – that underlie feelings, thinking, self-consciousness, and the development of a self. Thoughts

* For example, by Stuart Hampshire in *Thought and Action* (London: Chatto & Windus, 1959), chapter 1.

and emotions are physiological – bodily – occurrences and if I say, as I often do to students, that we play the piano with our entire bodies, not just our hands and fingers, then to be consistent I must say that we play the piano partly with our thoughts and emotions. That is true, and the conclusion is not really controversial; everyone acknowledges that a performer's emotions can affect his performance. My point in this section is this: if we are to perform successfully we must come to terms with our thoughts and emotions, accept and acknowledge them, modify them as necessary, and come to terms with revealing those thoughts and emotions to the world. This is as important as – and is similar to or even a part of – the discovering and correcting of the body map that I discussed in chapter 3.

I think it is reasonable to conclude from this discussion that in order to know the work and how to communicate it, we must know ourselves. But knowing ourselves is not something that can be done once and for all; it is an ongoing process in the life of any person who is at all reflective. Actively engaging in this process is what enables some performers to exhibit continual growth and development in the course of a long career. A young pianist, for example, may play fabulously well at twenty, winning competitions left and right and dazzling audiences. The same pianist, twenty or thirty years later, may play with all the same brilliance, but the music now seems to have deeper significance, more emotional power, and a greater sense of intimate communication. The transformation of her playing is not the result of her learning to play the piano better from a technical point of view; she was a virtuoso already. It is the result of learning more about life and about herself.

Loving Relationships

Love is complex, and it can take many forms. I shall not attempt to define it, nor am I certain that there is a definition that includes all aspects of it and is satisfactory in all respects. Nevertheless, there are four characteristics of loving relationships that I believe would surely have a place in a full analysis of the nature of love, and in this discussion I shall regard any relationship that exhibits them as a form of love.

Other-directed action. A lover acts in ways that benefit the beloved. He takes into account the other's preferences and aversions, he tries to please the other and protect the other from pain or disappointment. In this way, much of his action is directed toward the other; he acts *for* the other person.

Acceptance. A lover accepts the beloved. This does not mean being blind to the other's faults or approving everything about the other person; it means just what it says: *accepting.* A lover perceives the beloved as a complex individual with strengths, weaknesses, a mix of character traits and physical features; the lover perceives all that, accepts it, and says, "*That* is the one I love."

Exposure. A lover reveals or exposes himself to the beloved. In principle, nothing of consequence remains hidden. How he feels, what he values, his emotional states – all these are open, revealed to the other, or at least available to be revealed.

Reciprocity. All the characteristics I have listed are reciprocal. Exposing oneself to another means trusting the other with one's innermost self, and to do that one must count on the other's acceptance. There is thus a reciprocal relation between revelation and acceptance. One perceives the other and accepts what he perceives; conversely he reveals himself to the other and trusts the other to accept what is revealed. In short, lovers reveal themselves to *each other,* do things for *each other,* accept and trust *each other.*

I claim that both the relation between performers and audiences and the relation of performers to one another exhibit the four characteristics I have described. If so, and if we agree to regard a relationship with these features as a loving relationship, it follows that there is a loving relationship between performer and audience and a loving relationship of performers among themselves. Admittedly, it sounds odd to suggest that performer and audience fall in love, or that a fine performance is a love affair of sorts. Ordinary conversation often seems to imply a different relationship, one in which the proper stance for a member of the audience–or for anyone confronting an artwork–is one of passive receptivity. Art is supposed to have a special power to move us, and all we need to do is to receive its message, allow it to "speak" to us. But most people agree on reflection that passive receptivity doesn't take us very far, and they acknowledge that what we derive from an artwork depends on taking an active approach–questioning, reexamining, reflecting. This is especially important in performing art, for there the audience's doing or not doing its part makes a difference to the artwork that is offered them. In place of passive receptivity, the model I shall substitute is one of people observing and responding to one another on an emotional level–that is, observing the other's emotion directly and responding to it on the level of feeling, without recourse to words and, perhaps, without the ability to articulate verbally all the clues that reveal the other person's condition. The model I am proposing exhibits the four characteristics listed above of loving relationships.

One of the four characteristics, exposure, so far as it relates to the performer, has already been discussed in the first part of this chapter. I claimed that performance involves exposure and pointed out the courage and self-confidence that such exposure requires. But exposure does not occur in isolation; exposure means revealing or exposing oneself *to* another. It is therefore closely related to the first feature listed above, namely other-directed action. Let us turn, therefore, to other-directed action.

OTHER-DIRECTED ACTION

Performance is other-directed: it is for an audience. This could be taken simply as a recommendation, stating what performance should be but sometimes isn't. That is to say, it might just be saying that the performer ought to direct his activity toward the audience, ought to include the audience, although some performers seem to be wrapped in themselves, ignoring the audience entirely. Now, I agree with the recommendation that performers include the audience, but that is not what I mean by saying that performance is other-directed. I intend to be making a conceptual point and insisting that the *concept* of performance includes a relation with an audience. There *is* no performance except performance for an audience. I argued for that conclusion in chapter 1, and it might appear to have been settled, but it is worth developing because not everyone appreciates its importance or draws the appropriate conclusions from it. After all, from the performer's point of view, the presence or absence of an audience might seem to be a mere contingency. If the performer executes the bodily movements required to produce an instance of the work and accompanies those movements with attentive appraisal grounded in what I have been calling self-love or self-acceptance, then what else could be required? The presence or absence of an audience would seem not to matter one way or the other, the performer would do exactly the same thing in either case.

Indeed, the idea that the presence of an audience makes no difference, or that it *should* make no difference, is not only accepted, it is actively endorsed by some people. There are teachers who urge their students to "forget the audience is there." Such advice is sometimes offered as a way to overcome performance anxiety, on the assumption, I suppose, that the presence of an audience is the cause of the anxiety. In that case, forgetting about the audience, if performers could do it, would appear to be a remedy. A variant of this approach does not urge performers to forget about the audience, since that is hard or impossible to do, but to belittle the audience in their minds. The idea, I take it, is that if you cultivate thoughts that make your audience seem ridiculous or insignificant, then it will not seem threatening, its response will not matter to you, and you will not feel nervous. Advocates of this view say such things as,

"Imagine that everyone in the audience is asleep," or "Imagine that everyone in the audience is naked."* Now, there may be performers who can forget that the audience is there and perform as if in a space occupied by no one else, and there may be performers who can form a low enough opinion of their audience to erase all feelings of nervousness. But their performances, I claim, must suffer. Ignoring the audience causes performance to be wooden and dead, and no one will perform well for an audience he regards with contempt.

Suggesting that a performer should ignore the audience or that the presence of an audience is a mere contingency involves a misunderstanding of the other-directed activity that is performing. A performance is not "for" the audience merely in the sense of being something displayed in front of them. Performance is a kind of communication, but not in the sense of imparting information. It is communication in the sense of sharing experience. The performer does not merely exhibit an instance of a work of performing art, he *tells* it to us, as it were. He delivers it to us moment by moment *as experience*. The audience should have the sense that it is being communicated *to,* that it is included in what is going on, and it is the performer's responsibility to bring that about. This may seem a peculiar claim, difficult to establish. Reflection on some familiar experiences will make clear what I mean.

Imagine you are in a conversation with a friend who is describing a recent vacation trip. She tells you her story, replete with the usual hilarious incidents of lost luggage, missed connections, and surly taxi drivers, and when she has finished, the phone rings. She answers, and in response to a question from the caller, proceeds to describe the trip she has just described to you. Let us suppose that your friend gives exactly the same account on the phone that she gave to you a moment before (the story was so amusing that she can't bear to leave anything out). Suppose, further, that she uses the very same words

* According to someone I once met who had performed at a clothing-optional resort, this tactic does not work.

describing the trip to her friend that she used a moment ago to you. You have now heard the story twice. But the first time, the story was told to you, the second time to someone else.

I believe you would respond differently to the two accounts, and not just in the sense that you would recognize the second as a repetition of the first. That is, you would feel a difference between the situation in which your friend is talking to you and the one in which she is talking, in your presence, to someone else. By hypothesis, she uses the same words, so it might be hard to specify exactly how the two situations differ. They might be outwardly very similar. Perhaps she has a tiny cell phone nestled invisibly in her hair, so you can't easily see that she is on the phone. Nevertheless, I believe all of us feel that we know whether we are being addressed or not. Being part of a conversation is not the same as overhearing it.

Take a different example. You are relaxing with a cocktail at the kitchen table while your spouse or partner prepares dinner. Your partner is talking aloud, perfectly audibly, but not, initially, to you. You hear, "Let's see . . . a tablespoon of olive oil . . . that's the last of the olive oil, better put it on the shopping list . . . two cups of flour . . . now where's the flour got to . . . I bought flour yesterday, it must be here somewhere. . . . Say, where's the flour I bought yesterday?" The last question, unlike the rest of the speech, is directed at you. I believe that you would immediately know that you were being addressed. That is, although you heard the entire speech, you know that most of it was not directed at you, whereas the last question *was* directed at you. But how do you know that? The clue might lie in the tone of voice, or in your partner's speaking louder—but those changes could be very subtle. The change in tone of voice might be hard to describe, and the volume might not change very much either—you are, after all, in the same room. Still, you know perfectly well that you are being addressed, even if you have trouble stating *how* you know. Now, when you know that you are being addressed, whatever the source of that knowledge, you feel you are in a different relationship with the speaker and with what the speaker is saying. Obviously, you recognize that you are expected to reply to "Where's the flour I bought yesterday?" whereas you were not expected to reply to the rest of the speech, but that is not the difference I mean to point out. What I mean is that you now hear the words as having significance for you in particular. Also, you hear them as *intended* to have that significance. They are *addressed* to you. Your relationship with these words is quite unlike your relationship with mere words, not addressed to you, that you happen to overhear.

Imagine, now, that the situation is reversed. Instead of relaxing with your cocktail, you are the one preparing dinner and talking to yourself. You make the same speech quoted above, and when you get to the words, "Say, where's the flour I bought yesterday?" your partner responds, "It's still in the grocery bag, in the pantry," proving that he knew the words were addressed to him. The question is: what did you do to direct those words to him? Clearly, you articulated them in some way differently, with slightly different tone or inflection or volume. That there was *some* difference in the manner of saying the words is shown by the fact that your partner responded. Something called his attention from his cocktail to your question. Evidently, you moved your vocal chords or used your breath differently – in short, there was a change in how you used your body, but the difference might be difficult or impossible to describe precisely. Moreover – and more important – altering your movements is certainly not what you were thinking of when you shifted from talking to yourself to talking to your partner. You thought you would talk *to him* instead of just talking to yourself, and as a result you used your body in subtly different ways, causing words that might have been mere words to become communication.

Now imagine the same situation with one modification: your partner is not in the kitchen but in the next room with his cocktail. You make the same speech, but when you get to the end and ask, "Where is the flour?" you ask it of your partner *in the next room*. Again, your voice is altered by bodily changes that would be difficult to describe, but not exactly the same changes as when you addressed your partner in the same room, and, again, those changes are not what you consciously bring about. What you do, consciously, is simply address your partner, knowing that he is in the next room. In short, you speak *into a space that includes both you and your partner.* If you know that your partner is farther away, you speak into a bigger space. We can describe this situation using the terminology of mapping developed earlier, saying that your brain maps, or represents, the space into which you are speaking, bringing about changes in the way you use your voice and your body such that your partner in the next room knows you are speaking to him.* Alternatively, we could say that you deliberately *include* your partner in your activity, and your thought of including him brings about a change in the activity such that he knows he is included, although he was not included previously. Your activity formerly occurred in a space that you occupied alone, now it occurs in a space that includes you both.

The domestic scene we have been examining is not a performance, but the part of it we have been considering, the directing of our activity into a space that includes others, *is* what happens in performing. Performers must include their audience. They direct their activity not just at themselves or their fellow performers, but into a space that includes their audience. It is easy to offer examples of this. Imagine an opera singer waiting in the wings to go onstage. She is a little nervous; she fidgets and adjusts her costume while her hairdresser tucks a last curl into place. The moment arrives. When she walks on stage she is transformed. The nervous opera singer is now Violetta or Rosina or Leonora. She commands the attention of the entire opera house and when she sings, the patrons in the last row of the upper balcony feel that she is singing to them. By contrast, imagine the effect if instead of seeing Violetta or Rosina or Leonora emerge from the wings and take over the stage the audience saw a nervous woman fumbling

* This is similar to the way the tools we use become part of our body maps. Neurophysiologists have established that when I use, say, a hammer, my brain maps the hammer as if it were part of my body.

with her costume, pushing her hair into place, staring only at the conductor and waiting for her cue. Clearly, in the first case the audience feels included and in the second case it does not. My contention is that for the performance to succeed, indeed for it to count as a performance at all, the audience needs to feel included and that this is the responsibility of the performer. The performer must perform in a space—must command a space—that includes the audience. If the opera house holds 2,500 people, the singer must sing to a space containing 2,500 people.

Actors, opera singers, and dancers recognize the importance of including the audience, although not all use the same terminology. I think that when people talk of "stage presence," of "projecting the character," and so on, they are making a point similar to mine. The importance of including the audience is emphasized in the training of actors, but among instrumental musicians my impression is that the need to command or play to a space that includes the audience is less widely appreciated. Nevertheless, including the audience is as important for instrumental musicians as it is for other performers, and the difference it makes to the quality of the performance is just as great. As the above examples make clear, performers perform in subtly different ways when they play to a space including the audience. The audience feels the difference. People hear the music differently when they feel included; it becomes more significant and more personal. Audiences respond to performances that include them, even though they may not be able to explain what the performer is doing differently.

We can observe this even with performers of only modest accomplishment. I have several times demonstrated it to students (and their parents) in the following way. I prepare the student by saying, "Play as if you were in a tiny room, like a telephone booth, with barely room for you and the keyboard." The student plays. Then I say, "Now play in *this* room. Think of people in all the corners of the room and feel that you are playing to them." The student plays again. Then, with no further explanation or instruction to the student, I tell her I will call her parent from another room, and she should play twice, first to the phone booth, then to the room. When the parent arrives, I say that the student will now play twice. The difference is invariably striking. The piece played to the whole room is more authoritative, more expressive, more personal; the parent hears it and is astonished at the transformation without knowing how to describe or account for it.

Performing is a sharing or communicating, a kind of giving. But in order to give my listeners the Fourth Ballade as a sequence of sounds that generate a series of feelings that constitute an experience of the work, I must *also* respond to it myself. I must listen and test my responses to what I am doing, as described in the chapter on feeling and emotion. Thus in performing I am producing something – an instance of the Fourth Ballade – that is intended to bring about a set of feelings – an experience – in my audience and I do this by monitoring my own feelings, letting them become feedback for my activity. I observe and appraise my response and deliver music shaped by that response, with the intent that it will bring about an experience in my listeners. I am not merely producing the work; I am, literally, *sharing* it with my audience. Clearly, performing to an audience with the intent to include them requires a different attitude from merely playing. There is a turning of oneself outward, as it were, an intent to include, to share, to embrace. The performer *unfolds* the successive parts of the music or the dance, *shows* the work to the audience, *tells* them the story. The result for them is a more direct and personal involvement and a more significant experience of the work. Understood this way, performing is a case of the other-directed action that we earlier said is part of a loving relationship.

When a performer includes the audience, we in the audience feel it, just as we know, as in my earlier example, that we're being addressed when someone speaks to us. *How* we know this is hard to describe exactly. The performer who is including us must be doing *something* different from a performer who does not include us and whose work does not engage us. Alterations in gesture, articulation, or tone of voice on the part of the performer may be very subtle, too slight for us to describe in terms of movement. We experience a different feeling but we may not be conscious of what changes have brought about the different feeling. It may seem odd that we should do this, but in fact it is something we've practiced all our lives.

Humans, from birth onward, cultivate the ability to respond to subtle cues in other people's manner and actions. Babies respond to parental smiles and solicitude long before they can *say* what they are doing; indeed, before they can say anything at all. A parent imparts love and security and happiness to the infant; the infant receives comfort and reassurance. The infant communicates hunger or fatigue or contentment and the parent understands. All this happens without words, and in the case of the infant, without the capacity for words. Parent and infant share a conversation of gestures and feelings before there is a conversation in words. We discriminate subtle physical clues that reveal the changing emotions of people around us. We learn to do this before we can speak and such responses may remain unspoken even after we learn to talk. We *can* articulate them, at times, but usually we don't, and we don't need to. I know that you're angry or disappointed because I can see it; often I can see it even if you deny it in words. I suggest that the relation between performer and audience is like the relation between parent and infant—or, better stated, it is like the relation between any two people when they are observing and responding to one another's emotional states.

I believe, however, that to attempt to specify alterations in the performer's movements in order to explain the difference between being included and not being included is to look in the wrong place. The difference, I suggest, lies as much with us in the audience as it does with the performer, and it has a neurological foundation. The essential point is this: we should regard performance as an interaction, a conversation. It is known experimentally that most people find it easier to engage in a conversation than to deliver a monologue or listen to one. There is a neurological reason for this, and it lies in our mirror neurons. According to neuroscientist Marco Iacoboni, a conversation is "*exactly* the kind of social interaction that mirror neurons facilitate through imitation."* He suggests that "the way our brain perceives other people's speech is by simulating that we are talking ourselves,"† and this internal simulation appears to be a vital part of even *understanding* what someone else is saying.

I claim that the situation is similar at a performance. When we feel that the performance is addressed to us, we respond as if to a conversation. Thanks to the enhanced activity of our mirror neurons, we understand the work better, and it becomes emotionally significant. Iacoboni believes that "only through mirroring—through the simulation in our brain of the felt experience of other minds—do we deeply understand what others are feeling."‡ The role I am suggesting for mirror

* *Mirroring People,* p. 98. Italics in original.

† *Mirroring People,* p. 103.

‡ *Mirroring People,* p. 126.

neurons in responding to performances seems persuasive to me, although I am not aware of scientific studies that would confirm the importance of mirror neurons in the relation between performer and audience. However, Iacoboni does cite studies that show increased activity of mirror neurons in dancers watching videos of dance performances, and this activity is greater the more familiar the dancer is with the type of dance being shown. I believe that the different significance we attribute to a work when we think a performer is addressing us is not an illusion. It is grounded in the makeup of our brains.

If this is true, then my admonition to performers to play and practice with full intention to communicate becomes all the more compelling. A performer might imagine that his intention to communicate makes no difference – "if I play the piece flawlessly, what difference does it make what my intentions are? Who can tell the difference?" Well, we might not be able to articulate the difference in words, but it doesn't follow that we can't *feel* the difference – that is exactly what mirror neurons do. Thus, the discovery of mirror neurons reinforces the intuitive belief that how the performer thinks of relating to the audience is important, and it corroborates the experience and the practice of many performers, who consciously address themselves to their audience. Many performers have been quite explicit about this – Renée Fleming, Artur Rubinstein, and countless others. They don't need to know about mirror neurons to know that they are right, but the discovery of mirror neurons helps us better to understand what is going on.

RECIPROCITY

The performer performs for the audience, but what does the audience do for the performer? Some audience responsibilities are universally acknowledged. Everyone agrees that members of the audience should be courteous and not distract or irritate others. Consequently, people stop talking, they turn off their cell phones, and they try not to cough. But I do not think they do those things because they consider that as members of an audience they actually have a role in the performance, let alone a responsibility for its success. They don't believe that the quality of the performance depends in any way on themselves. They are simply being courteous. But in fact, the audience member who sits reading the program or fumbling for a mint or whispering to a companion is not just being rude and annoying people nearby. Such behavior *is* rude, but more than that, it undermines the performance. Because of it, the performance may not be as good as it could have been. Performers can't perform their best in a vacuum, and there are two ways to create a vacuum. One way, which we have already discussed, is by the performer's not including the audience. The other is by the audience not including the performer. I conclude from all this that the role of the audience goes beyond mere courtesy: the audience should act so as to enhance the performance.

This may seem a surprising claim. Most people, I think, assume that the audience receives what the performer gives, but does not really contribute anything. On the contrary, the audience has an important role. Indeed, it would be astonishing if this were not the case. Imagine the following situation: you are sharing some personal experience with a friend, describing a situation that, for you, is emotionally charged and deeply personal. It involves exposing some of your most private thoughts and feelings. While you tell your story your friend sits impatiently drumming his fingers, glancing at his watch, yawning, and looking sideways at his newspaper. Now imagine a second situation, like the first except that your friend sits with full attention. You can see in his face that he is absorbing your story and understands its emotional significance. He may make slight gestures, his face may undergo changes of expression, but he does not interrupt. He shows by his manner that he is utterly absorbed and sympathetic.

In the first of the situations described above I am certain you would feel hurt, disappointed, insulted; your willingness and perhaps your ability to complete your story would be impaired. Even to attempt it might seem pointless and you might be unable to communicate adequately the subtle personal concerns that you intended to share. In the second situation you would feel better. More important: you would be motivated to tell your story and your ability to do so would be greater. Knowing that your listener was following attentively and sympathetically would give a purpose to your undertaking. You could feel free to describe your experience accurately. Just as we hear things differently when we believe we are being spoken to, so we speak differently to an attentive listener. The same holds for performance. The quality of the performance can change, depending on the quality of the audience. None of this comes as news to performers. They know it very well. They often speak of the difference an audience can make, or of a particular audience being "hard" or "easy;" they talk of having – or not having – the audience "with" them. Every performer who offers the same program to various audiences is aware of different responses from one audience to the next, and knows that these differences influence the performance.

Members of the audience know this, too; or, at any rate, they are aware of the difference it makes to be part of one audience or another. Being part of an audience where everyone sits in rapt attention, absorbed by the performance, is not at all like being part of an audience that is bored or distracted or hostile, just as watching a funny movie in a theatre filled with laughing people is different from watching the same movie alone at home on a video. But people do not always conclude from this that they have a responsibility beyond mere courtesy. I claim that each individual has the responsibility to constitute the sort of audience that will enable the performer and enhance the occasion. Performance is not just display, it is interaction. The performer must include the audience, but he also responds to the feedback – sometimes overt, sometimes subtle – that he gets from the audience. Therefore, the audience must provide that feedback. It does that in two principal ways: by being attentive, and by being receptive. Attention and receptivity correspond, from the audience's point of view, to the other-directed action and the acceptance involved in a loving relationship.

6 • *Love*

ATTENTION

Vladimir Horowitz is said to have asserted that what he treasured from his audience was not the applause, but the silence. I do not know for certain what Horowitz had in mind, but I choose not to suppose he meant merely that his playing had stunned his audience dumb. I prefer to think he meant that the attention from the audience, silently communicated, created an opening for him to play his best, and for the audience, consequently, to have the best experience of the work. Let me explain. Every now and then, special moments occur in concerts or in the theatre, when the audience sits in an extraordinary silence while something wonderful happens on the stage. Such occasions can live in memory for decades. In my mind I can still hear Artur Rubinstein spinning the descending arpeggios at the end of Chopin's Nocturne in F-sharp Major, surrounded by a rapt and tangible silence in Carnegie Hall. I remember Beverly Sills, in *Julius Caesar*, singing "Piangerò la sorte mia" in a barely audible pianissimo, to an audience that seemed scarcely to breathe. Both performances occurred long ago, in the 1960s, but they left an enduring impression. I believe that anyone who attends performances with any frequency has had similar experiences.

We assume, I think, that such things happen because the performer in that moment soars to an unusual height of achievement and grabs the full attention of the audience. That is doubtless true, but I think it is only part of the story. I suspect that something else is at work here: the performer is enabled, empowered, by the quality of attention. Just as the audience needs to feel spoken to, the performer needs to feel listened to. Could Rubinstein have played *that* well or Beverly Sills have achieved *quite* such ethereal sounds if women in the audience had been groping through their purses while their husbands perused the schedule of the Long Island Rail Road? The performer plays to the audience, and the audience, through its attentive silence, communicates its involvement in what is happening. The special moments I have described are an interaction.

Both the occasions I recalled above were very quiet moments – Beverly Sills singing, Artur Rubinstein playing, *pianissimo*. The sound was perfectly audible throughout the hall, but it was quiet, so the audience had to pay close attention, resulting in the relationship with the performer that I call "interactive listening." The British pianist Paul Roberts writes, "Yes, I definitely hear the silence, which in a paradoxical way I associate with 'hearing' the inaudibility of an audience, when I perform. And I consciously play to it, and it is thrilling."* But interactive listening should not be confined to quiet moments. On the contrary, I believe that it ought always to occur. Nevertheless, I think that quiet moments may be the occasions when people are most likely to become vividly aware of the rapt attention of others in the audience, resulting in a shared experience of interactive listening. The fact that such experience is shared alters its quality and increases its significance. Not all audience members seem to realize this, but some music critics do; David Stabler, for example, writes

> Communal listening is a joy shared, and living through a performance together touches something deep within us. The perfect listening experience for me is when I can feel people around me giving their full attention to the performers.†

We can conclude from this that not only do members of the audience have a responsibility to the performer to enable the best possible performance, they also are responsible to each other for the quality of their shared experience. The lady who sits reading her program may imagine that she is not disturbing anyone or detracting from the performance or the enjoyment of others, but she is wrong. She is making herself an obstacle to the shared experience that – when it occurs – makes performance special and thus she is spoiling the occasion for audience members nearby. I have used musical examples in this discussion, but the same points apply to dance and the-

* Personal communication.

† *The Oregonian*, Tuesday, August 16, 2011, p. C6.

atre, where we could talk of "interactive watching." Clearly, the proper response from the audience varies with the kind of performance; sitting in determined silence at a comedy is no more appropriate than chatting during a symphony. The responsibility of audience members, to the performers and to one another, is to know the appropriate behavior in different situations, and to understand that fulfilling their responsibility as audience contributes not only to their own and others's enjoyment, but influences the quality of the performance.

Performances are not like works of music or paintings, both of which exist before they are presented to an audience or shown to a viewer. The performance does not exist beforehand. It comes into being at the same moment that it is seen or heard by its audience. It is never experienced in the state of having been completed, only in the state of becoming. The interaction of performer and audience – indeed, their collaboration – is critical in a way that does not arise in nonperforming art. What, as audience, we derive from an artwork – any artwork, whether of performing or nonperforming art – depends very much on taking an active approach – questioning, examining, reexamining, exploring, reflecting – but in the case of a nonperforming art, painting for example, how well we do our part does not affect the artwork; the painting is the same whether we view it insightfully or perfunctorily. Likewise with works of performing art: Beethoven's work remains unaltered whether we listen or not. But with performances the situation is different, for there the audience's doing or not doing its part makes a difference not just to how much the audience derives from the work, but to the performer's artwork itself; at a performance the audience partly determines the artwork that is set before them.

Being consistently attentive is not easy. How often have you given your unbroken attention to an entire performance with not a moment's distraction? Most people, I suspect, would admit that their attention occasionally wanders. But each moment of the performance occurs exactly once and there can be no going back. A moment's inattention means that part of the performance has been irretrievably missed. I think inattention is particularly common in the case of music. In part, that is no doubt because music is the most abstract of the performing arts. It is easier to follow the concrete unfolding of a dance or a play than to follow the abstract structure of a complex work of music. A more important point is this: there are cultural factors that condition us not to attend to music.

We are constantly surrounded by recorded music in the supermarket, in elevators, in stores, in restaurants, and in our cars. Listening attentively in most of these surroundings is impossible, and most of the music is not intended to be listened to anyway. It is "background" music, put there to set a mood or because some marketing executive believes it will cause people to spend more money. In self-defense we cultivate inattention and pursue our activities–shopping, conversing, reading–oblivious to the music. We teach ourselves to shut out music that surrounds us. But, surely, conditioning ourselves to regard music as wallpaper, even if we do not do so on purpose, makes it harder to attend to music in a concert. The result is a disservice to both composers and performers. Much of the best music we have was composed with the expectation that people would listen attentively, and much of it requires close attention from anyone who hopes to hear what is going on. In the days before recordings, when music of any kind was a special occasion, requiring that one be within earshot of someone playing or singing, or else play or sing oneself, it was more likely that people would give music their attention when they had the chance. Today the situation is reversed. Music is everywhere but attentive listening is rare. I offer two examples, one hypothetical and the other real, to bring that out.

The hypothetical example is this: suppose you enjoy reading but find turning pages a nuisance. To spare yourself that annoyance, you devise a machine to turn pages automatically, coordinating the rate of page turning with your reading speed. Suppose, now, that you are reading, the phone rings, you answer, and chat on the phone while your machine continues to turn pages at the same rate. The question is this: after you

end your conversation, would you, with no sense of having missed anything, simply continue reading on whatever page was now open before you? No one, I think, would do that. But it is easy to imagine someone putting on a recording of a symphony, then chatting on the phone and returning five minutes later without giving a thought to what happened in the music in the meantime. That this is easy to imagine reveals the extent to which we are in the habit of not attending to the music around us, even in the case of symphonies whose creators intended them to be heard without interruption. If we are in the habit of treating music thus casually, we may find it difficult suddenly to switch gears and pay attention.

My real example is this: several times, when teaching an introductory music class, I tried the following experiment. I told the students I would play a short recording, they were to listen carefully and describe to me what they heard. I chose a recording of Beethoven's 8th Symphony, one in which I knew that Beethoven's instruction to repeat the exposition in the first movement was observed, and I played the exposition and the repeat of the exposition. The exposition lasts just over two minutes, so with the repeat the students heard a little more than four minutes of music. I tried this experiment on several occasions, with several different classes, but never once, when I asked, "What did you hear?" did anyone say anything equivalent to, "We heard a stretch of music and then we heard the same music repeated," and when I pointed out that they had heard the same music twice, they were astonished.

I have described this experiment to people who have said, "Oh, that's really unfair. How could you expect them to notice that?" (As if it were an obscure detail!) I could have defended my experiment by pointing out that these were college students, at a good college, and they should be able to pay attention for four minutes. Moreover, the attention my students lacked was something *Beethoven* took for granted, something his symphonies depend on for their effect.* I do concede, however, that my experiment was unfair in the following way: nothing in my students's cultural upbringing had prepared them to pay uninterrupted attention to four minutes of music and emerge with a sense of where the music had been and where it was going. Our culture does not encourage us to treat music as something to occupy the full attention of an intelligent person. The great English musician and critic Donald F. Tovey claimed that there were two requirements of a good listener: 1) That the person know, at each moment, whether what he is hearing is new or is something heard before, and 2) if it is something heard before, the person should know whether it occurs exactly as before or is altered in some way. A moment's reflection is enough to recognize that these requirements are quite demanding, and no

* Consequently it is inexcusable, with composers like Beethoven, Brahms, and others, to omit repeats. Repeats, in their minds, were not optional or inserted casually just to make the piece longer. (Beethoven was livid when someone omitted the first movement repeat in the Eroica Symphony on grounds that the movement was long enough without it.) It is important to understand that the works of Beethoven, Brahms, and others are architectural structures that depend very much on contrasts between various key areas, on the length of time spent in one key area or another, and whether a particular key becomes firmly established or is simply passed through. Omitting a repeat completely undermines these proportions.

one could possibly meet them who did not pay careful attention at every moment. Surrounding ourselves in our daily lives with music that we ignore makes them still more difficult. This means, however, that we are likely to have trouble fulfilling our responsibility as members of an audience.

RECEPTIVITY

Receptivity, the second responsibility of the audience that I shall discuss, is analogous to the acceptance that I have claimed is part of a loving relationship. The analogy is not exact, however. In a loving relationship, what we accept is a person. When we attend a performance, what we need to accept is not a person but the nature and conditions of artistic performance. Let me explain. When a pianist plays the Fourth Ballade she is, of course, giving us Chopin's work. But she is also giving us herself. For the time of the performance, as we saw in chapter 6, she is making herself into the Fourth Ballade. But at the same time, as we saw in connection with Renée Fleming's Marschallin, she remains herself even while being the Fourth Ballade. Her Fourth Ballade will reflect that; it will be hers as well as Chopin's. It will not sound exactly like anyone else's Fourth Ballade, nor should we expect or desire it to. This follows from recognizing and accepting the nature of artistic performance itself, which entails that every instance of a work of performing art is under an interpretation. This is where the analogy with love comes in. Because the pianist must necessarily offer the work under her interpretation, we must give her room to be herself, just as, because of what love is, I must give my lover room to be himself.

Accepting the conditions of performance does not mean we must approve of the performer's interpretation. It does not mean that we should be undiscerning or refrain from evaluating. It just means we should give the performer room, which amounts to saying we should not have preformed ideas of what the performance should be like. We should not attend a performance hoping for something as close as possible to an admired recording or exactly like some other performance of the same work. We attend a performance to hear or see an individual, and part of the interest derives from there being no way to know what we will encounter. Evaluation should be based on what the performer actually does and what feelings the performance evokes in us, not on how closely the performer matches an expectation formed ahead of time.

Receptivity is required of audiences for the same reason that attention is required: it is part of the audience's role in the interaction – the collaboration – that artistic performance involves. It enables the performer to give a better performance, because a performer obviously has a far more difficult time doing her best if she feels that the audience is hostile, or hopes she will fail, or is predisposed to complain or criticize, or has a rigid conception of what the interpretation should be. Paul Roberts points out that the sense of being judged by external, arbitrary standards formulated in advance often prevents conservatory students from performing their best for a jury. The same is true in a public performance. Some people attend a performance expecting to find fault, like the judges of Olympic events who scrutinize an athlete's routine looking for opportunities to take deductions. Some people think that finding fault shows their own perspicacity and cleverness. Some are convinced from the outset that the performer will not – cannot possibly – meet their expectations, and their dismissive attitude, conveyed as it inevitably is, in subtle ways, to the performer, may help to ensure that their pessimism is borne out. Under such conditions, the performance may easily fall short of what the same performer could achieve with proper audience support. Imagine someone who goes to hear Natalie Dessay as Lucia while insisting that no soprano can possibly equal Joan Sutherland in the role. His lack of receptivity serves no one. He cheats himself, because he may miss something wonderful, his attitude adds no extra luster to the memory of Joan Sutherland, and worse, he does disservice to Natalie Dessay because by withholding the support that might enable or inspire her to sing her best, he makes her task more difficult. Thus he also cheats others in the audience, since the performance may not be as good as it might have been. Granted, no single member of the audience will alone make a decisive difference to the performance, but the more members of the audience come with the attitudes I am describing, the more certain it becomes that the performance will suffer, as any performer can testify.

Some comments or criticisms leveled at performers betray ignorance of the points we have been making. Someone who says, "I wouldn't play it that way," or, "I hear it differently," may, on the one hand, be merely uttering a tautology. *Of course* you wouldn't play it that way, because you are you, and you would be yourself, not the pianist on stage, in the Fourth Ballade. On the other hand, someone who says, "I wouldn't play it that way," with the implication, "That's the wrong way to play it," or someone who objects to a performance merely because it is different or because it departs from some supposed standard, betrays ignorance of what performing is about. The goal is not to play like someone else, not even to play exactly like the composer or some famous pianist. Such a thing is impossible in any case. The goal is to give an instance of the work, and since each performer remains himself even while giving an instance of the work, his instance will not be identical to anyone else's. We ought not to desire or expect two performances of the Fourth Ballade to sound exactly alike or exactly like some recording any more than we should expect Ian McKellen's Lear to look and sound just like John Gielgud's. A prominent exponent of the music of Bach is alleged to have said, "You play it *your* way, I'll play it *Bach's* way." The remark is variously attributed, and it may never actually have been made. One hopes it was not, because if it was, the person who made it exhibited appalling arrogance.* What matters for our purpose, however, is that such remarks betray a fundamental misunderstanding of the nature of artistic performance.

* The remark is also pointless because no one really *knows* exactly how Bach played.

I have grounded the need for receptivity on the nature of artistic performance, but even without that argument, many people would doubtless agree that receptivity is desirable simply because we should be open to new artworks and new interpretations. Nevertheless, just as full attentiveness is a demanding goal, so is receptivity. This is particularly true with performances of well-known works. The better we know a work, the more likely we are to think we know how it should be performed, and to object to what is set before us if it departs from our expectation. It is difficult to put one's knowledge and experience aside and listen or look with genuine receptivity. We must do so, however, if we are to enable the performance to be the best possible, and if we ourselves are to derive the best experience from the performance.

The points I have been making are important, but they are not the whole story. The receptivity required of an audience goes beyond mere open-mindedness. Theorists have long talked about the "suspension of disbelief" that is a part of some aesthetic experience. That was Coleridge's description of what happens in the theatre when an audience willingly believes—or at least, provisionally accepts—things it knows to be fictitious. What happens when attending an artistic performance is similar, but it goes deeper. If in a performance a portion of our experience—a bit of ourselves—is to be shaped into an artwork, then we must suspend more than mere belief or disbelief in this or that matter of fact. We must suspend our very selves. We temporarily surrender ourselves, our autonomy, to another to be refashioned into an artwork. Surrendering ourselves this way is part of what is involved in accepting the nature of artistic performance.

I have characterized the relation between audience and performer as involving other-directed action and reciprocity, two of the features I earlier attributed to loving relationships. The other two were acceptance and exposure. The receptivity I have demanded of the audience is similar to acceptance, and I consider that the self-surrender described in the last paragraph corresponds, from the audience's point of view, to the exposure undergone by the performer, discussed in the first part of this chapter. I think the correspondences here are close enough to justify us in concluding that the relation of audience to performer exhibits the four characteristics of loving relationships. Putting all this more briefly—and picturesquely—we can say that artistic performance is a love affair between the performer and the audience.

I am aware that the situation I have described in which performer and audience interact to produce a magical experience is an ideal; it happens occasionally, not all the time. A great performance may be like a love affair, but many actual performances can scarcely be called love affairs; some are more like unsuccessful blind dates. Sometimes the performer seems contemptuous of the audience. Sometimes the audience is imperfectly attentive, with cell phones going off and people whispering to their companions. Such things unfortunately do occur, but they are irrelevant to the view we have been developing. Our task is not to describe what happens all or most of the time, or to extrapolate from the routine and the mediocre. We achieve insight by formulating and examining ideals.

My claim that the audience—or the viewer or the reader—must take an active role in responding to an artwork is not a novel proposal; on the contrary, it is more like a commonplace than a controversial point. Arthur C. Danto puts it this way: "The spectator stands to artist, or reader to artist, in a kind of spontaneous collaboration."* Ordinarily, however, this collaboration is indirect, in the sense that the artist is not personally present to the spectator. The painter collaborates through his painting, not through his presence; he may, after all, be long dead. A writer likewise communicates indirectly, through his novel. Creators of works of performing art also collaborate indirectly: Beethoven speaks to us through a symphony or sonata, Balanchine through *Jewels* or *Pavane*. In none of these cases is there communication, or any possibility

* *The Transfiguration of the Commonplace* (Cambridge, Massachusetts: Harvard University Press, 1981), p. 119.

of communication, in the opposite direction, from spectator to artist. Beethoven may speak to us, but we cannot speak to him. That, however, is what does occur in a performance, where performer and audience are present to one another. *Their* collaboration is not indirect; it is an interaction. The performer receives and responds to feedback from the audience while he simultaneously offers his artwork. We have yet to determine exactly what artwork it is that the performer creates, my point in this chapter is that whatever exactly the performer's artwork turns out to be, it occurs in a context of communication and sharing; in short, within a loving relationship.

A crucial moment for establishing the relationship of audience and performer is immediately before the performance begins. Let me explain. People arrive, find their seats, and begin to turn their thoughts from daily affairs to the performance ahead. At last, the house lights go down. Everyone falls silent. That is the magic moment, the short period in which the audience adopts an attitude of attentive receptivity, thereby opening a space for the performers to appear and create something wonderful, a space in which audience and performers collaborate to enter the world of Shakespeare or Beethoven or Balanchine. That's what *should* happen. Unfortunately, what actually does happen far too often, at least in the small city where I live, is something else. Instead of allowing the performance to begin, the chairman of the board or the executive director or someone appears with a microphone and makes a fatuous speech. "Welcome ladies and gentlemen . . . blah blah blah . . . [insert a lame joke here] . . . blah blah blah . . . CDs available in the lobby . . . blah blah blah. . . . The annual patron's reception . . . blah blah blah. . . . Thanks to our sponsors . . . blah blah blah. . . . Turn off your cell phones . . . blah blah blah. . . . Thank you, and enjoy the performance." Not so easy, any longer. Anticipation, attention, and receptivity have given way to irritation and impatience. The magic moment has been irretrievably shattered, leaving performers and audience to pick up the pieces as best they can. This kind of disregard for the conditions of artistic performance by the very people who organize the event is unpardonable. When it happens audiences and performers are entitled to complain vigorously.

Collaborative Performance

Our discussion of loving relationships has focused on the relation between a performer and the audience, but in most performances there is another relationship involved that should also be regarded as a kind of love. I am thinking of the relations of performers with one another. So far in this book I have spoken of performers as individuals, as if performance were always a matter of a single performer producing an instance of a work and communicating it to an audience – in short, as if all performers were soloists. That is a useful model, because it simplifies discussion and helps illuminate the points I have been trying to make. In addition, it is sometimes true. Pianists do give solo recitals; there are plays that use only one actor and dances choreographed for a solitary dancer. I have taken such situations as a paradigm, and I shall continue to do so. Nevertheless, most performances are not the work of a single performer; they are collaborations. Five musicians, not one, are needed to generate an instance of Schubert's *Trout* Quintet, and an entire ballet company is needed for *Swan Lake*. I claim that the relationship of performers among themselves in a performance exhibits the characteristics of loving relationships that we identified earlier, and therefore it, too, can be regarded as a form of love. In speaking of "the relation of one performer to another in a performance" the qualification "in a performance" is essential. I am not talking about performers's relationships with one another in their daily lives. In daily life, anything is possible. In their ordinary lives, performers can regard one another with love, hate, envy, admiration, contempt, or whatever. But, the moment the curtain goes up or the first chord is sounded, a different set of relationships must come into play among them.

Other-Directed Action. Performance is a collaboration, which means that in a performance, as in a loving relationship, one acts to benefit others. A particular scene requires one actor to deliver a line in a way that sets up the reply of another actor, since only then can the scene achieve the appropriate dramatic level. We could say that the performer does this in order for the scene to be successful. This brings out a way in which performance, though it is a kind of loving relationship among the performers, is different from the way we ordinarily think of a loving relationship between two individuals. I believe that we tend to think of a loving relationship between two people as involving those two people only. A better way to think of a loving relationship, which makes it more like collaborative performance, is one I once heard from a person who had a long-standing intimate and successful partnership. He said, when asked his secret of success, "There are really three of us. There's me, there's him, and there's our relationship. Sometimes I do things for him, sometimes he does things for me, and sometimes we both do things for the sake of the relationship." Performers do things for each other in performance, and they also do things for the sake of the performance (although we could also say that *everything* they do is, ultimately, for the sake of the performance).

Acceptance. Performers must accept one another. Just as the lover, seeing flaws and shortcomings as well as virtues in the beloved, accepts the entire individual, warts and all, and says "that is the one I love," so a performer, seeing the strengths and weaknesses of his colleagues must accept and work with them, as if to say, "For this performance, we're in it together and we'll do what we can to make it work. Whether we see or speak to one another after the performance, whether we like or dislike one another after the show closes is irrelevant; for now, we focus on the job at hand."

Exposure. We spoke earlier about how a performer must reveal or expose himself to his audience and we saw that this requires courage and a sort of self-love. But a performer also exposes himself to his colleagues, and the apprehension and uncertainty that this involves can be just as great as it is when exposing oneself to an audience, likewise the courage it requires. "What will they think when they hear me play, or watch me dance, or hear me speak my lines? Will they think I'm good enough? Will they want to work with me?" No performer, I believe, is entirely immune to such worries. Nevertheless, it is essential to overcome them and stand naked, as it were, before one's colleagues. It is essential because performers must know one another's strengths and weaknesses, as if to say, from the first rehearsal, "This is who and where we are; this is what we have to work with." Only then can they achieve the collaboration that will be the performance.

Reciprocity. Clearly, the elements I have described are reciprocal. Performers reveal themselves to one another, they accept one another, and their actions are directed to one another. Obviously, all of these things go both ways.

The sort of collaboration that I am describing was vividly illustrated for me by the following experience. I was to play Schubert's *Trout* Quintet with a group of musicians of whom I had previously performed with only one, the violist. At the first rehearsal it was clear that the violinist and the cellist were excellent players, but the bass player, whom I'll call John, was not really up to the demands of the score. The other players could have adopted a critical attitude or behaved like prima donnas, but that is not what happened. Instead they undertook to get John through the performance. The cellist was particularly active in this, going over passages with him and giving him encouragement. In the end, we gave a creditable performance, better than I thought at first we could possibly pull off. It happened that the scores we were using belonged to me and when the cello part was returned to me after the performance I saw that the cellist had marked her part in pencil with instructions like "cue John." Privately, she acknowledged John's deficiencies, and I doubt she would agree to play with him again. But she did not let those feelings get in the way of doing what she could to put together the best possible performance, as if to say at the outset, "OK, this is what we have to work with, how can we make the most of it? Let's get to work."

A relationship among performers that includes self-exposure, acceptance, other-directed action, and reciprocity is needed, first, in preparation and rehearsal. Its presence is necessary if a group of actors or musicians or dancers who may never even have met one another before assembling for the first rehearsal are to achieve a good performance. What happens when we get to the performance itself? The relationship is still important, but there is more to add. Let us return to the example of the *Trout* Quintet.

Ordinarily, the players of a work of chamber music see only their own part. The pianist has a full score, and is the only one who has the luxury of seeing his own part and all the others as well. In chamber music without piano, no one plays from a score that includes the parts of the other instruments. I recounted above how, when the parts of the *Trout* Quintet were returned to me after the performance, the cellist had marked her part with reminders to help the bass player. But she had marked her part in other ways as well. In various places she had written the names of other players in the group—"Tom," "Jane," "Ann"—referring to the pianist, the violinist, and the violist (fictitious names except for my own). She was identifying places where she wanted to be particularly attentive to one of the other parts. If she had an accompanying figure she wanted to know which part had the melody—"whom am I accompanying now?" If she was doubling one of the other parts, or answering it, or accompanying it, she needed to know which other part to attend to in order to shape her playing in relation to that part. In short, she was not simply learning notes, she was mapping her part in relation to the work and that activity of mapping was an aspect of learning her own part. Moreover, it was significant that she mostly did not use the names of the other instruments. She wrote not "violin" but "Jane"; not "piano" but "Tom." In other words, she was not thinking of the work as just a collection of parts or an ensemble of instruments, she was thinking of the performance as a human interaction, a conversation. She was thinking the way every performer in a collaborative performance needs to think.

Thinking of chamber music as a conversation is a helpful way to think of it (although in real life a conversation among several people all speaking simultaneously is not considered an example of good breeding). A play is a conversation in a literal sense: the actors exchange speeches and normally listen and respond to the replies to those speeches. But all ensemble performances are conversations in the following way: they are all human interactions made possible by the reciprocal relations of exposure, acceptance, and other-directed action. Now, the performers stand in these relationships to one another, but at the same time they communicate with the audience, as described in the first part of this chapter. Ensemble performance is for an audience, just as solo performance is. If the audience does not feel it is being spoken to (or played to or danced to), if it feels that the performers communicate only with each other, then the performance is unsuccessful.

Performers work within a loving relationship, and they also perform for their audience. But although they work within a loving relationship with the other performers, *that* is not what they mainly communicate to the audience. What I mean is this. If I am playing a sonata with a violinist named Sally, then Sally's and my collaboration must have the earmarks of a loving relationship, as described above. Nevertheless, what we communicate to the audience is not—or is not only—a relation between Tom and Sally, it is a musical relationship between a piano and a violin. We give the audience the work. This is even more obvious in drama. Two actors must have a loving relationship to work effectively together, but their characters, which is what they offer to the audience, may hate each other. The actor who plays Lear must have a relationship with the actress who plays Regan, they may like and respect each other.

Nevertheless the relation between Lear and Regan that they offer to the audience is something else entirely, with emotions ranging, on Lear's side, from uncritical acceptance to baffled outrage, and on Regan's side, from hypocritical flattery to selfish cruelty.

Every performance of a work of chamber music or a play or a ballet requires this kind of collaboration among the performers. Personal worries, insecurities, strengths, and weaknesses must be acknowledged, accepted, and set aside. Performers do this for each other, but even more for the sake of the performance. I know that my account of performers working within a loving relationship is a description of an ideal. It is what should happen, not what happens always. In real life there are prima donnas, actors who try to call attention to themselves at the expense of others or even to undermine others' work, and musicians who are unforgiving of others' shortcomings and unwilling to sacrifice their vanity for the sake of collaboration. It is tempting to say that such performers are not engaged in artistic performance at all, if artistic performance is taken in the sense we have taken it all along, as an activity aimed at offering an instance of a work of performing art. Performers who try to call attention to themselves at others's expense, or undermine the work of others, are not directing their activity at producing an instance of the work, but at some self-serving goal of their own. Nevertheless, as I pointed out when talking about the relation of performer and audience, our task here is to examine the concept of performance, not to say what happens every day. Reality may fall short of an ideal, but that does not impugn the validity of the ideal.

Cap. Cerimonia.
Sig.a Lauinia.

7 • *Performers as Artists*

I have assumed throughout this book that performers are artists, but I have also pointed out that their status as artists in their own right is precarious. It is time now to take up that question. Performers are sometimes referred to as "interpretive" artists, as if to separate them from "creative" artists. They are also said to "serve" the creators of the works they perform. Such descriptions cast doubt on whether they create anything themselves. Now, there is an obvious way in which performers do depend on the artists whose works they perform: they depend on those artists to create the works in the first place. A pianist couldn't play the Fourth Ballade if Chopin hadn't composed it, so in that logical sense the pianist does depend on Chopin. It is also true that performers interpret the works they perform, because as we have seen, every instance of a work of performing art is under some interpretation. But none of this implies anything about the comparative artistic status of composer and performer, or playwright and actor, or choreographer and dancer. Composer and performer have different functions, as do playwright and actor, choreographer and dancer. What counts is the achievement of each individual in his particular sphere, and the question before us is whether the sphere of the performer falls within the category of creative artist. In this chapter I argue that performers are indeed artists in their own right, and I make clear what their artworks are.

It will be essential in this discussion scrupulously to observe the distinctions laid down in chapter 1 between 1) a work of performing art, 2) an instance of that work, 3) a performance of that work, and 4) an interpretation of that work.

Let us quickly review those distinctions. A *work of performing art* is a musical composition, a dance, or a play. It is not a physical object, and therefore cannot be directly perceived. To be apprehended in the intended way it must receive a physical embodiment that makes it perceptible to the senses. That physical embodiment is an *instance*. It is a series of sounds, or a series of movements, or movements together with speeches, that meet the requirements of the work performed. Sounds and movements and spoken words have physical reality and they can be perceived. A *performance* is a series of intentional actions that produces an instance of a work of performing art. *Interpretation* refers to the ways in which instances can differ one from another while remaining instances of the same work.

Many discussions of performing art, including critical discussions, ignore these distinctions. Consequently, it is sometimes hard to know what people are talking about and easy to doubt whether they know it themselves. Suppose someone says, "Stephen Hough gave a wonderful performance of the Fourth Ballade." That might mean 1) that he managed to include his audience, draw and hold its attention, and create the sort of communicative interaction we discussed in chapter 6. In that case, the statement refers to the *performance*. On the other hand, it might mean 2) that the quality of the sound was exemplary – rich without being harsh, with ravishing shades of color and dynamics. In that case, the statement refers to the *instance*. Or, finally, it might mean 3) that his choice of tempi and layering of dynamics revealed the structure of the Fourth Ballade in a particularly lucid and compelling way. In that case, the statement refers to the *interpretation*. It is possible that the person who makes the statement means all of these things. It is also possible – and more likely – that he doesn't actually know which of them he means. The lumping together of three different concepts under the single word "performance" is what makes this likely. When several things are given the same name it is easy to lose sight of the differences among them.

Because of the extent to which the word "performance" has been co-opted to refer to instances and interpretations, we encounter yet an additional expression: "live performance." This is an odd expression because it suggests that there could be some other kind. But what could that be? Dead performance? In fact, there isn't any other kind of performance. Performing is the human action of making the sounds or executing the movements that constitute an instance of a work of performing art, which can only be done in the moment. I suspect that the term "live performance" comes about because people have become accustomed not to distinguish among performances, instances, and interpretations. They have come to imagine that what is available from a recording is appropriately called a "performance." Consequently, when they want actually to speak of *performance*, they think they need a new term, hence "live performance." (In fact, a recording cannot possibly give the performance, which may have occurred years earlier. It does offer an instance under a particular interpretation, and the instance it offers is a *reproduction* of the instance produced previously by the performer.)

Of the four concepts distinguished three paragraphs back, two are a kind of universal, and two are not. The work of performing art is universal in the sense that it can be embodied in an unlimited number of instances while remaining the same work, and an interpretation is likewise universal because it, too, can be embodied in an unlimited number of instances. On the other hand, a performance and the instance it generates are both unique occurrences. I can perform the Fourth Ballade over and over, but each performance is a unique series of intentional actions, numerically distinct from every other, and each performance generates an instance that is likewise numerically distinct from every other instance of the work.* Since the work performed and the interpretation, as universals, are independent of any particular performance and any particular performer, neither of them will illuminate for us what

* Confusion is easy here, because works of performing art, unlike performances, *can* be repeated. It makes sense to say, "As an encore, the pianist repeated the finale of the sonata." But although the pianist repeated the finale, she didn't repeat her *performance* of the finale; she gave *another* performance of the same finale.

is special about artistic performance or reveal to us the sense in which performers are creative artists. We must examine the other two concepts before us: the period of activity that constitutes a performance and the instance generated by that activity.

Artistic Making

The instance that a performer produces, I claim, is an artwork by the performer. This is because the activity of performers is similar in crucial ways to the activity of any creative artist. Like other creative artists, performers engage in what I call an *artistic making*. I shall describe this first on an intuitive level, and then in more detail.

Consider a painter. He makes a picture by applying paint to canvas. Applying paint is a bodily movement that can be observed. But applying paint to make a picture is not just any movement, it is movement guided by taste, judgment, intention, and skill, and those things are not directly observable. During the activity of making, the painting gradually emerges. When the making ends, the painting is finished. The activity of performing is analogous: the performer engages in a series of movements which, like the manipulation of the painter's brush, are observable, and those movements, again like the painter's movements, are guided by taste, judgment, intention, and skill. The instance he produces has physical reality and is perceptible to the sense of hearing or sight. A painting is also a physical object perceptible to the sense of sight. The painting and the instance differ, however, in that the painting continues to exist as a physical object after the making has been completed, whereas the instance ceases to exist when the performance ends. Nevertheless, despite the brief existence of their product, performers engage in an activity of making similar to that of a painter or sculptor. Moreover, like painters and sculptors, they engage in that activity with the intent and expectation that the product will be regarded as an artwork. My claim in this chapter is that because the instance is produced by a process of artistic making, it is properly regarded as an artwork.

Let us examine the concept of artistic making more closely. Ordinarily, the making of an artwork has three phases. The first is making in the sense of constructing or manufacturing the object. It may be the physical work of putting paint on canvas, shaping porcelain, or carving marble, or it may be the abstract work of devising relationships among sounds or words and notating those relationships. Eventually, the maker judges that the process has gone far enough and pronounces the work to be finished. The object is as he wanted or planned it to be, or as close as he can come to what he wanted; in any case it will remain as it is. This judgment amounts to a declaration, "It is finished," and it constitutes the second phase of making. The third phase is an additional declaration: "This is an artwork." It amounts to a claim or a demand that the object should be accepted as an artwork. Completion of the three phases is what makes something, potentially, an artwork.*

During the first phase, the object is simply a work in progress. Completing the second phase – declaring that the object is finished – yields an artifact, but not necessarily an artwork. To see this, consider a craftsman who makes a bed by attaching pieces of wood together in a certain way. He is engaged in the first phase of making, and the bed is in progress. At some point he says, "It is finished," thereby completing the second phase. We could say that he has produced an instance of the Platonic idea "bed." But his declaration, "It is finished," simply says, in effect, "There it is, that's what I wanted to make. A bed." His bed is an artifact, a piece of furniture, but not an artwork. To establish it as an artwork would require something more than just making and completing the bed – it would require completion of the third phase.

By contrast, suppose Monet sees the mist on the Seine and decides to make a painting. He sets to work applying paint, bit by bit, to a canvas (first phase). At a certain point, he steps back

* I say "potentially" because the object's status as an artwork does not depend exclusively on the artist. It depends also on its reception by its audience. We could describe this by saying that the object must not only be declared an artwork, it must also be received into the artworld.

and says, "finished" (second phase). But unlike the craftsman he also makes the additional claim that the painting should count as an artwork (third phase). He may not make the claim verbally, he may make it implicitly through his actions, perhaps by delivering the painting to his dealer, Paul Durand-Ruel, who exhibits it and offers it for sale as an artwork. Thus, Monet completes all three phases of artistic making and his painting, accepted into the artworld, is an artwork, not just an artifact.

Performers likewise offer what they do as artworks. Obviously, a pianist who plays the Fourth Ballade is offering an instance of Chopin's work, but she is not just offering Chopin. Her relation to the work is not merely that of an exhibitor, although that is part of what she does; she does say, in effect, "Here is Chopin's Fourth Ballade." But she also says, "*I* am producing, or making, an instance of the Fourth Ballade." She offers it as her doing, which is shown by the fact that she takes credit after the performance for what she has done. The audience directs applause at her, not just at Chopin. She is thus engaging in artistic making. She manipulates the keys of the piano (first phase), she appraises the quality of the sounds she makes and launches them into the world (second phase), and she offers the sounds as an artwork of her own making (third phase). That these things occur simultaneously should not obscure the fact that they do all occur. Thus, she launches what she does not just into the world but into the *art*world, and the audience shows its acceptance of the instance as her artwork by directing applause at her.

The instance offered is an artwork by the performer and no one else, no matter how much assistance the performer may have received in preparing the performance. A singer may have worked intimately with a coach over every nuance, every ornament; a dancer may have meticulously prepared every movement according to the instructions of the choreographer; a dictatorial director may have insisted on the exact manner in which an actor is to play the scene. Nevertheless, all the coach or choreographer or director can do is to instill an interpretation. In the moment of performance, it is up to the performer alone to sing the aria, dance the dance, or act the scene. The instance that emerges, moment to moment, is the work of the performer. No one else can do the job; none of those others is out there on the stage. The interpretation might be that of the director or the choreographer, but the instance is the work of the performer; it is his artwork.

Once we recognize that an instance produced in performance is an artwork by the performer we can resolve a question that sometimes seems puzzling, the question why the value of a performance is not simply a function of the value of the work performed. It might seem odd that we can be moved by performances of works that we know to be inferior and would not contemplate for their own sakes. Why, for example, should we flock to hear a soprano who at great expense to the opera company has revived a third-rate *bel canto* opera? Or a pianist who fills her program with Czerny studies? One reply is that such works are "surefire" and "can't miss." But that is certainly false. Such works, in fact, are less surefire, and more risky, than greater works would be. When I listen to a Beethoven sonata, my attention may focus as much on Beethoven as on the performance. If the performance is uninspired, there remains Beethoven, whose musical ideas sustain interest on their own. Provided the performance does produce an instance of Beethoven's sonata, there is plenty for me to think about besides the performance. But what could be more boring than an uninspired performance of Czerny? If the performer is not so supremely skilled as to attract all our attention to the performance, we are left with just Czerny, whose musical interest is negligible. The performer who undertakes such works is claiming, in effect, to be able to produce an instance so breathtaking that it alone will hold our interest. Quite the opposite of "surefire," this is like cutting away the safety net. We go to hear the *bel canto* opera or the Czerny studies because we are interested in performance, and we believe this particular soprano or pianist is able to sing or play these works not just acceptably but in a way that puts us in the immediate presence of an artistic making so completely integrated as to yield an instance that is a fully realized artwork in its own right.

Vladimir Horowitz furnishes a striking example of this sort of thing. No one, I think, would contend that his arrangement of "Stars and Stripes Forever" or his *Carmen* Fantasy are great works of music. But his performances of those pieces were absolutely electrifying. I think it is not too much to claim that although the compositions were not profound, or particularly distinguished as music, the instances Horowitz produced of them were masterpieces of the performer's art. Other examples are easy to come by, such as Stephen Hough's arrangement of "My Favorite Things." "My Favorite Things" is an insipid tune if ever there was one, but Hough's performance of his virtuoso arrangement is pianistically thrilling.*

It is worth a brief digression to point out that although the paradigm of artistic making that I have offered fits most cases, there are artworks in which the three phases of making are differently related. There are artworks in which someone other than the one who completes the first two phases completes the third phase, and there are artworks in which the first two phases are missing altogether. Marcel Duchamp's notorious *Fountain* is an example of the first of these situations. In 1917 Duchamp took a urinal, titled it "Fountain," signed it "R. Mutt," and displayed it as an artwork. The construction and completion of the urinal (first two phases) and the declaration that it is an artwork (third phase) were performed by different people. The manufacturer constructed the urinal (first phase) and determined that it was finished (second phase). At that point, it was simply an artifact, a piece of restroom equipment. Later, Duchamp declared, "This is an artwork." His declaration was controversial but eventually accepted and the object was taken into the artworld. This situation is not

* Here I think that the banality of the tune is part of the point of the piece: using such a silly tune as a vehicle for virtuosic display turns the whole thing into a joke, like heaping truffles on an Egg McMuffin. Many people for whom I have played Hough's recording simply burst out laughing, and the one time I heard Hough perform it, as an encore, it drew chuckles from the rather staid audience.

rare. Numerous objects in art museums were not designated as artworks by their makers; they were accorded that status by others. Native American baskets, for example, were first produced as utilitarian objects, or as having ritual significance. Chinese funerary pottery was not intended to be seen at all, let alone as art. Only later, having been taken up by a different culture, were these objects pronounced to be artworks.

The scholar's rocks admired in Chinese culture furnish an example of the unusual situation in which the first two phases of making are absent altogether. These are rocks with unusual, intricately eroded shapes. When a rock is found with a particularly pleasing shape it is placed on a specially carved stand where it becomes an object of aesthetic contemplation. The natural object, a stone, has been elevated into an artwork. There is no human activity of manufacturing, no physical carving of stone that caused it to be shaped as it is (at least, there is not supposed to be). The human activity that accounts for its being an artwork is simply the decision to treat it as one.* The concept of artistic making that I have offered does not address what many people rightly consider to be important parts of artistic creation, such as originality, profundity, inspiration, imagination, or other topics. But those are not the concepts that will yield insight into the special nature of artistic performance. That insight will come from exploring the phases of making that I have just described.

Let us consider the temporal relation between a finished artwork and the artistic making that produces it. In a performance, the first phase of making is what I have called "the activity of performing," namely the movements executed by the performer to create an instance of the work. But the making that

* Speaking of a simple decision here makes the establishing of something as an artwork sound like an arbitrary matter. I leave it at that for the moment, in order to bring out the ways in which the artistic making that produces instances differs from the making that produces other sorts of artworks. A more interesting and penetrating account of the process that lifts an object out of reality and places it in the artworld rests on the object's receiving an appropriate interpretation, and in the final chapter I shall apply that analysis to instances.

occurs in performance is not related temporally to the resulting artwork in the same way that the making is related to its product in nonperforming art. I shall list the points of difference, taking paintings as representative of artworks that are physical objects. The features of paintings that I shall describe characterize all artworks that are physical objects—paintings, sculptures, buildings, etc.—as well as some artworks that are not physical objects—novels, plays, works of music—but none of them are found in the works of performers.

1) With a painting, the first phase of making—the putting of paint on canvas—occurs at a particular time, or over a period of time, and the painting does not exist as an artwork until this phase has been completed. Until then, the painting is "unfinished" or "in progress."* There is no temporal overlap between the making of the artwork and the existence of the artwork, no moment when making and existence as an artwork occur together. The making must end before the artwork can take its place in the artworld. But in works produced by performers, the making and the existence *do* occur simultaneously: there is complete temporal overlap, no moment when making and existence do *not* occur together. When the making ends, so does the existence of the artwork. Completion of the work coincides with the end of its existence.

2) With a painting, the first phase of making need not be continuous. It can be interrupted and resumed later. Cézanne is said to have chosen apples as subjects for his still-life paintings because they could last for days without spoiling, permitting him to work on a painting intermittently, and even to have used wax fruit, because it took him so long to finish a painting. But performances must be continuous (except, of course, for

* It is true that some works left unfinished by their makers are nevertheless regarded as artworks. The most famous portraits of Mozart and George Washington were not finished by the artists who painted them. They count as artworks, but the decisions so to regard them, that is, the decisions to elevate them from the status of "unfinished portrait" to "artwork," were not made by the artists, but by others who came later. Thus, these portraits count as examples of the situation already considered in which two phases are carried out by different people.

interruptions designated in the work – intermissions between acts of a play, pauses between movements of a symphony). A pianist must play the Fourth Ballade all the way through without interruption in order to perform it. A dancer in the role of the Black Swan cannot say, "I'm exhausted after sixteen *fouetées*. I'll rest and do the other sixteen later."

3) With a painting, there is no limit to the length of time that can elapse between the beginning of the making and the completion of the work. A painter can begin a work and finish it days, months, or even years later,* but performances occur within very narrow constraints of time. Producing an instance of the Fourth Ballade takes approximately eleven minutes. If it takes very much more or less – if it takes one minute, or four hours – it ceases to give an instance of the ballade.

4) With a painting, there is no particular order in which parts of the work must be made. A painter can begin with the sky and then paint the foreground, or he can begin with the foreground and do the sky last, whereas a performer must give the different parts of the work in the precise order prescribed in the score or script. When I perform the Fourth Ballade I can't begin with the coda, technically the hardest part, "to get it over with," and then proceed to less difficult sections.

5) In the course of the first phase, a painter can evaluate what he has done, and go back and alter any parts of it that he does not like. Eventually, he judges the making to be over. He pronounces the painting "done" (second phase), and, immediately or later on, declares it an artwork (third phase). The three phases are temporally separable. Performers also judge their work, but they are obliged to do so in the moment of producing it. They cannot alter what has already occurred or delay offering it to the audience, which means that at each moment of performing the performer is producing the work (first phase), judging its acceptability (second phase) and also

* Admittedly, there are types of nonperforming art in which the making has some temporal constraints. A ceramicist must complete a work before the clay hardens, for example. Nevertheless, even here there is considerable latitude; the ceramicist can do things to retard the drying of the clay.

offering it to the audience (third phase). The three phases occur simultaneously.

6) After a painting is finished, its existence does not depend on any continued action by the artist. It can exist for an indefinite period of time, even after the artist is dead. Artworks produced in performance, by contrast, do not exist apart from the performance. When the performer's activity ends, the artwork ends. The pianist stops playing and the music is over; the dancer stops moving, assumes her final pose, and the dance is over. There is then no way except in memory or reproduction to experience or have access to the artwork produced in performance. It no longer exists.

Instances as Artworks

If an instance produced in performance is an artwork by the performer, then it counts as two artworks at once, by two different artists. When a pianist performs the Fourth Ballade the sounds she intentionally produces are her artwork, but they also are an instance of the Fourth Ballade, which is by Chopin. So the instance is simultaneously her creation and a creation of Chopin's; it is two artworks at once. Similarly in other cases. If Patricia McBride, in *Pavane,* produces a series of bodily movements, that physical sequence of movements is her product, her artwork, but the same sequence is also an instance of *Pavane,* an artwork by Balanchine. That a single sequence of sounds or movements should count as two different artworks may seem paradoxical at first. In fact, however, the situation is not especially rare and it can occur in nonperforming, as well as performing, art. As an example in nonperforming art, consider etchings. An artist makes an etching by preparing a plate. He etches a *matrix* in the plate. At some point, he makes an artistic decision that the plate is finished. Prints can then be made from the plate. Each print is a separate physical object, but each print is an impression of the same matrix. We can describe this by saying that each print is an instance of the etching. Now, each print is individually made, and "pulling" a print is a different process from etching a plate. Moreover, there is an exercise of skill, taste, and intention in pulling the print. Each print must be examined and approved, the judgment pronounced, "that's good, it's finished." Thus, there is an artistic making and pronouncement concerning each print, separate from the artistic making and pronouncement that produced the plate and declared *it* to be finished. Because of this separate making and pronouncement, the print can be regarded as a separate artwork. So we can say that the etching is an artwork, but each impression is also an artwork. Moreover, each print is a different artwork from every other print, even though every print is an instance of the same matrix. So each print is two artworks at once, and the relation between the matrix and the individual impression is like the relation between a work of music and an instance generated by a performance.

In the case of etchings, the artist who etched the plate is often the one who also makes the prints. A similar identification can occur in performing art. Some composers perform their own compositions, and some choreographers dance their own ballets. But it is also possible that the artist who etches the plate is not the artist who makes the prints. There could even be several different artists who each made prints of the same etching, using the same plate. Although the person who makes the print may be called a "master printer" rather than an artist, I contend that making a print requires taste, skill, judgment, and so on, and can plausibly be regarded as an separate exercise of artistic making. With that understanding, we can say that each print is an artwork by the master printer, and each print is simultaneously an instance of the matrix, which is an artwork by a different artist. That is analogous to the situation in music, where a sequence of sounds is an artwork by the pianist who produces it, and also an instance of a musical work.

Not all artworks that admit of multiple instances are such that the instances count as artworks in their own right. Works of literary art can have many instances; each copy of a novel, for example, is an instance of the novel. However, a copy of a novel is not two artworks at once. That is because copies of novels are simply run off a printing press; they are not products of a separate activity of artistic making. Nevertheless, we can imagine instances of a literary work that would count as artworks in their own right. Suppose a calligrapher makes a beautifully lettered copy of a Shakespeare sonnet and meticulously illuminates the page in the manner of a medieval manuscript. That copy might count as an artwork, and as such it would be an artwork by the calligrapher. At the same time, however, it would be an instance of a different artwork, namely, the Shakespeare sonnet. What separates the copy of the sonnet that is an artwork from copies that are not artworks is that the special copy we have imagined was produced by an activity of artistic making distinct from the activity of making that produced the sonnet.

Ordinarily, when an object is simultaneously two different artworks, one of the works involved is a work that admits of numerous instances, as do works of music, literature, dance, or drama. That is, one of the two works will be present as an instance, but the instance, because it is individually produced by a separate activity of artistic making, is also an artwork. However, this may not always be the case. An example of an object that is simultaneously two artworks but where neither artwork admits of numerous instances is perhaps found in the work of Robert Rauschenberg. In 1953, Rauschenberg—famously—took a drawing by Willem de Kooning, erased it meticulously, and exhibited it as *Erased de Kooning Drawing*. It is tempting to regard this as an example of two artworks at once, one by Rauschenberg and one by de Kooning. Clearly, Rauschenberg's work requires that the piece of paper be de Kooning's drawing, therefore it is the work of de Kooning, as well as a work by Rauschenberg. There can be no denying that de Kooning's drawing is necessary for Rauschenberg's artwork. On the other hand, the drawing has been erased. We do not confront de Kooning's drawing but the *absence* of his drawing, which muddies the picture. Indeed, someone might claim that Rauschenberg's artwork *is*

the absence of de Kooning's drawing. But it is not just any absence. De Kooning's drawing, having been erased, is absent everywhere in the universe, but only one absence, the absence from this particular paper, has any significance. I am, I confess, not certain whether to regard this as an example of an object that is simultaneously two different artworks, though I think it may be, and it would not surprise me if this uncertainty were part of Rauschenberg's intent.

Having become accustomed to the idea that a sequence of sounds or movements can count as more than one artwork, we can observe that the examples I have offered, though valid, represent only the simplest cases. I have talked of works for a single performer, whereas many works of performing art, perhaps the majority, require more than one performer. The analysis I have offered does apply to works involving several performers, but the situation is complex and it is worth examining. Let us return to Schubert's *Trout* Quintet, which we considered earlier in connection with love. The *Trout* Quintet is, obviously, a single artwork by Schubert, but producing an instance of it requires a collaboration among five musicians.

To produce an instance of the *Trout* Quintet, the violinist produces an instance of the violin part, the pianist produces an instance of the piano part, likewise for the other performers. Now, the violinist produces an instance of the violin part by an activity of artistic making, and the instance, therefore, is an artwork by the violinist. The instance of the piano part is likewise an artwork by the pianist, and the same holds for the viola, cello, and bass parts. There are, therefore, five separate artworks, produced simultaneously, and what justifies us in calling them separate artworks is that each is produced by a separate activity of making. They are not unrelated, however; they combine to make an instance of the complex artwork that is the *Trout* Quintet.

Now, Schubert composed the parts in such a way that they would fit together to form a quintet, but his composing them that way does not guarantee the success of a particular performance. In performance, something else is needed, and what is needed becomes obvious when we consider performances in which it is lacking. We have all heard performances in which the performers play simultaneously, but each is entirely wrapped up in his separate part, with little awareness or consideration of what the others are doing. In such a performance, the parts do not come together to make a satisfactory whole. Merely playing the five parts simultaneously is not sufficient; the players must actively combine their parts, attentively relating them to each other. The catalyst of this combination, as we saw in chapter 6, is love. When it succeeds, the result is magical. At a successful performance of the *Trout* Quintet, we in the audience experience an artwork that is a whole in itself, but is also an amalgam of five other artworks, by five different artists united in a relationship of love. This has no analogue in nonperforming art.

The same thing occurs in opera and dance and drama. Renée Fleming's Marschallin is her artwork, as we have seen, but it is not sufficient in itself to give us *Der Rosenkavalier*; the opera requires contributions from many other performers as well. All of those performers – the other soloists, the chorus members, the dancers, the orchestral players – produce instances of their own parts. Each of those instances is an artwork by an individual performer and they all combine, united by love, to make an instance of *Der Rosenkavalier.* It is worth a brief digression to point out the implication of these conclusions concerning the role of the conductor. The conductor does not produce an instance of anything—at least not in the way the other performers do, by singing, playing an instrument, or dancing. He is essential, however, to coordinate the activities of the performers, to create a context, we could say, in which their separate artistic activities can come together into a larger whole. And it seems to follow from what we have observed that an essential part of his role must be to encourage and enable the performers, giving each a space in which to function as an artist, even while overseeing and directing the way their individual contributions relate to each other.

Originals and Reproductions

A performance lasts only a short time, but technology enables us to offset its transience and preserve it on a recording. We can record sounds, and we can make a video of a dance or play. But obviously, the sounds from a CD player or the movements shown on a DVD are not the same individual sounds and movements that were produced by the pianist or the dancer or the actor. They may sound or look similar, but even if they were perceptibly indistinguishable they would still be different individual sounds, different individual movements, and therefore they are not the artwork produced by the pianist, actor, or dancer. They have a different causal history. In short, they are a *reproduction*. Recorded music can sound similar to music actually played, similar enough that some people lose sight of the difference between a musical performance and a reproduction, and confusion here is made easier by the ambiguity of the word "performance" as commonly used. In dance and drama the confusion between performance and reproduction does not arise, or at any rate, it is not acute. That is because musical works receive physical embodiment in series of sounds whereas works of dance or drama receive their physical embodiment in series of movements. Sounds can be recorded and then reproduced by a machine, but movements cannot be prized off the bodies that execute them and then reproduced by some other causal mechanism. The closest we can come is with a video, which, although it can reveal things about the movements of a dancer or actor, does not resemble those movements closely enough to be confused with them. Consequently the need to distinguish instances produced in performance from instances produced by reproduction is not pressing in the case of dance and drama. Nevertheless, in order to maintain the conceptual parallel among the performing arts of dance, music, and drama, I shall, in what follows, treat videos as reproductions, analogous to sound recordings.

Suppose that a pianist produces an instance of the Fourth Ballade. That instance is her artwork. The instance—that series of sounds—can be recorded. But we cannot record the *performance*. The performance is an action, or a series of actions. It is the activity of producing the sounds. The activity causes the sounds, and in that activity lies the causal history that makes those particular sounds into an artwork. We can record the sounds but not the activity of making them. The situation is exactly analogous to what we find in nonperforming art, painting, for example. The reproduction of a painting reproduces the painting but not the artistic activity of producing it, although it is that activity that accounts for its being the artwork it is, or being an artwork at all. We could put the point slightly differently this way. A description of *Bathsheba* is "a painting made by Rembrandt." This description has two parts, the "painting" part and the "made by Rembrandt" part. The "painting" is a product, a physical object, and it is easily imitated; we may even be able to make another physical object that is perceptually indistinguishable from the painting. However, the "made by Rembrandt" part of the description refers to the causal history of the object, the artistic making that produced it, and *that* cannot be reproduced, although it is essential to the artwork's being the artwork it is. When we reproduce an artwork, all we can reproduce is the product; we cannot reproduce the making, although the making is what causes the product to be an artwork. This applies to artworks produced in performance as much as it does to paintings.

Reproductions have their value. Through them it is possible to know something about an artwork without having access to the original. If the sounds from a recording are like those a pianist produced in performance, they can reveal something about the pianist's artwork. They can have a similar expressive quality to the sounds she got from the piano, reveal her choice of tempo and dynamics and thus convey her interpretation. Similarly, a reproduction of Rembrandt's *Bathsheba* can reveal important aspects of Rembrandt's art: the visual composition, the use of light and shade, the choice of colors, and other features.

Reproductions are especially valuable in the case of performances. The performance may be far in the past, but the reproduction gives some inkling of what once was. Through recordings we can form a notion of the stature and achievement of such legendary performers as Sergei Rachmaninoff and Josef Lhevinne, in the same way, perhaps, that Roman marbles give us a notion of Greek bronzes. That is to say, the access a recording offers to a performance is like the access a reproduction offers to a painting that has been destroyed. In the spring of 1958 a fire at the Museum of Modern Art in New York destroyed one of Monet's paintings of water lilies. Also in the spring of 1958 Van Cliburn, on his triumphant return from Russia, performed Tchaikowsky's Piano Concerto no. 1 in Carnegie Hall. Neither of those artworks, neither Monet's painting nor Van Cliburn's instance of the concerto, exists today. We can have access to them only through reproductions. Nevertheless, despite their value, reproductions are not the originals, and they are not ordinarily artworks.

When I listen to a recording of the Fourth Ballade, the sounds emerging from the CD player have the same pitches and the same relations to one another as those generated in the performance, and if the relations of sounds and pitches are the same, so is the musical work they instantiate. So I *am* hearing Chopin's composition. Therefore, although the sounds from the CD are a reproduction with respect to the pianist's artwork, with respect to the *ballade* they are *not* a reproduction. Indeed, the distinction between original and reproduction makes no sense in the case of the ballade. *Any* sequence of sounds that satisfies the prescriptions laid down in the score counts as the actual ballade, not a mere reproduction of the ballade. In just the same way, any copy of the words that make up a novel counts as the novel, not a reproduction of the novel. The recording gives us Chopin's artwork, and if the sounds from the machine are sufficiently like those produced by the pianist, it gives it under the same interpretation.

We can summarize these conclusions as follows. Attending a performance of the Fourth Ballade we are in the presence, first, of a performance, which is a period of artistic making in which the pianist produces sounds by pushing down the keys of a piano. We are in the presence, second of the sounds themselves. They are what the pianist makes, they are her artwork, and they are an instance of the Fourth Ballade. We are in the presence, third, of the Fourth Ballade, set before us in a particular instance. The Fourth Ballade is an artwork by Chopin; this instance of it is an artwork by the pianist. The features of this instance that distinguish it from other instances of the same work are part of the pianist's interpretation of the Fourth Ballade. When we listen to a recording we are again in the presence of an instance of the Fourth Ballade, and consequently in the presence of Chopin's artwork. If the recorded sounds are sufficiently like those produced in concert, the instance from the recording will be under the same interpretation as the one in concert. But the instance from the recording is not the pianist's artwork, it is the *reproduction* of the pianist's artwork. The recording gives us one artwork, not two.

What does it matter whether we are in the presence of an actual performance or just a reproduction? That depends on which artwork we are interested in. If we are interested in the work by Chopin it may make no difference whether we listen to a recording or attend a performance, since we can have access to Chopin's work either way. If we are interested in the interpretation, we can likewise have access to that through the recording. But what if our principal interest is in the performance? Most people take for granted that original artworks should be preferred to reproductions, and they would object–indeed, they would consider it a fraud–if a museum displayed a reproduction of a painting instead of the original.* We might conclude from this alone that instances generated in performance, which are the originals, are preferable to recordings, which merely reproduce those instances.

But it is still fair to ask why this should be so. Why should we prefer an original artwork to a reproduction? It is tempting to reply that we prefer it because we can perceive it to be superior. The sounds generated in actual performance, we may say, are better than those from a recording, the colors in the painting are better than those in a reproduction, and so on. But this is not a satisfactory answer, because it may not be true. There is no necessity that a reproduction will in every case have inferior perceptible qualities. What if its perceptible qualities were the same? What if they were better?† Someone might hold that even if the reproduction did possess all the perceptible qualities of the original, we would still prefer the original, on grounds that it *is* the original. On this view, preferring the

* It is a curious fact that many people who would shrink from confusing a reproduction with an original painting are much more complacent when dealing with performances and will speak confidently about Artur Rubinstein's piano playing or Maria Callas's singing although they never heard either artist, only some recordings.

† This, or something like it, actually happens in commercial recordings in which wrong notes are edited out and the best parts of different takes are pasted together. As an instance of Chopin's work, the doctored recording may be better than the performance, because it gives a more accurate instance of the score. However, in relation to an instance produced in performance (and it is the *instance* that is the performer's artwork), it is worse: it is no longer even a reproduction of an instance; it is more like a collage of reproductions. In a phrase I wish I had thought of myself, Frank R. Wilson refers to commercial recordings as "the wholesale *misrepresentation* of performance," *The Hand* (New York: Pantheon Books, 1998), p. 214. Italics in the original.

original to a reproduction is not something for which we need a reason; that it is the original *is* the reason. But that is not an explanation; it merely begs the question. What is it about the original that justifies our attitude? What does an original offer that a reproduction, assuming it to be perceptually indistinguishable from the original, cannot offer? I do not propose to answer this question with respect to nonperforming art, but in the case of instances generated in performance I shall offer an explanation in chapter 8.

In this chapter I have argued that performers do produce artworks: the instances they make are their artworks. This justifies us in regarding performers as artists in their own right. I have further pointed out that in the artworks of performers, the making of the work and the existence of the work are differently related temporally from the way they are related in nonperforming art. I shall summarize their temporal relations by saying that in the work of performers, the existence of the work and the making of the work are simultaneous. That formulation does not capture all six of the differences pointed out earlier, but it gives us a convenient phrase to use in our discussion.

It might seem that simultaneity of making and existence would explain what is special about performance, but in fact it is not enough. After all, a CD player also exhibits simultaneity of making and instance. The speakers vibrate, causing sound, and the instance takes shape simultaneously with the making of it by the speakers. Consequently, simultaneity alone is not enough. Now, the instance produced by the CD player could be indistinguishable from one produced in performance. Because the two instances may be perceptually identical, it is not by examining *them* that we shall discover what is special about performance. We must look elsewhere. The CD player produces sounds by a causal, mechanical process. It is a machine and as such it is reminiscent of the golden harp we considered in chapter 1. The instance that occurs in a performance, by contrast, is the result of an artistic making. That performers engage in artistic making was our principal reason for claiming that they are artists in their own right. Therefore, to discover what is special about performers as artists and what is special about their artworks, we must look more closely at the process of artistic making. More specifically, we must consider the significance of an artistic making that coincides in time with the existence of the artwork it produces, and, as we shall see, we must consider the context in which that making occurs.

Pulliciniello. Sig.ª Lucretia.

8 • *Performance and the Human Condition*

When a performance occurs, there is a period of artistic making that coincides in time with the existence of the artwork it produces. Describing this situation as a *period* of artistic making reminds us that performances occur over a stretch of time, and so do the instances they generate. We in the audience experience the instance bit by bit, not all at once, which is also the way the performer makes it. This means that performance involves uncertainty or contingency, of several kinds.

Uncertainty and Contingency

First, there is uncertainty what will happen. Will Lear and Cordelia escape their enemies and live happily ever after?* Will the Fourth Ballade end quietly, like the Second Ballade, or will it build to a fiery climax, like the First Ballade? Obviously, we can be in doubt about such things only on a first encounter with the work, when, not knowing what comes next, we must wait and find out. I call this the *uncertainty of ignorance*. We are in doubt, but not because the events are actually undetermined – only because we don't know yet what they are. Shakespeare did provide an ending, and Chopin did write a coda, which will unfold in due course. We can also experience the uncertainty of ignorance when we listen to recording or video. If I am unfamiliar with *King Lear* or the Fourth Ballade I can watch a video or listen to a recording with the same uncertainty

* For many decades, Shakespeare's ending was considered *too* tragic, and a version was substituted with a happy ending in which Cordelia marries Edgar.

about the outcome that I would have at a performance. The uncertainty of ignorance is a central ingredient in many works, as in mystery stories and suspense movies where the creator of the work and the actors and directors do all in their power to heighten the uncertainty and anticipation of the audience. Composers do the same. There are moments in Beethoven symphonies when a sudden shift of harmony takes the piece in an unexpected direction making us wonder what will happen next.

Once we are familiar with a work we are no longer uncertain about the outcome, but there is another kind of uncertainty, namely, uncertainty as to just how the performer will present the work. We know that an actor performing Lear will say, at a particular point in the play, "I have ta'en too little care of this." We know that a pianist performing the Fourth Ballade will begin with three octave Gs, not three Cs. But we do not know the exact manner in which the performer will do these things. We must wait until it is revealed to us. The different ways in which performers meet the demands of a work are differences of interpretation, so we can refer to this as "the uncertainty of interpretation." The uncertainty of interpretation can occur when we listen to a recording or watch a video. If I don't know how a certain pianist interprets the Fourth Ballade, I can listen to a recording and find out (at least, I can find out how she interpreted it at the time of making the recording) and if I don't know how a certain actor plays Lear I can watch a video, if one is available. My uncertainty regarding what interpretation will emerge from a recording or video is really just a variety of the uncertainty of ignorance, since the interpretation is there, embedded in the upcoming tracks of the recording or the frames of the video.

At a performance, the situation is different. The audience does not know how the performer will interpret the work, but this uncertainty of interpretation is not a case of the uncertainty of ignorance, because *neither does the performer know this.* For one thing, the performer can change his mind in response to unexpected circumstances or the inspiration of the moment.

Indeed, this happens often. A performer must be able to respond, in the course of performing, to unforeseen events or situations. The stage is smaller than expected, so a dancer must adjust the length of his leaps. The hall is not very resonant, so the musician or actor must adapt to the space. Sometimes, interpretive choices are made in the moment of performing. A pianist chooses to take a bigger ritard than usual in a particular place, because in the moment it seems the right thing to do, which may suggest or inspire other effects of rubato elsewhere in the piece, leading to an interpretation different from the way she's played the piece before, and different from her expectation at the beginning of the performance. In performance, therefore, we do not merely experience the uncertainty of ignorance. We confront actual contingency.

The performer doesn't know exactly what he will do because he *hasn't decided*. He *can't* decide ahead of time, and the reason he can't is that performance, as we have shown previously, cannot be guided by intentions articulated beforehand. In performance, the vital intention is the one that actually generates the movement, moment to moment, and *that* intention, which amounts to a decision what exactly to do, is formed together with the execution of the movement. From this it follows that performance is an ongoing exercise of freedom and choice. It is an exercise of freedom because it is intentional action and to act according to intention *is* to act freely. Moreover, each movement is the result of choice, not in the sense that the performer is constantly deliberating between alternatives, but in the sense that the performer forms an intention in the moment, which governs a particular movement and determines a particular result, and the result would be different if the performer had formed a different intention. Thus, in performance, the *events themselves* are contingent. Moreover, the audience, knowing that the events are not determined beforehand, experiences the emerging work, at each moment, as something brought about by intention and choice, in short, by human action. This means, however, that there is another sort of contingency involved.

Intentions are not always realized. They can fail. Indeed, the idea of any action at all includes the possibility that it may fail – the possibility, that is, of intending but not succeeding. Consequently, there may be doubt not only about what the performer's intentions will be at each moment, but whether the performer will successfully carry out those intentions. Since it is entirely possible that the performer will fail, this doubt is not based on ignorance; it is a genuine contingency. This is especially evident in works that emphasize the technical skill of the performers. A virtuoso performance is thrilling because the performer is doing something that is obviously very difficult, testing the limits of technique and, as it were, courting disaster. Part of the thrill depends on knowing that he is not doing it as an automaton but as a free agent, with every note or every movement the result of intentional action. Consequently, there is a sense of triumph, combined, perhaps, with an element of relief, when the performer is successful. The virtuoso performance, by heightening our awareness of the contingency that is a precondition of any action at all, dramatizes the human choice that underlies the production of an artwork. Many works of performing art are deliberately constructed so as to call attention to the skill of the performer. The display of skill is part of the content of the work. Any number of works – piano pieces by Chopin, Liszt, and others; opera arias by Mozart, Bellini, Verdi; some ballets by Balanchine – can serve as examples.*

The contingencies we have just been discussing, which are essential features of performance, cannot occur in recordings or videos; they occur only in performance. That is really just another way of pointing out that the instance that comes from a CD player or video is completely determined beforehand. The recording or video is not an action, even though it may have been produced by an action. It is not the product of an artistic

* Works intended to call attention to the skill of the performers are one category of what I call *works of virtuosity* and they can be found in all the arts, not just performing art. They have philosophically interesting features, which I discussed in "On Works of Virtuosity," *Journal of Philosophy*, 77:1 (January 1980), pp. 28–45. That paper is available on my website, www.pianomap.com.

making occurring simultaneously with itself. Recognizing that any uncertainty associated with a recording or video is simply one or another form of the uncertainty of ignorance, whereas performance involves genuine contingency, gets us partway to fulfilling the promise made earlier, namely, to explain the superiority of originals to reproductions. But there is more to be said.

Consciousness and Intention

We concluded in chapter 5 that performing must be intentional action. That conclusion enables us now to uncover a connection between performance and consciousness, but to explain the connection we must briefly discuss consciousness and clarify some features of intention. I begin with consciousness.

To be conscious is to have a sense of oneself as an agent in the world, a sense of oneself acting. I shall occasionally refer to this sense of oneself as an agent as *the foundation of consciousness.* Now, the expression "foundation of consciousness" can also be taken another way, to refer to the *neural* foundation of consciousness, which Antonio Damasio describes as "the process whereby neural representations, which consist of biological modifications created by learning in a neuron circuit, become images in our minds; the process that allows for invisible microstructural changes in neuron circuits . . . to become a neural representation, which in turn becomes an image we each experience as belonging to us." He calls this "the center of neurobiology."*

I mention this alternative in order to make clear that it is not what I shall discuss. I mean to speak not of the neural foundation but of what we might call the *experiential* foundation of consciousness: how do we experience ourselves as conscious beings? We could call this the *conceptual* foundation of consciousness, in one sense at any rate, since to say how we experience ourselves as conscious beings is to say what

* *Descartes' Error,* p. 90.

it means to be conscious. In other words, I am taking a first-person perspective and considering what consciousness is like to the person whose consciousness it is, whereas a neurobiologist takes a third-person perspective and attempts to describe the neural processes that, when they occur, constitute a person's being conscious.

The approach I am taking is different from the one most common in empiricist philosophy. According to the empiricist tradition, consciousness is a state of awareness; to be conscious is simply to receive and register impressions, and it can be largely passive. This view of consciousness is perhaps modeled on the experience of seeing, where seeing is understood as the receiving of visual impressions. The opposite of this kind of consciousness is unconsciousness, which is lack of awareness, as in sleep. Consciousness as awareness admits of degrees or kinds; researchers speak of "core consciousness," "extended consciousness," and others. It is not limited to humans; other creatures, too, can be in a state of awareness. By contrast, the view I am adopting, which grounds consciousness on a person's sense of agency, refers specifically to human consciousness and it is construed not on the model of seeing but that of doing or acting.

Such an approach may seem odd to someone steeped in the empiricist assumption that consciousness is a state of passive awareness or receptivity, but it has a respectable philosophical tradition of its own and it has been persuasively developed by a number of philosophers, among them Stuart Hampshire, on whose analysis I draw in this section. He writes, "A man's present intentions and his beliefs about his present situation and environment, taken together, constitute his present state of consciousness."* We move from one moment to the next by doing things. We carry out our plans, we realize or fail to realize our intentions, we walk, we converse, we ponder, and it is in the doing of such things that we are conscious. Even time itself, as we actually experience it, is the result of act-

* *Thought and Action* (London: Chatto & Windus, 1959), p. 101.

ing, doing one thing after another, not something flowing by externally, chopped into equal bits by the ticking of a clock. A piano teacher of mine once urged that the tempo is not something "out there" to which I must match my playing; instead I *create* the tempo by playing one note after another.* That is an important pedagogical and philosophical point, but reality goes further: we don't just create the tempo, we create *ourselves* by doing things.

If a person is conscious at a certain time, he is engaged in some activity at that time. There is something he is doing, although "what he is doing" may not include overt bodily movement. Thinking, planning, deciding, and attending to sensations count as activities in this context, no less than walking or opening the door. That there is something a conscious person is doing is true even in moments of indolence when he sincerely replies, "Nothing" to the question, "What are you doing?" He is "musing," or "contemplating," or something; he is not literally doing nothing. We can also put the point this way: if a person is conscious, there is an answer to the question, "What is he doing?" There is some verb that accurately describes his activity. Moreover, there is some description of his activity that he would accept, because a conscious person knows what he is doing. This is true even if he has not formulated a verbal description of his activity and even if he would have trouble formulating such a description. His activity may be "hard to put into words" without its following that he doesn't know what he is doing or couldn't recognize and accept a description if it were offered. In addition, if he is acting purposively he knows whether or not his action is meeting its purpose. Summing up: if a person is conscious at a particular time, there is something he is doing, which he also knows himself to be doing, and the action he knows himself to be doing is the action *in virtue of which* he is conscious at that time.

* This relates to the experimental discoveries about time perception cited in chapter 4, p. 108.

Now, if a person knows what he is doing, then if his action is purposive, that action is intentional. Hampshire offers a helpful formulation of intention as a "thought that guides and accompanies deliberate action."* Clearly, if someone knows what he is doing and is acting with a purpose then there must be a thought that guides and accompanies his action, which amounts, on this definition, to saying that the action is intentional. That the action is intentional need not imply that he *likes* what he is doing or would choose it if he could avoid it. He may be acting unwillingly or under duress and yet be acting intentionally. The bank teller does not *want* to hand over the cash, but staring into the barrel of a gun he does it, and does it intentionally.

Let us turn now to intention, and remind ourselves of the point made in chapter 4 that any action is intentional only in relation to a description, because any action can be described in an unlimited number of ways and it may be intentional under one description and not under another. Suppose someone raises his arm in a manner that could be described either as "pointing to a rainbow" or "making an obscene gesture." Which of those was an intentional action? If he doesn't know that raising his arm in that manner could be construed as an obscene gesture, then "making an obscene gesture" cannot be a description of his intention, even if the same movement, under the description "pointing to a rainbow" *was* intentional. If one description is part of someone's answer to "what are you doing?" and another is not, then that person's action is intentional under the first description only. If neither of them is part of his answer, his action is not intentional under either one, since an action cannot be intentional if the person does not know that he is doing it.

This point is worth elaborating a bit. Whenever I act, there are indefinitely many things I can truly be described as doing. Suppose I am planting a rose bush. I may at the same time be "getting a sunburn," "frightening the squirrels from

* *Thought and Action*, p. 92.

the birdbath," and "destroying the dahlia tubers buried in the garden." Any one of those is something I could do intentionally, but only one – planting a rose bush – is such that there is at that moment a thought guiding and accompanying it; it alone would be my answer to "What are you doing?" so it is the action that is intentional at that moment. But the intentional action, the one that is my answer to "What are you doing?" is also the one that accounts for my being conscious at that time; it is the action *in virtue of which* I am conscious at that time. Another way of putting the point is this: at any moment there may be many things I can truly be said to be doing, but some of them may not be things that in the moment I know myself to be doing. Only an action that I know myself to be doing can be the action in virtue of which I am conscious.

The kind of intention that concerns us, which I earlier described as "the thought that guides and accompanies action," occurs simultaneously with the action it guides and accompanies. In chapter 4, I described "fully intentional" activity as "moment-to-moment direction of each movement in the context of a heightened awareness of the entire body, as well as ongoing appraisal and adjustment" (p. 106) and said that it is the kind of intentional activity needed in performance. I mentioned above that a conscious person knows what he is doing but even though there is a description he would accept, were it offered, he may find it hard or impossible to *say* what he is doing. That is the condition of a performer engaged in fully intentional activity. Hampshire's example of this is an actor who knows precisely how he intends to play a character or scene but can't *say* how he will do it; the only way to convey his intention is to *do* it. Another example is a pianist playing the Fourth Ballade with full intention. For the actor, as for the pianist, there is at each moment a thought that guides and accompanies action; the performer knows what he is doing, and knows whether the action matches the intention, but the thought that guides and accompanies action may not be precisely expressible in words. It is revealed by the action it guides.

In addition to the intention that guides and accompanies action, there is another kind of intention, formed separately from the action that fulfills it. We could call this an intention *to* do something, as in "I intend to go to the bank this afternoon" as contrasted with an intention *in* doing something. I shall call the intention to do something a "fixed" intention. Fixed intentions are similar to beliefs in that a person can have them over a period of time and at moments when he is not consciously thinking about them, just as one can hold a belief even at moments when one is not thinking about that belief. For example, I may be fully engaged over lunch in conversation with a friend, but it can be true throughout the conversation that I intend to go to the bank in the afternoon.

Ordinarily, when I carry out an action that fulfills a fixed intention, the action is intentional in the way described earlier, that is, I am aware of my action under a description that characterizes it as fulfilling my intention. Thus, in the above example, when I do go to the bank in the afternoon I know that I am doing so and I know that I am fulfilling my previously formed intention. It is essential for our discussion of performance to notice, however, that this may not always be true, because it is possible to carry out an action that fulfills a fixed intention, but to do so unintentionally. For example, suppose I intend to trespass on some property, perhaps as a political protest. On my way to the protest I cross onto the property without knowing I am doing so, because I am mistaken about the boundary. I am trespassing, thereby fulfilling my fixed intention, but I am doing so unintentionally. Another way to unintentionally fulfill a fixed intention, more relevant to our discussion of performance, is through the activation of dispositions that function automatically. For example, we have all had the experience of walking while thinking of other things. That is, our brains contain dispositions that can direct the movements of walking even while our conscious thoughts are elsewhere. In such a situation it is possible temporarily to forget where one is, even to pass one's street without noticing.

Suppose, therefore, that I intend to go for a walk in order to get some much-needed exercise. At the start of my walk, I meet a friend who joins me, we fall into an absorbing conversation, and after half an hour one of us says, "Oh my goodness! Here we are, back already! I had no idea." In this example I intended to go for a walk and get some exercise; I did go for a walk and I did get some exercise, fulfilling my fixed intention, but I was not aware in the moment of my actions and therefore not aware of myself fulfilling my intention. I fulfilled my intention unintentionally.

The discussion of the last few pages enables us to offer a better analysis of the requirement that performing be intentional. Let us recall to the stage the distracted pianist playing the Fourth Ballade whom we met in chapter 4 (pp. 112–4). She has a set of dispositions established in her brain that can direct her fingers to produce the Fourth Ballade, and these dispositions are secure enough that if an irrelevant thought distracts her attention, her fingers continue to play the notes although her attention at that moment is elsewhere. Now, even while she is distracted, she is still playing the Fourth Ballade. Moreover, her playing satisfies a fixed intention, because she has had the intention of playing the Fourth Ballade at this recital ever since she put together the program, and the notes she is now playing do fulfill that fixed intention. But in the moment of distraction, "playing the Fourth Ballade" cannot be her answer to the question "what are you doing?" since by hypothesis she is not aware, at that moment, that she *is* playing the Fourth Ballade. Perhaps her true answer to the question would be "thinking about my dinner." Therefore, her playing of the Fourth Ballade is not intentional in the sense that matters to us: the thought that *accompanies* her action does not also *guide* it. Now, by our previous argument, to answer the question "what are you doing" is to name the activity in virtue of which one is conscious at that time. Therefore, we can say about our pianist that she *is* conscious and she *is* playing the Ballade, but her activity of playing the Fourth Ballade is not the activity *in virtue of which* she is conscious at that moment. *That* activity is "thinking about my dinner." We can now restate the requirement that performance be intentional: in order to count as a performance, the activity of performing must be the activity in virtue of which the person is conscious during that period. This is the link between intention and consciousness that I promised at the beginning of this section.

The formulation just offered is illuminating and will lead to additional insights about performance, but it requires clarification. To count as a performance, the "activity in virtue of which the person is conscious" must be more than just the activity of playing the piece or acting the scene. Take our pianist, who while playing the Fourth Ballade suddenly thinks about dinner, but suppose that instead of playing mindlessly while thinking of food, she immediately dismisses the thought of dinner and redirects her focus to the central thought of herself playing the Fourth Ballade. If she can do that her performance will not suffer. Now, recovering focus as quickly as one loses it is *also* intentional. That is, the pianist's intention to play the Fourth Ballade is part of a more comprehensive, overriding intention to remain focused, and recover focus immediately should she lose it momentarily. We described this in chapter 4 as a "second-order" intention and insisted that this second-order intention is what performance requires (p. 114). Consequently, when we now conclude that the activity of performing must be the activity in virtue of which the person is conscious, the activity we have in mind is the one governed by this second-order intention. The activity of performing in virtue of which the person is conscious includes the intention to remain focused, remain in the moment, and immediately recover focus if necessary.

We are at last in a position to describe what is special about artistic performance, how the artworks of performers differ from those of other artists, and what makes an instance produced in performance superior to a reproduction.

Life is built from daily experience. Events occur from day to day, we do one thing after another, and the accumulation of

events and actions makes up our life. Many things that occur in life are not particularly significant. They may have no intrinsic connection with one another and it does not usually seem essential that they should occur just as they do or in the order they do. I went to the bank today and the supermarket yesterday, but I could have reversed the order; it wouldn't have made much difference. In themselves, such events do not seem to be connected to one another causally or logically or in any other way. What ties them together is just the thread of my life. My ongoing sense of myself as an agent is a constant that leads from one to another, but that ongoing sense may be the only link between disparate events and actions.

The situation is different when we confront an instance of a work of performing art. Then a bit of our life is shaped a special way. When I hear an instance of a Chopin ballade, sounds occur generating feelings – experiences – in me. *Those* feelings are not unrelated to one another. They are linked by relationships of anticipation, imitation, repetition, and others; they cohere among themselves. As the work unfolds, the feelings generated in me by the sounds reflect the formal structure and expressive content of the ballade, which is thus instantiated in me as experience. The situation is similar when I see a work of choreography built by one movement leading to another, or an instance of a drama taking shape in a succession of words and movements. The result is an experience with greater intensity and a more coherent structure than the ordinary experiences of life. We do not so much contemplate the work as we experience it; our experience during that stretch of time takes the form of an artwork. This kind of experience can result from any encounter with an instance of a work of performing art. Recordings do give instances; therefore, such experience is available from a recording as well as from a performance. But performance offers something more.

A performance is a period of intentional human action that results in an instance of a work of performing art. The instance and the intentional activity of producing it unfold together. But intentional action, as I argued earlier in this chapter, is also the foundation of human consciousness. Therefore, we can characterize what happens in performance as "the foundation of consciousness shaped into an artwork," fulfilling, at last, the promise made in chapter 1.

We can reach this conclusion another way. When intentional action is shaped into an artwork, we can say that it becomes an object of contemplation in its own right, something to be viewed aesthetically. Now, regarding something as an object of aesthetic contemplation is often described as regarding it "in itself," separating it from its ordinary purposes and from any use to which it might be put. But intentional action cannot be separated from its purpose; its *nature* is to have a goal or purpose. To act intentionally is, necessarily, to be doing *something*. Making intentional action an object of aesthetic contemplation, therefore, does not mean that we contemplate the action separated from any purpose, to contemplate it *is* to contemplate its purpose, or, if you like, to contemplate it in relation to its purpose, and its purpose, in this case, is the creation of an artwork. But since intentional action is the foundation of consciousness, this amounts, once again, to saying that in artistic performance the foundation of consciousness is shaped into an artwork.

I suspect that the view I am presenting is unfamiliar to many readers, so I shall offer yet another way of describing it. If performing art essentially involves the idea of intentional action, we can say it rests on something fundamental to our conscious being. But it does not involve intentional action in the sense of holding it up to us as a goal or ideal or something to aspire to in our daily lives; instead it takes intentional action itself, and shapes out of it an artwork. Performance is free human action made into an object of contemplation. But the way performance accomplishes this is by taking individual free actions, occurring in real time, and making them into an instance of *another* artwork. We experience that other artwork both in itself—we hear the work by Beethoven or Chopin, we see the work by Balanchine—and as a product of a coherent and focused period of free human action. Thus action, the foundation of consciousness, is made into an artwork.

It may seem that the intentional action that is shaped into an artwork is the action engaged in by the performer. True, but the audience also engages in intentional action: it pays attention, which counts as an action and can be done intentionally. Therefore, the consciousness of the audience, like that of the performer, is shaped into an artwork in the course of the performance. The artwork comes into being in the consciousness of the audience simultaneously with its emergence in the consciousness of the performer. Now, to act according to intention—to do as one wills—is to act freely. Performance, therefore, is a case of free action; we can regard it as an exercising of human freedom. The ability to act freely is unique to humans. Only humans, who possess language, are capable of forming intentions, and hence of acting according to intention. Therefore, only humans have the possibility of acting freely. Other creatures can have desires, and some of their activity may be purposive, but their desires and purposes are not mediated by thought or formulated as intention. It makes no sense to say of them that they act with intention, or freely. Since the possibility of free action separates us from other creatures, we can regard it as part of what defines us as human; it lies at the heart of our humanity. Therefore, at a performance, which is a period of free intentional action shaped into an artwork, we can say that what defines us as humans, the center of our humanity, is presented to us in the form of an artwork and made an object of aesthetic contemplation. We are shown the defining nature of our selves.

We can sum up the conclusions we have reached as follows. At a fine performance of a masterpiece like the Fourth Ballade we confront, first, a great artwork: the Fourth Ballade. Our consciousness during the performance takes the form of the ballade, so the ballade is not merely present as an object of contemplation but becomes part of our experience, part of ourselves. Now, the ballade is made available to us by another artwork, namely the instance created simultaneously with our experience of it, by a pianist whose activity of artistic making is an exercise of free human action. Thus, free action, which defines us as human, is exhibited to us in the form of an artwork – the instance – and it gives us another artwork – the ballade – that is simultaneously realized as experience in ourselves. We participate in two extraordinary artworks at once, the ballade and the instantiation of it through an exercise of intentional free action, that is, through an exhibition of the essence of our humanity. All this occurs, moreover, in a context of sharing. The performance is directed at us in the audience, and we feel included. It speaks to each of us individually, but it speaks simultaneously to the rest of the audience, and we are aware of that. This adds another dimension to the occasion: the significance of what happens is enhanced by its being shared, by its being a communal experience.

Performances at which all these elements come together at a high level in the manner I have described are rare occasions. They are supreme moments. When we are lucky enough to encounter them they can remain in our thoughts for years and enrich our lives. However, even performances that do not reach this pinnacle can still have value. The significance of a performance does not depend entirely on the quality of the work being performed or the skill of the performer; indeed, even the performances of only modestly skilled performers may have something worthwhile to offer. Imagine a nine-year-old pianist playing a sonatina by Clementi. Now, the Clementi sonatinas are not masterpieces of music, although they do count as artworks. They are pleasant, trivial teaching pieces, and they make only slight technical demands on the pianist. In playing her sonatina, therefore, our nine-year-old will not be displaying virtuosic skill or offering an instance of a profound musical work. Let us suppose, however, that her activity is fully intentional, fully in the moment, and therefore is a case of free action, which she shapes into an artwork. Suppose further that our pianist plays with intent to share, including her audience in her activity.

Under those suppositions, I claim, her performance has a significance and power independent of her technical accomplishments and the quality of the work performed. It becomes an example of the free human action that lies at the heart of our humanity and is part of the defining nature of ourselves. Therefore her performance can provide us, her audience, with a profound and moving experience. There is, after all, something compelling about a child, who in a spirit of sharing is completely absorbed in a complex task, and part of what moves us is the evidence that this child has passed beyond infancy and is capable of engaging in fully realized human action. That this can happen—that a nine-year-old pianist might perform with full intention—does not in my opinion require argument. It may be rare but I believe we have all of us observed it from time to time. It is easy to imagine other examples, such as a nine-year-old dancer performing with focused intention, including her audience as she executes the movements of her dance. The possibility of focused intention in young children has obvious implications for other fields than performance, such as education, which it is not my purpose to explore here.

The nine-year-old's performance is significant in another way. It makes clear what is all too often missing in the case of older, more accomplished performers. It is very easy for performers as they move from childhood to adulthood to become absorbed in the technical demands of their activity, or preoccupied with competition for jobs and engagements, or dedicated to display and self-promotion. They may overlook or forget the importance of communicating, sharing, including the audience, and even if they acknowledge it in words, they do not always cultivate it, or perhaps they imagine that communication will somehow happen automatically. In fact, however, it usually needs to be cultivated, and performers who neglect it would benefit from the example of our nine-year-old, whose performance, however naïve, shows us – or reminds us – what artistic performance is really about.

Performance and the Human Condition

We saw earlier in this chapter that performance involves contingency. Now, contingency is not confined to performances or to the artworld. On the contrary, it is the stuff of our daily lives, which consist, after all, largely of voluntary actions that are undetermined until they occur, are governed by intention, and admit of being otherwise. This is just the human condition, how life is. In adopting the expression "human condition," I am not using it to refer to people's social, political, or economic situation, which is the more common use of the expression. Instead I am referring to what might be called humanity's *metaphysical* condition. Events and actions no sooner occur than they become past, and they are then irretrievable, knowable only in recollection. We live in the present, in the elusive moment that separates future and past, at the moving boundary between potentiality and actuality. *That* is the human condition, metaphysically speaking, and performance occurs in the same space. At each moment in the performance, actuality emerges from possibility and we move from uncertainty to fact. The amount that remains to be determined diminishes as the performance progresses, and when no uncertainty is left, the performance is over. The same is true of life.

To the extent that artistic performance exhibits voluntary action involving choice and freedom, it offers something we all are familiar with. Our daily lives are filled with conscious intentional action, but such action becomes extraordinary, indeed it stands as a supreme human achievement, when it results in something as complex, expressive, and profound as an instance of the Fourth Ballade, *Jewels*, or *King Lear*. All artistic creation involves an exercise of freedom, skill, intention, choice, and emotional insight, but in performance we confront these things not through their results but in their actual occurrence. Skill, intention, choice, and insight are immediately and actively present. Moreover, as they combine in a performance they are present at that moment only. This performance is happening now and never again. We confront an artwork whose creation and existence occur together, and both endure for a moment only. Performance thus makes art out of the uncertainty of the human condition.

In nonperforming art—art in which the making and the existence of the work are separate—artists produce artworks that stand outside the human condition. Paintings can depict or represent many aspects of human life, but they are not *made* out of life. They hang on the wall and remain unchanged while life goes on around them. A painting or a statue can endure through many generations, whereas performances occur in time, have a beginning and an end, and when they end, they cease to exist. They do not escape the human condition, nor do they seek to escape it. Instead, the performer shapes experience *within* the human condition into an instance of an artwork.

The result is a reciprocal communication: a performer producing by conscious intentional action an instance that evokes feelings in the audience, and the audience conveying, through unbroken attention, its receiving and responding to those feelings. This interaction gives urgency and immediacy to performance. Only in the performing arts do audience and artist simultaneously experience the emergence of an artwork. At a performance we experience the work being performed, but we experience it as created in that moment by the performer who through intention and choice determines the precise nuances of the instance he is making; those nuances constitute his interpretation of the work he is performing. This situation reminds us of the famous description of art by Emile Zola:

Une œuvre d'art est un coin de la création
vu à travers un tempérament.

An artwork is a corner of reality
seen through an individual temperament.

We can apply Zola's description to the relation between an instance and the work being performed, and say that the relation of the instance to the work performed is the same relation in which, according to Zola, art stands to reality. Thus, an instance of the Fourth Ballade created by Stephen Hough would stand to the Fourth Ballade in the same relation that Monet's *Morning on the Seine, near Giverny* (1897) stands to the actual morning on the Seine near Giverny. In each case we are offered a bit of reality seen through an individual temperament.

The analogy holds, but there is a vital difference between the two situations. In the case of Monet, there is a bit of reality – some trees and mist along a river – of which he makes a representation out of paint and canvas. In the case of Stephen Hough's performance, what stands in the place of reality – the Fourth Ballade – is not a physical object like trees and a river, it is an artwork and its reality is that of an abstract object. It can't be visually represented; it must be sensuously realized – instantiated – under a particular interpretation. Moreover, the scene that Monet represented is no longer available as reality, since the trees, I assume, have long since died or been cut down and the mist has dissipated. Neither Monet nor anyone else can put us in touch with those actual trees and mist, because they no longer exist. That means that the "corner of reality" that Monet depicted has disappeared; all that is left is his view of it, embodied in his painting. But in Stephen Hough's performance, what stands in the place of reality *does* still exist and *is* available. Moreover, Stephen Hough gives us that *actual object*, namely, the Fourth Ballade. Thus, in a performance a nonphysical object that is also an artwork is taken as reality, and that very reality is what the performer presents to us, under an interpretation, in an instantiation that is *another* artwork. We experience the Fourth Ballade through Stephen Hough's instance of it, but that instance embodies his individual interpretation of the ballade, which matches Zola's account: we experience the ballade through the individual temperament of Stephen Hough.

There is a trap here, however. In saying "we experience the ballade through the individual temperament of Stephen Hough," it is perhaps tempting to conclude that we experience the work indirectly as through a lens, the lens being the temperament of Stephen Hough. But that is not right. Experiencing Chopin through sounds made by Stephen Hough is analogous instead to experiencing the Grand Canyon under a particular condition of light. The Grand Canyon varies in appearance as it is variously illuminated, and Stephen Hough's relation to the Fourth Ballade is like that of the sun to the Grand Canyon. He illuminates it for us in a particular way at a particular moment.

In chapter 7 I claimed that an instance produced in performance is an artwork by the performer and I based that claim on the observation that it is the result of an artistic making. I promised, however, to take up the question from a different, more penetrating perspective, in which an object's being an artwork is a consequence of its receiving an appropriate interpretation. Arthur C. Danto developed this approach in his book *The Transfiguration of the Commonplace*,* which offered an exceptionally profound and illuminating philosophy of art. His analysis took as its point of departure the fact that there can be cases, both real and imagined, in which two objects

* (Cambridge, Massachussetts: Harvard University Press, 1981)

may be perceptually indistinguishable from one another and yet one of them is an artwork and the other is not, or less commonly, both are artworks, but different artworks. Duchamp's *Fountain* can serve as an example. It has, let us assume, exactly the same perceptible features as another urinal from the same manufacturer, and yet it is an artwork and the other just a piece of useful plumbing. Danto argued that something is an artwork if it occurs in a culture that has a concept of reality as distinct from unreality, and then, within that culture, it receives an interpretation that lifts it from reality, the world of ordinary things, into unreality, one form of unreality being the artworld. The object is transfigured into an artwork. If only one of two indiscernible objects receives such an interpretation then only it is an artwork; if two indiscernible objects are both artworks but their status as such is the result of receiving different interpretations, then they are different artworks. Danto uses examples almost exclusively from visual art, but examples of the sorts of indiscernible objects that interest him can also be imagined in performing art.

Consider the case described above of Stephen Hough's presentation of the Fourth Ballade. I claimed that he gives us his interpretation of the ballade; through it we hear the ballade, and this, I said, is similar to Zola's account of art as a bit of reality seen through an individual temperament, with the ballade standing in the place of reality. Danto at one point describes the appreciation of art almost exactly as Zola does: he says it is "as if the work of art were the externalization of the artist who made it, as if to appreciate the work were to see the world through the artist's sensibility and not just to see the world" (p. 160). Now, Stephen Hough's presentation of the Fourth Ballade presents the ballade to us in exactly this way. We hear the ballade, to use Danto's expression, "through the sensibility of Stephen Hough" (although, as I insisted above, we must take this to mean something like "illuminated by the sensibility of Stephen Hough"). Now, let us suppose Hough's ballade is recorded, and that the sounds emerging from the CD player are indistinguishable from those produced in concert.* Both instances, the one produced in performance and the one emerging from the CD player, give us Chopin's ballade. And both give us Stephen Hough's interpretation. Therefore we can say of both of them that they give us instances of the Fourth Ballade through the sensibility of Stephen Hough. We therefore have two instances of the ballade, under the same interpretation. There is nevertheless a profound difference – an ontological difference – between the two.

A performance gives an instance of Chopin under a particular interpretation, but that instance simultaneously receives an interpretation of a different kind, the sort of interpretation that, in line with Danto's theory, transforms – transfigures – it into a different artwork from a recorded instance, even though the two might, by hypothesis, be perceptibly indiscernible. The audience at a performance interprets what it sees or hears as resulting from a *performance,* that is, as resulting from the moment-to-moment creation of sounds or movements by intentional human action. To hear or see it that way is to attribute to it properties that are not perceivable; after all, I cannot *see* or *hear* your intention or know by observation whether your words or movements are actions or mere bodily movements. I must attribute intention to you, however, in order to attribute any meaning to your words or movements. The same holds when attending a performance. But to regard the instance produced in performance as resulting from a series of intentional actions occurring moment to moment is to place it within the human condition, within life itself. Moreover, the instance occurs, I have insisted, in a context of sharing, of communication, of love. It does not seem a stretch to say, then, that the instance is about, or partly about, that communication; it has communication as its artistic subject, or one of its subjects; that's what it's about. If that is true, then the interpretation that attributes that artistic subject to the instance is sufficient to

* Obviously, *establishing* that the two instances are perceptibly indistinguishable would be a practical impossibility, since the sounds produced in concert no longer exist, but let us assume for the purpose of argument that the two sequences of sounds are perceptibly identical.

make the instance produced in performance count as a different artwork from the perceptibly identical instance coming from a CD player. Performance offers an experience of whatever the work performed is about, whether *King Lear, Jewels,* or the Fourth Ballade. But it gives us that as part of the human condition, within a shared experience of communication and love, and this has no counterpart in nonperforming art.

Because the existence and the making of the artwork generated in performance are simultaneous, a performance is a period of uninterrupted artistic creation. We in the audience are present at the creation of an artwork. We encounter artistic creation in "real time." The performer molds our feelings into a coherent experience of the artwork within the context of a loving relationship and our experience ends when the performance ends. What is created passes out of existence as fast as it is created. This may be felt as a loss. It seems unfortunate—tragic, even—that something wonderful should pass out of being the moment it happens, which perhaps accounts for the element of sadness or regret that some people feel at the end of a fine performance, as if to say, with Wordsworth,

> *But yet I know, where'er I go,*
> *That there hath past away a glory from the earth.* *

Performances are not the only things that pass out of being the moment they occur. *All* of our experience is like that. Things happen, and then they are over, like life itself. That, too, is part of the human condition, which, ending as it inevitably does in death, has been a perennial subject of art. Throughout history, art has offered various perspectives on the human condition. It may point to the human condition simply as a fact:

> *Alles endet, was entstehet.*
> *Alles, alles rings vergehet.*†

* "Ode: Intimations of Immortality from Recollections of Early Childhood."

† "Everything ends which comes to be. Everything everywhere passes away." Walter Heinrich Tornow, "Alles endet, was entstehet," based on a poem by Michelangelo and set to music by Hugo Wolf.

Art may point to the human condition in order to exhort us to mend our ways—think of the *vanitas* still lifes in seventeenth-century Dutch painting, which remind us of the impermanence of earthly things and urge us to contemplate the hereafter—or it may portray death as a release from the human condition:

> *Man comes and tills the field and lies beneath,*
> *And after many a summer dies the swan.* *

Or locate happiness in an escape from the human condition:

> *Ah, happy, happy boughs! that cannot shed*
> *Your leaves, nor ever bid the spring adieu.*†

But representing, depicting, or referring to something, for whatever purpose, which is what occurs in nonperforming art, is different from *being* that thing, which is what occurs in performance. Performance does not attempt to escape or transcend the human condition, nor to describe it; performance is *within* the human condition. It is part of life, not something outside. When a part of one's life becomes an experience of Chopin's Fourth Ballade brought into being moment to moment by intentional free action in a context of love, the occasion is something to treasure.

We have arrived at last at the goal announced at the beginning. I promised to show that performers are artists in their own right, to explain what their artworks are, and describe how performance offers a kind of experience unlike what is available from nonperforming art. The conclusions I have presented have been drawn partly from a clarification of the relation between works of performing art and performances of those works, and partly from an extended examination of motion—not mere motion but intentional bodily movement directed so as to evoke emotion and feeling. I have pointed out along the way that these ideas are of more than theoretical interest; they make a difference in the way performers practice,

* Tennyson, "Tithonus."
† Keats, "Ode on a Grecian Urn."

teach, and perform, and in the way the audience interacts with the performer. Performance is a communication, a sharing. Attending a performance, I not only experience an instance of a work as created in the moment, I experience it created *for me*. I am part of the event; the event is an interaction. My experience takes the shape of an artwork, but it is at the same time an experience I share with the performer and the rest of the audience. An artistic performance is a bringing together. In saying that, I am simply pointing out that everything I have said about performance must be understood in the context of the loving relationships described in chapter 6. Love is all too easily forgotten, by performers and audience alike. Performers can become wrapped up in the technical demands of their work; the audience can arrive with preconceptions or preoccupations that stand in the way of proper acceptance and attention. Under such conditions, performance becomes cold and lifeless and the audience remains unmoved. Love is stifled. But love is not just one element among others in a performance; it is a *precondition* if artistic performance is to provide the sort of experience I have described in this chapter. I claim that artistic performance is motion, emotion, and love. But motion, if not directed to an expressive purpose, is meaningless, and emotion, if not communicated, availeth nothing. And so, completing the paraphrase, I conclude that performance is indeed motion, emotion, and love,

*but the greatest of these is love.**

* I Corinthians 13.

PRODUCED BY Marquand Books, Seattle

DESIGNED BY Tina Henderson

TYPESET IN Fournier, a Monotype font based on types cut by Pierre Simon Fournier, circa 1742, and called "St Augustin Ordinaire" in Fournier's *Manuel Typographique*

PRINTED AND BOUND IN The United States of America by RR Donnelley

PRINTED ON Glatfelter offset B-18 Antique

DUST JACKET ON Neenah's Classic laid solar white, an FSC-certified, acid-free paper